IN THE
PRESIDENT'S
SECRET SERVICE

Inside the White House:
The Hidden Lives of the Modern Presidents and
the Secrets of the World's Most Powerful Institution

The FBI:
Inside the World's Most Powerful Law Enforcement Agency

Inside the CIA:
Revealing the Secrets of the World's Most Powerful Spy Agency

Escape from the CIA:
How the CIA Won and Lost the Most Important
KGB Spy Ever to Defect to the U.S.

The Spy in the Russian Club:
How Glenn Souther Stole America's Nuclear War Plans
and Escaped to Moscow

Moscow Station:
How the KGB Penetrated the American Embassy

Spy vs. Spy:
Stalking Soviet Spies in America

The Richest Man in the World:
The Story of Adnan Khashoggi

The Life Insurance Game

IN THE PRESIDENT'S SECRET SERVICE

BEHIND THE SCENES WITH AGENTS IN THE LINE OF FIRE AND THE PRESIDENTS THEY PROTECT

RONALD KESSLER

BROADWAY PAPERBACKS
NEW YORK

Published in the United States by Broadway Paperbacks, an imprint of
the Crown Publishing Group, a division of Random House, Inc., New York.
www.crownpublishing.com

Broadway Paperbacks and its logo, a letter B bisected on the diagonal are trademarks of
Random House, Inc.

Originally published in hardcover in slightly different form in the United States
by Crown Publishers, an imprint of the Crown Publishing Group, a division of Random House, Inc.,
New York, in 2009, and in paperback in the United States by Three Rivers Press, an imprint of the
Crown Publishing Group, a division of Random House, Inc., New York, in 2010.

Library of Congress Cataloging-in-Publication Data is available upon request.

ISBN 978-0-307-46136-0

Printed in the United States of America

Design by Leonard W. Henderson

14 16 18 20 19 17 15

First Broadway Paperbacks Edition

For Pam,
Greg, and Rachel Kessler

Contents

Contents

Prologue

LL EYES IN THE crowd were on the new president and first lady as they smiled and waved and held hands, celebrating the moment. But the men and women who walked along Pennsylvania Avenue with them never looked at the couple, only into the crowd.

The temperature was twenty-eight degrees, but the Secret Service agents' suit jackets were open, hands held free in front of the chest, just in case they had to reach for their SIG Sauer P229 pistols. On television as the motorcade proceeded, the world could sometimes catch a glimpse of a man's silhouette on top of a building, a countersniper poised and watching. But that was just a hint of the massive security precautions that had been planned in secret for months.

The Secret Service scripted where Barack and Michelle Obama could step out of "the Beast," as the presidential limousine is called. At those points, counterassault teams stood ready, armed with fully automatic Stoner SR-16 rifles and flash bang grenades for diversionary tactics.

If they spotted any hint of a threat, the grim-faced agents never betrayed it. It is the same when they see what goes on behind the scenes. Because Secret Service agents are sworn to secrecy, voters rarely know what their presidents, vice presidents, presidential candidates, and Cabinet officers are really like. If they did, says a former Secret Service agent, "They would scream."

Pledged to take a bullet for the president, agents are at constant risk. Yet the Secret Service's own practices magnify the dangers to its agents, the president, the vice president, and others they protect. These lapses could lead to an assassination.

IN THE
PRESIDENT'S
SECRET SERVICE

1

Supervise

EVEN BEFORE HE took the oath of office, Abraham Lincoln was the object of plots to kidnap or kill him. Throughout the Civil War, he received threatening letters. Yet, like most presidents before and after him, Lincoln had little use for personal protection. He resisted the efforts of his friends, the police, and the military to safeguard him. Finally, late in the war, he agreed to allow four Washington police officers to act as his bodyguards.

On April 14, 1865, John Wilkes Booth, a fanatical Confederate sympathizer, learned that Lincoln would be attending a play at Ford's Theatre that evening. The president's bodyguard on duty was Patrolman John F. Parker of the Washington police. Instead of remaining on guard outside the president's box, Parker wandered off to watch the play, then went to a nearby saloon for a drink. As a result of Parker's negligence, Lincoln was as unprotected as any private citizen.

Just after ten P.M., Booth made his way to Lincoln's box, snuck in, and shot him in the back of the head. The president died the next morning.

Despite that lesson, protection of the president remained spotty at best. For a short time after the Civil War, the War Department assigned soldiers to protect the White House and its grounds. On special occasions, Washington police officers helped maintain order and prevented crowds from assembling. But the permanent detail of four police officers that was assigned to guard the president during Lincoln's term was reduced to three. These officers protected only the White House and did not receive any special training.

Thus, President James A. Garfield was unguarded as he walked through a waiting room toward a train in the Baltimore and Potomac Railway station in Washington on the morning of July 2, 1881. Charles J. Guiteau emerged from the crowd and shot the president in the arm and then fatally in the back. Guiteau was said to be bitterly disappointed that Garfield had ignored his pleas to be appointed a consul in Europe.

Alexander Graham Bell, inventor of the telephone, tried to find the bullet in the president's back with an induction-balance electrical device he had invented. While the device worked in tests, it failed to find the bullet. All other efforts failed as well. On September 19, 1881, Garfield died of his wounds.

While the assassination shocked the nation, no steps were taken to protect the next president, Chester A. Arthur. The resistance came down to the perennial question of how to reconcile the need to protect the country's leaders with their need to mingle with citizens and remain connected to the people.

In fact, after Garfield's assassination, the *New York Tribune* warned against improving security. The paper said that the country did not want the president to become "the slave of his office, the prisoner of forms and restrictions."

The tension between openness and protection went back to the design of the White House itself. As originally proposed by Pierre L'Enfant and approved in principle by George Washington, the White House was to be a "presidential palace." As envisioned, it would have been five times larger than the structure actually built. But Republican opposition, led by Thomas Jefferson, discredited the Federalist plan as unbefitting a democracy. The critics decried what was known as "royalism"—surrounding the president with courtiers and guards, the trappings of the English monarchy.

To resolve the impasse, Jefferson proposed to President Washington that the executive residence be constructed according to the best plan submitted in a national competition. Washington endorsed the idea and eventually accepted a design by architect James Hoban. Workers laid the cornerstone for the White House on October 13, 1792. When the building received a coat of whitewash in 1797, people began referring to it as the White House.

Given the competing aims of openness and security, it's not surprising that the Secret Service stumbled into protecting the president as an afterthought. The agency began operating as a division of the Department of the Treasury on July 5, 1865, to track down and arrest counterfeiters. At the time, an estimated one third of the nation's currency was counterfeit. States issued their own currency printed by sixteen hundred state banks. Nobody knew what their money was supposed to look like.

Ironically, Abraham Lincoln's last official act was to sign into law the legislation creating the agency. Its first chief was William P. Wood, a veteran of the Mexican-American War, a friend of Secretary of War Edwin Stanton, and the superintendent of the Old Capitol Prison.

One of the Secret Service's first targets, William E. Brockway, was doing such a good job creating bogus thousand-dollar treasury bonds that the treasury itself redeemed seventy-five of them. Chief Wood personally tracked Brockway to New York, where he was living under a pseudonym. Known as the King of Counterfeiters, he was convicted and sent to jail.

By 1867, the Secret Service had brought counterfeiting largely under control and had won acclaim in the press.

"The professional criminal never willingly falls in the way of the Secret Service," the *Philadelphia Telegram* declared. "The chase is as relentless as death, and only death or capture ends it."

With the agency's success, Congress gave the Secret Service broader authority to investigate other crimes, including fraud against the government. In 1894, the Secret Service was investigating a plot to assassinate President Grover Cleveland by a group of "western gamblers, anarchists, or cranks" in Colorado. Exceeding its mandate, the agency detailed two men who had been conducting the investigation to protect Cleveland from the suspects. For a time, the two agents rode in a buggy behind his carriage. But after political opponents criticized him for it, Cleveland told the agents he did not want their help.

As the number of threatening letters addressed to the president increased, Cleveland's wife persuaded him to increase protection at the White House. The number of police assigned there rose from three to twenty-seven. In 1894, the Secret Service began to supplement that protection by providing agents on an informal basis, including when the president traveled.

It did not help the next president, William McKinley. Unlike Lincoln and Garfield, McKinley was being guarded when Leon F. Czolgosz shot him on September 6, 1901. McKinley was at a reception that day in the Temple of Music at the Pan-American Exposition in Buffalo, New York. Long lines of citizens passed between two rows of policemen and soldiers to shake his hand. Two Secret Service agents were within three feet of him when the twenty-eight-year-old self-styled anarchist joined the line and shot the president twice with a pistol concealed in a handkerchief. Bullets slammed into McKinley's chest and stomach. Eight days later, he died of blood poisoning.

Still, it was not until the next year—1902—that the Secret Service officially assumed responsibility for protecting the president. Even then it lacked statutory authority to do so. While Congress began allocating funds expressly for the purpose in 1906, it did so only annually, as part of the Sundry Civil Expenses Act.

As protective measures increased, President Theodore Roosevelt wrote to Senator Henry Cabot Lodge that he considered the Secret Service to be a "very small but very necessary thorn in the flesh. Of course," he wrote, "they would not be the least use in preventing any assault upon my life. I do not believe there is any danger of such an assault, and if there were, as Lincoln said, 'Though it would be safer for a president to live in a cage, it would interfere with his business.'"

Unsuccessful assassination attempts were made on President Andrew Jackson on January 30, 1835; President Theodore Roosevelt on October 14, 1912; and Franklin D. Roosevelt on February 15, 1933, before he had been sworn in. Even though Congress kept considering bills to make it a federal crime to assassinate the president, the legislative branch took no action. Members of the public continued to be free to roam the White House during daylight hours. In fact, back when the White House was first opened, a deranged man wandered in and threatened to kill President John Adams. Never calling for help, Adams invited the man into his office and calmed him down.

Finally, at the Secret Service's insistence, public access to the White House grounds was ended for the first time during World War II. To be let in, visitors had to report to gates around the perimeter. By then, Congress had formally established the White House Police in 1922 to guard the complex and secure the grounds. In 1930, the White House Police became part of the Secret Service. That unit within the Secret Service is now called the Secret Service's Uniformed Division. As its name implies, the division consists of officers in uniform.

In contrast to the Uniformed Division, Secret Service agents wear suits. They are responsible for the security of the first family and the vice president and his family, as opposed to the security of their surroundings. They also are responsible for protecting former presidents, presidential candidates, and visiting heads of state, and for security at special events of national significance such as presidential inaugurations, the Olympics, and presidential nominating conventions.

By the end of World War II, the number of Secret Service agents assigned to protect the president had been increased to thirty-seven. The stepped-up security paid off. At two-twenty P.M. on November 1, 1950, two Puerto Rican nationalists tried to force their way into Blair House to kill President Harry S. Truman. The would-be assassins, Oscar Collazo, thirty-six, and Griselio Torresola, twenty-five, hoped to draw attention to the cause of separating the island from the United States.

The two men picked up a couple of German pistols and took a train from New York to Washington. According to *American Gunfight* by Stephen Hunter and John Bainbridge, Jr., they took a cab to the White House. It turned out that the White House was being renovated, and their target was not staying there. The building was in such poor condition that Margaret Truman's piano had begun to break through the second floor. From the cab driver, Collazo and Torresola learned that during the renovation, Truman—code-named Supervise— was staying at Blair House across the street. They decided to shoot their way in.

Getting out on Pennsylvania Avenue, Torresola walked toward the west side of Blair House, while Collazo approached from the east. They planned to arrive at the mansion simultaneously with guns blazing, take down the security, and then find the president. As marksmen, Torresola was by far the better shot; Collazo was engaged in on-the-job training. But for the two men, fate would have its own plans.

Secret Service Agent Floyd Boring and White Hou
cer Joseph Davidson were manning the east security
west security booth was White House Police Officer Leslie Co
White House Police Officer Donald Birdzell was standing on the front
steps under the mansion's canopy, his back to the street, when Collazo
came up behind him.

Unfamiliar with the automatic pistol he carried, Collazo tried to
fire. The gun clicked, but nothing happened. Birdzell turned at the
sound, to see the gunman struggling. Then the pistol cracked. A round
tore into Birdzell's right knee.

Leaving the east security booth, Agent Boring and Officer Davidson drew their pistols and opened fire on Collazo. Hearing the shots,
Secret Service Agent Stewart Stout, who was inside Blair House,
retrieved a Thompson submachine gun from a gun cabinet. He had
been standing post in a hallway, guarding the stairs and elevator leading to the second floor, where Truman was napping in his underwear.
Bess Truman—code-named Sunnyside—as usual was out of town.
She hated Washington.

Standing in front of the west security booth, Torresola whipped
out his Luger and pumped rounds into Officer Coffelt's abdomen.
Coffelt slumped to the floor. Torresola came around from the guard-
house and encountered another target—White House Police Officer
Joseph Downs, who was in civilian clothes. Torresola hit him three
times—in the hip, the shoulder, and the left side of his neck.

Then Torresola jumped a hedge and headed toward the entrance
where wounded officer Birdzell was aiming his third or fourth shot at
Collazo. Spotting Torresola, Birdzell squeezed off a round at him and
missed. Torresola fired back, and the shot tore into the officer's other
knee.

In a last heroic act, Coffelt leaped to his feet and propped himself
against his security booth. He pointed his revolver at Torresola's head

and fired. The bullet ripped through Torresola's ear. The would-be assassin pitched forward, dead on the street.

The other officers and agents blasted away at Collazo. He finally crumpled up as a shot slammed into his chest. Meanwhile, Secret Service Agent Vincent Mroz fired at him from a second-floor window.

The biggest gunfight in Secret Service history was over in forty seconds. A total of twenty-seven shots had been fired.

Having killed Torresola, officer Coffelt died in surgery less than four hours later. He earned a place on the Secret Service's honor roll of personnel killed in the line of duty. Collazo and two White House policemen recovered from their wounds. Truman was unharmed. If the assassins had made it inside, Stout and other agents would have mowed them down.

Looking back, agent Floyd Boring recalled, "It was a beautiful day, about eighty degrees outside." He remembered teasing Coffelt. "I was kidding him about getting a new set of glasses. I wanted to find out if he had gotten the glasses to look at the girls."

When the shooting stopped, Boring went up to see Truman. As Boring recalled it, Truman said, "What the hell is going on down there?"

The next morning, "Truman wanted to go for a walk," says Charles "Chuck" Taylor, an agent on his detail. "We said we thought it was not a good idea. The group might still be in the area."

The following year, Congress finally passed legislation to permanently authorize the Secret Service to protect the president, his immediate family, the president-elect, and the vice president if he requested it.

"Well, it is wonderful to know that the work of protecting me has at last become legal," Truman joked as he signed the bill on July 16, 1951.

But it would remain up to the president how much protection he would receive. By their very nature, presidents want more exposure, while Secret Service agents want more security. As President Kennedy's aide Kenneth O'Donnell said, "The president's views of his responsibilities as president of the United States were that he meet the people, that he go out to their homes and see them, and allow them to see him, and discuss, if possible, the views of the world as he sees it, the problems of the country as he sees them."

Yet there was a fine line between those worthwhile goals and recklessness.

2

Lancer

AT SEVEN AGENTS per shift, John F. Kennedy's Secret Service detail consisted of about twenty-four agents, including supervisors. Before being hired, they were taken to a range for target practice with a pistol and handed a manual. There was no other initial training.

"On my second day on the job as an agent, they put me in the rear seat of the president's limousine," says former agent Larry D. Newman. "A supervisor on the detail placed a Thompson submachine gun on my lap. I had never seen a Thompson, much less used one."

Over the next several years, Newman received a total of ten weeks of training, consisting of four weeks on law enforcement procedures at the Treasury Department and six weeks of Secret Service training. But he never could figure out why locked boxes of shotguns were kept in the White House for the Secret Service, yet only the White House police had the keys.

Newman was told to take a bullet for the president and keep his mouth shut about the president's personal life. Human surveillance cameras, Secret Service agents observe everything that goes on behind the scenes. To this day, Secret Service directors periodically remind agents that they must not reveal to anyone—let alone the press—what they see behind the scenes. Usually the directors cite a phrase about trust from the commission book that agents carry with their credentials. The book says the agent is a "duly commissioned special agent of the United States Secret Service, authorized to carry firearms, execute warrants, make arrests for offenses against the United States, provide protection to the president and others eligible by law, perform other such duties as are authorized by law, and is commended as being worthy of trust and confidence."

Newman and other agents assigned to guard Kennedy soon learned that he led a double life. He was the charismatic leader of the free world. But in his other life, he was the cheating, reckless husband whose aides snuck women into the White House to appease his sexual appetite.

Former agent Robert Lutz remembers a gorgeous Swedish Pan Am flight attendant who was on the press plane that was following Kennedy on Air Force One. She seemed to take a liking to Lutz, and he planned to invite her out to dinner. The detail leader noticed that they were getting chummy and told the agent to stay away.

"She's part of the president's private stock," he warned Lutz.

Besides one-night stands, Kennedy had several consorts within the White House. One was Pamela Turnure, who had been his secretary when he was a senator, then Jackie's press secretary in the White House. Two others, Priscilla Wear and Jill Cowen, were secretaries who were known as Fiddle and Faddle, respectively. Wear already had the nickname Fiddle when she joined the White House staff, so Kennedy aides applied the name Faddle to Cowen.

"Neither did much work," says former agent Larry Newman, who was on the Kennedy detail.

They would have threesomes with Kennedy.

"When Jackie was away, Pam Turnure would see JFK at night at the residence," says former Secret Service agent Chuck Taylor.

"Fiddle and Faddle were well-endowed and would swim with JFK in the pool. They wore only white T-shirts that came to their waists. You could see their nipples. We had radio contact with Jackie's detail in case she came back."

One afternoon, Kennedy was cavorting in the pool with young women when Secret Service agents on Jackie's detail radioed that she was returning to the White House unexpectedly.

"Jackie was expected back in ten minutes, and JFK came charging out of the pool," says agent Anthony Sherman, who was on his detail at the time. "He had a bathing suit on and a Bloody Mary in his hand."

Kennedy looked around and gave the drink to Sherman.

"Enjoy it; it's quite good," the president said.

According to Secret Service agents, Kennedy had sex with Marilyn Monroe at New York hotels and in a loft above the Justice Department office of then Attorney General Robert F. Kennedy, the president's brother. Between the fifth and sixth floors, the loft contains a double bed that is used when the attorney general needs to stay overnight to handle crises. Its proximity to a private elevator made it easy for Kennedy and Monroe to enter from the Justice Department basement without being noticed.

"He [Kennedy] had liaisons with Marilyn Monroe there," a Secret Service agent says. "The Secret Service knew about it."

If Kennedy was reckless in his personal life, he was also rash when it came to security. Before his trip to Dallas on November 22, 1963, he received warnings about possible violence there. United Nations Ambassador Adlai Stevenson called Kennedy aide Arthur Schlesinger, Jr., and urged him to tell the president not to go to Dallas. He said he had just given a speech in Dallas and had been confronted by demonstrators who'd cursed at him and spat on him. Stevenson said Senator J. William Fulbright also warned Kennedy.

"Dallas is a very dangerous place," Fulbright told him. "I wouldn't go there. Don't you go."

Nonetheless, Kennedy aide O'Donnell told the Secret Service that unless it was raining, the president wanted to ride in an open convertible, according to the Warren Commission Report, which was largely based on the FBI's investigation. If it had rained, Kennedy would have used a plastic top that was not bulletproof. Kennedy—code-named Lancer—himself told agents he did not want them to ride on the small running boards at the rear of the car.

Shortly after eleven-fifty A.M., Kennedy's limousine proceeded from Love Field toward a scheduled luncheon at the Trade Mart. The car made a gradual descent on Elm Street toward a railroad overpass before reaching the Stemmons Freeway at Dealey Plaza. The Texas School Book Depository was on Kennedy's right.

Only two Secret Service agents had gone ahead to Dallas to make advance preparations for the trip. As is true today, the agency relied a great deal on local police and local offices of other federal agencies. At the time, the advance protocol did not include an inspection of buildings along the motorcade route, which was publicized in advance.

At twelve-thirty P.M., the president's limousine was traveling at about eleven miles per hour. Shots resounded in rapid succession from the Texas School Book Depository. A bullet entered the base of the back of the president's neck. Another bullet then struck him in the back of the head, causing a massive, fatal wound. He fell to the left onto his wife Jackie's lap.

Agent William R. Greer was driving the limo, and Agent Roy H. Kellerman was sitting to his right. But neither could immediately leap to Kennedy's assistance, as would have been the case if agents had been allowed to ride at the rear of the car. Making things more difficult, the president's limousine had a second row of seats between the front and rear seats, where Kennedy sat. The "kill shot" to the president's head came 4.9 seconds after the first shot that hit him.

Greer had no special training in evasive driving. After the first shot, he did not immediately accelerate or take evasive action. In fact, he momentarily slowed the car and waited for a command from Agent Kellerman.

"Let's get out of here! We are hit," Kellerman yelled.

Agent Clinton J. Hill, riding on the left running board of the follow-up car, raced toward Kennedy's limousine. He pulled himself onto the back of the car as it gained speed. He pushed Jackie—code-named Lace—back into the rear seat as he shielded both her and the president.

"If agents had been allowed on the rear running boards, they would have pushed the president down and jumped on him to protect him before the fatal shot," Chuck Taylor, who was an agent on the Kennedy detail, tells me.

Confirming that, Secret Service Director Lewis Merletti later said, "An analysis of the ensuing assassination—including the trajectory of the bullets which struck the president—indicates that it might have been thwarted had agents been stationed on the car's running boards."

Taken to Parkland Memorial Hospital four miles away, Kennedy was pronounced dead at one P.M. Agents throughout the Secret Service were devastated.

Once again, an assassin had changed the course of history. For the Secret Service, the question was how well it would learn lessons from the assassination in order to prevent another one.

3

Volunteer

IF SECRET SERVICE agents found Kennedy to be reckless, Lyndon B. Johnson was uncouth, nasty, and often drunk.
Agent Taylor recalls driving Johnson, who was then vice president, with another agent from the U.S. Capitol to the White House
for a four P.M. appointment with Kennedy. Johnson—code-named
Volunteer—was not ready to leave until three forty-five P.M. Because
of traffic along Pennsylvania Avenue, they were going to be late.

"Johnson said to jump the curb and drive on the sidewalk," Taylor
says. "There were people on the sidewalk getting out of work. I told
him, 'No.' He said, 'I told you to jump the curb.' He took a newspaper
and hit the other agent, who was driving, on the head. He said, 'You're
both fired.'"

When they arrived at the White House, Taylor told Evelyn
Lincoln, Kennedy's secretary, "I've been fired."

Lincoln shook her head in exasperation. Taylor was not fired.

After becoming president on November 22, 1963, Johnson had
affairs with several of his young, fetching secretaries. When his wife,
Lady Bird Johnson, was away, the Secret Service would take him to the

home of one secretary. He would insist that the agents depart while he spent time with her.

"We took him to the house, and then he dismissed us," Taylor says.

At one point, Lady Bird Johnson—code-named Victoria—caught him having sex on a sofa in the Oval Office with one of his secretaries. Johnson became furious at the Secret Service for not warning him.

"He said, 'You should have done something,'" recalls a supervisory Secret Service agent.

After the incident, which occurred just months after he took office, Johnson ordered the Secret Service to install a buzzer system so that agents stationed in the residence part of the White House could warn him when his wife was approaching.

"The alarm system was put in because Lady Bird had caught him screwing a secretary in the Oval Office," a former Secret Service agent says. "He got so goddamned mad. A buzzer was put in from the quarters upstairs at the elevator to the Oval Office. If we saw Lady Bird heading for the elevator or stairs, we were to ring the bell."

Johnson did not limit himself to the women he hired for his personal staff. He had "a stable" of women with whom he had sex, including some who stayed at the ranch when Lady Bird was home, another former agent says.

"He and Lady Bird would be in their bedroom, and he'd get up in the middle of the night and go to the other room," the former agent says. "Lady Bird knew what he was doing. One woman was a well-endowed blonde. Another was the wife of a friend of his. He had permission from her husband to have sex with her. It was amazing."

"We had gals on my staff he screwed," says Bill Gulley, who headed Johnson's military office. "One . . . showed up [for work] when she wanted to show up. I couldn't tell her to do anything."

Johnson "would screw anything that would crawl, basically," says William F. Cuff, Gulley's executive assistant in the military office. "He was a horny old man. But he had a totally loyal White House staff. There was one common enemy everyone in the White House had, and that was him [Johnson]. Therefore, everyone got along fine because they were afraid of him."

Asked in a 1987 TV interview about her husband's rumored infidelities, Lady Bird Johnson said, "You have to understand, my husband loved people. All people. And half the people in the world were women."

Air Force One crew members say Johnson often closed the door to his stateroom and spent hours alone locked up with pretty secretaries, even when his wife was on board.

"Johnson would come on the plane [Air Force One], and the minute he got out of sight of the crowds, he would stand in the doorway and grin from ear to ear, and say, 'You dumb sons of bitches. I piss on all of you,'" recalls Robert M. MacMillan, an Air Force One steward. "Then he stepped out of sight and began taking off his clothes. By the time he was in the stateroom, he was down to his shorts and socks. It was not uncommon for him to peel off his shorts, regardless of who was in the stateroom."

Johnson did not care if women were around.

"He was totally naked with his daughters, Lady Bird, and female secretaries," MacMillan says. "He was quite well endowed in his testicles. So everyone started calling him bull nuts. He found out about it. He was really upset."

Johnson was often inebriated. He kept bottles of whiskey in his car at the ranch. One evening when Johnson was president, he came back to the White House drunk, screaming that the lights were on, wasting electricity.

"He is the only person [president] I have seen who was drunk," says Frederick H. Walzel, a former chief of the White House branch of the Secret Service Uniformed Division.

"He had episodes of getting drunk," George Reedy, his press secretary, told me. "There were times where he would drink day after day. You would think, 'This guy is an alcoholic.' Then all of a sudden, it would stop. We could always see the signs when he called for a Scotch and a soda, and he would belt it down and call for another one, instead of sipping it."

Johnson's drinking only fueled his outbursts.

"We were serving roast beef one time," says MacMillan. "He [Johnson] came back in the cabin. Jack Valenti [Johnson's aide] was sitting there. He had just gotten his dinner tray. On it was a beautiful slice of rare roast beef."

Johnson grabbed the tray and said, "You dumb son of a bitch. You are eating raw meat."

Johnson then brought the food back to the galley and said, "You two sons of bitches, look at this. This is raw. You gotta cook the meat on my airplane. Don't you serve my people raw meat. Goddamn, if you two boys serve raw meat on my airplane again, you'll both end up in Vietnam."

Johnson threw the tray upside down onto the floor and stormed off.

A few minutes later, Valenti went back to the galley.

"Sorry about your dinner, Mr. Valenti," MacMillan said.

"Do we have any more rare?" Valenti asked.

"We have plenty of rare," MacMillan said.

"Well, he won't be back. He's done his thing. Don't serve me any fully cooked meat."

Gerald F. Pisha, another Air Force One steward, says that on one occasion when Johnson didn't like the way a steward had mixed a drink for him, he threw it onto the floor.

"Get somebody who knows how to make a drink for me," Johnson said.

At his ranch in Texas, Johnson was even more raunchy than at the

White House. At a press conference at his ranch, Johnson "whips his thing out and takes a leak, facing them [the reporters] sideways," says D. Patrick O'Donnell, an Air Force One flight engineer. "You could see the stream. It was embarrassing. I couldn't believe it. Here was a man who is the president of the U.S., and he is taking a whiz out on the front lawn in front of a bunch of people."

A Secret Service agent posted to his ranch recalls that Johnson would take celebrities on a tour of the ranch in a car that—unknown to them—was amphibious. As he approached the Pedernales River, he would drive the vehicle into the river, terrifying his guests.

At six one morning, the agent was posted outside a door that led directly to Johnson's bedroom.

"I'm looking at the sun coming up and listening to the birds, and I hear this noise," the former agent says. "I turn around, and here's the most powerful man in the world taking a leak off the back porch. And I remembered a saying down in Texas that I heard when I first got on that detail: When LBJ goes to the ranch, the bulls hang their heads in shame. This guy had a tool you wouldn't believe."

The former agent was present when LBJ held a press conference with White House pool reporters as he sat on a toilet, moving his bowels. He had discarded his girdle, which he wore to hide his girth.

"I just couldn't believe that this stuff was going on," the former agent says. "But this was an everyday thing to the guys that were with him all the time."

After Robert F. Kennedy was assassinated, an agent was told to wake Johnson in the morning so he could meet with his press secretary.

"I tapped on his bedroom door," the former agent says. "Lady Bird said to come in."

"He's in the bathroom," she said.

"I tapped on the bathroom door," the former agent says. "Johnson was sitting on the can. Toilet paper was everywhere. It was bizarre."

"If Johnson weren't president, he'd be in an insane asylum," former agent Richard Roth says he thought to himself when he was occasionally on Johnson's detail.

Johnson kept dozens of peacocks at his ranch.

"One night at midnight, one of these peacocks was walking around," says David Curtis, who was temporarily assigned to Johnson's Secret Service detail at his ranch. "It was a moonlit night, and an agent picked up a rock just intending to scare the darn thing. He lobbed it over in the direction of the peacock and hit him right in the head. The peacock went down like a ton of bricks."

After an agent relieved him at his post, the agent told other agents, "Oh, my God, I've killed a peacock. What do you think we should do?"

"The consensus was, there were so damn many of them around, no one would miss one," Curtis says. "Just drag him down to the Pedernales River and throw him in. So that's what they did."

At the break of dawn, the day shift relieved the midnight people. One of the day shift agents called the command post on the radio.

"My God, you've got to get out here!" the agent said. "Looks like a drunken peacock. He's all wet. He's staggering from one foot to the other, feathers askew. He's walking back up toward the house."

Somehow, the peacock had recovered and managed to drag itself out of the river. Johnson never found out about the incident.

"Johnson was the grand thief," Gulley, his White House military aide, says. "He knew where the money was. He had us set up a fund code-named Green Ball. It was a Defense Department fund supposedly to assist the Secret Service to purchase weapons. They used it for whatever Johnson wanted to use it for. Fancy hunting guns were bought. Johnson and his friends kept them."

All the while, Johnson fostered the image of a penny-pincher who was saving taxpayer money. As part of an economy drive, Johnson announced he had ordered the lights turned off inside the ladies' room in the press area.

When Johnson left office, Gulley says he arranged for at least ten flights to fly government property to Johnson's ranch. O'Donnell, the Air Force One flight engineer, says he flew three of the missions, shipping what he understood were White House items back to the Johnson ranch.

"We flew White House furniture back," O'Donnell says. "I was on some of the missions. The flights back were at seven-fifty or eight-fifty P.M. and early in the morning. . . . I think he even took the electric bed out of Walter Reed army hospital. That was a disgrace."

Johnson's greatest achievement was overcoming Southern resistance to passage of civil rights legislation, yet in private, he regularly referred to blacks as "niggers."

After Johnson died, Secret Service agents guarding Lady Bird were amazed to find that even though their home was crammed with photos of Johnson with famous people, not one photo pictured him with JFK.

4

Threats

EVERY DAY, THE Secret Service receives an average of ten threats against any of its protectees, usually the president. Ironically, until after the Kennedy assassination, murdering the president was not a federal crime. Yet in 1917, Congress made "knowingly and willfully" threatening the president—as opposed to killing him—a federal violation. As later amended, the law carries a penalty of up to five years in prison and a fine of $250,000, or both. The same penalty applies to threatening the president-elect, the vice president, the vice-president-elect, or any officer next in the line of succession.

To ensure that an attack on a protectee—called an AOP—does not take place, the Secret Service uses a range of secret techniques, tools, strategies, and procedures. One of those tools is the extensive files the Secret Service Protective Intelligence and Assessment Division keeps on people who are potential threats to the president.

To most potential assassins, killing the president would be like hitting the jackpot.

"We want to know about those individuals," a former agent who worked intelligence says. "Sooner or later, they will direct their attention to the president if they can't get satisfaction with a senator or governor."

The Secret Service may detect threats anywhere, but those directed at the White House come in by email, regular mail, and telephone. Upon hearing a threatening call, White House operators are instructed to patch in a Secret Service agent at headquarters. Built in 1997, Secret Service headquarters is an anonymous nine-story tan brick building on H Street at Ninth Street NW in Washington. For security reasons, there are no trash cans in front of the building. An all-seeing security camera is attached below the overhang of the entrance.

Just inside is a single metal detector. On the wall in big silver letters are the words "Worthy of Trust and Confidence." No mention of the Secret Service, not even on the visitor's badge that the security officer issues. It is just when you get into the inner sanctum that you see a wall announcing the United States Secret Service Memorial Building, a reference to the thirty-five agents, officers, and other personnel who have died in the line of duty.

Inside, around a central atrium, catwalks link the rows of offices behind glass walls. For agents too pressed to wait for an elevator, open staircases within the atrium offer vertiginous looks down during the climb to another floor. The hallways are lined with candid photos of presidents being protected. A display commemorates those who have died in the line of duty, with spaces left for more.

An exhibit hall features first chief William P. Wood's 1865 letter of appointment from the solicitor of the treasury, a copy of Lee Harvey Oswald's gun, and examples of counterfeit bills alongside real bills.

The nerve center of the Secret Service is on the ninth floor. Here, in the Joint Operations Center, a handful of agents monitor the movements of protectees, whose code names and locations are displayed on light panels on the walls. When a protectee arrives at a new location, the agent who is assigned to intelligence and is traveling with him informs the Joint Operations Center. When protectees make unexpected trips, agents refer to the new assignment as a pop-up. Next to the Joint Ops Center, as agents refer to it, the Director's Crisis Center is used to direct operations in emergencies such as the 9/11 attack.

When a suspicious call comes in to the White House and an agent at headquarters listens in, the agent may pretend to be another operator helping out.

"He is waiting for the magic word [that signifies a threat to the president]," a Secret Service agent explains. "He is tracing it."

The Forensic Services Division matches a recording of the call with voices in a database of other threat calls. No threat is ignored. If it can locate the individual, the Secret Service interviews him and evaluates how serious a threat he may be. Agents try to differentiate between real threats and speech that is a legitimate exercise of First Amendment rights.

"If you don't like the policies of the president, you can say it. That's your right," a Secret Service agent assigned to the vice president's detail says. "We're looking for those that cross the line and are threatening: 'I'm going to get you. I'm going to kill you. You deserve to die. I know who can help kill you.' Then his name is entered into the computer system."

Arrests for such threats are routine. For example, the Secret Service arrested Barry Clinton Eckstrom, fifty-one, who lives in Upper St. Clair, Pennsylvania, after a Secret Service agent, alerted that the man was sending threatening emails, saw him type the following into an email he was sending from a Pittsburgh area public library: "I hate and despise the scum President Bush! I am going to kill him in June on his father's birthday." Eckstrom was sentenced to two years in prison and two years of supervised release.

If there is a problem at the White House, the Joint Ops Center can view the scene by remotely controlling surveillance cameras located outside and inside the complex. Any threatening letter or phone call to the White House is referred to the Secret Service. Most threats are in the form of letters addressed to the president, rather than emails or calls. Potential assassins get a great sense of satisfaction by mailing a letter. They think that if they mail it, the president will personally read it.

If a letter is anonymous, the Secret Service's Forensic Services Division checks for fingerprints and analyzes the handwriting and the ink, matching it against the ninety-five hundred samples of ink in what is called the International Ink Library. To make the job easier, most ink manufacturers now add tags so the Secret Service can trace the ink. The characteristics of each specimen are in a digital database. Technicians try to match the ink with other threatening letters in an effort to trace its origin. They may scan the letter for DNA.

The Secret Service's Protective Intelligence and Assessment Division categorizes individuals according to how serious a threat they may pose.

"There's a formula that we go by," says an agent. "It's based on whether this person had prior military training, firearms training; a prior history of mental illness; and how effective he would be in carrying out a plan. You have to judge these things based on your interview with the subject, and then evaluate the seriousness of the threat."

Class III threats are the most serious. Close to a hundred people are on the list. These individuals are constantly checked on. Courts have given the Secret Service wide latitude in dealing with immediate threats to the president.

"We will interview serious threats every three months and interview neighbors," an agent says. "If we feel he is really dangerous, we monitor his movements almost on a daily basis. We monitor the mail. If he is in an institution, we put in stops so we will be notified if he is released." If an individual is in an institution and has a home visit, "We are notified," the agent says. "I guarantee there will be a car in his neighborhood to make sure he shows up at his house."

"If a call comes here, if you get a piece of correspondence, any form of communication, even a veiled threat, we run everything to the ground until we are certain that we either have to discontinue the investigation or we have to keep monitoring a subject for a prolonged period of time," says Paula Reid, the special agent in charge of the Protective Intelligence and Assessment Division.

If the president is traveling to a city where a Class III threat not confined to an institution lives, the Secret Service will show up at his door at some point before the visit. Intelligence advance agents will ask if the individual plans to go out and, if so, his destination. They will then conduct surveillance of the house and follow him if he leaves.

Even if a Class III threat is locked up, an intelligence advance agent will visit him. Nothing is left to chance.

"If they aren't locked up, we go out and sit on them," former agent William Albracht says. "You usually have a rapport with these guys because you're interviewing them every quarter just to see how they're doing, what they're doing, if they are staying on their meds, or whatever. We knock on their door. We say, 'How're you doing, Freddy? President's coming to town; what are your plans?' What we always want to hear is, 'I'm going to stay away.'"

"Well, guess what," an agent will say. "We're going to be sitting on you, so keep that in mind. Don't even think about going to the event that the president will be at, because we're going to be on you like a hip pocket. Where you go, we go. We're going to be in constant contact with you and know where you are the entire time. Just be advised."

John W. Hinckley, Jr., is still considered a Class III threat. In March 1981, he was found not guilty by reason of insanity in the shootings of President Reagan, Reagan press secretary James Brady, Secret Service Agent Timothy McCarthy, and D.C. police officer

Thomas Delahanty. Since then, he has been confined to St. Elizabeth's Hospital in Washington. But Hinckley is periodically allowed to leave the psychiatric hospital to visit his mother in Williamsburg, Virginia. If he visits Washington, his family notifies the Secret Service, and agents may conduct surveillance of him.

In contrast to a Class III threat, a Class II individual has made a threat but does not appear to have the ability to carry it out.

"He may be missing an element, like a guy who honestly thinks he can kill a president and has made the threat, but he's a quadriplegic or can't formulate a plan well enough to carry it out," says an agent.

Class II threats usually include people who are confined to a prison or mental hospital. According to a virulent rumor in state prisons, if a prisoner threatens the president and is convicted of the federal crime, he will be moved to a federal prison, where conditions are generally more favorable than in state prisons. For that reason, the Secret Service often encounters threats from prisoners. For example, in November 2008, Gordon L. Chadwick, age twenty-seven, threatened to kill President George W. Bush while serving a four-year state prison term in Houston for threatening a jail official. As happened in Chadwick's case, a federal prison term for threatening the president is tacked on to the state prison term.

After another state prisoner wrote a threatening letter to Bush, an agent arranged to meet with him. After driving three hours to the prison, the agent asked him if he knew why the agent was there.

"Yep. When do I go to federal prison?" the man said.

The prisoner added that he hoped to "see the country" and, since he was serving a life term, this would be his best opportunity. When the agent explained that he would be serving his state term first, the man said he had heard that threatening the president was the way to be transferred to a federal prison.

"I could have strangled him," the agent says.

A Class I individual—the least serious threat—may have blurted out at a bar that he wants to kill the president.

"You interview him, and he has absolutely no intention of carrying this threat out," an agent says. "Agents will assess him and conclude, 'Yeah, he said something stupid; yeah, he committed a federal crime. But we're not going to charge him or pursue that guy.' You just have to use your discretion and your best judgment."

In most cases, a visit from Secret Service agents is enough to make anyone think twice about carrying out a plot. When Pope John Paul II visited Saint Louis in January 1999, the Secret Service, which was protecting him, received a report about a man seen driving a camper in the city. On the sides of the camper were inscriptions such as "The Pope Should Die" and "The Pope Is the Devil."

Through the reported license plate number, the Secret Service tracked the man to an address, which turned out to be his mother's home not far from Saint Louis. When interviewed by Secret Service agents, the man's mother said her son was driving to the mountains in western Montana near Kalispell to see his brother.

Norm Jarvis, the resident agent in charge, drove to the Kalispell area where the brother was supposed to be living. The forested area is vast. Like many who live in the area, the brother did not have an address. Jarvis hoped local law enforcement would know where he could start looking.

"I was driving down the road, and lo and behold, coming the other way down the street, is this camper," Jarvis says. "The Pope Should Die" and "The Pope Is the Devil" were written on the sides of the vehicle. The man driving the camper fit the description of the suspect. Jarvis could not believe his luck.

"I spun my car around and turned on my lights and siren," Jarvis says. "I got up alongside him and waved him over."

With the man's wife sitting beside him, Jarvis interviewed the man, who said he had been in mental institutions and was off his medication. The man had no firearms, and Jarvis decided he was not capable of harming the Pope. Thus, he was a Class II threat. Jarvis took his fingerprints and photographed him. He warned him to stay away from Saint Louis during the Pope's visit, and he suggested the man get some help.

Jarvis called headquarters to report his contact with the suspect and the results of his initial findings. Within a few days, he finished writing a report and called the duty desk to say he was going to be sending it.

"They told me the guy had killed himself with his brother's pistol," Jarvis says. "His brother reported that he was so shook up after talking to me that he decided to end his life. He felt that he couldn't escape the devil; the devil was going to find him. And then he shot himself."

5

Searchlight

IF LYNDON JOHNSON was out of control, the Secret
Service found Richard Nixon and his family to be the strangest
protectees. Like Johnson, Nixon—code-named Searchlight—did
not sleep in the same bedroom with his wife. But unlike Johnson, who
consulted Lady Bird on issues he faced, Nixon seemed to have no relationship with his wife, Pat.

"He [Nixon] never held hands with his wife," a Secret Service agent
says.

An agent remembers accompanying Nixon, Pat, and their two
daughters during a nine-hole golf game near their home at San
Clemente, California. During the hour and a half, "He never said a
word," the former agent says. "Nixon could not make conversation
unless it was to discuss an issue. . . . Nixon was always calculating, seeing what effect it would have."

Unknown to the public, Pat Nixon—code-named Starlight—was
an alcoholic who tippled martinis. By the time Nixon left the White
House to live at San Clemente, Pat "was in a pretty good stupor much
of the time," an agent on Nixon's detail says. "She had trouble remembering things."

"One day out in San Clemente when I was out there, a friend of mine was on post, and he hears this rustling in the bushes," says another agent who was on Nixon's detail. "You had a lot of immigrants coming up on the beach, trying to get to the promised land. You never knew if anybody's going to be coming around the compound."

At that point, the other agent "cranks one in the shotgun. He goes over to where the rustling is, and it's Pat," the former agent says. "She's on her hands and knees. She's trying to find the house."

Pat, he says, "had a tough life. Nixon would hardly talk. The only time he enjoyed himself was when he was with his friends Bebe Rebozo and Bob Abplanalp, when they would drink together."

Nixon often spent time with Abplanalp on his friend's island, Grand Cay in the Bahamas.

"Just to give you an idea of his athletic prowess, or lack of it, he loved to fish," a former agent says. "He'd be on the back of Abplanalp's fifty-five-foot yacht, and he would sit in this swivel seat with his fishing pole. Abplanalp's staff would hook Nixon's hook and throw the hook out. And Nixon would be just sitting there, with both hands on the pole, and he'd catch something, and the staff would reel it in for him, take the fish off, put it in the bucket. Nixon wouldn't do anything but watch."

During Watergate, "Nixon was very depressed," says another former agent. "He wasn't functioning as president any longer. [Bob] Haldeman [Nixon's chief of staff] ran the country."

Milton Pitts, who ran several barbershops in Washington, would go to a tiny barbershop in the basement of the West Wing to cut Nixon's hair.

"Nixon talked very little," Pitts told me. "He wanted to know what the public was saying. We had a TV there. But he never watched TV. All the other presidents did."

During Watergate, Nixon would ask Pitts, "Well, what are they saying about us today?"

Pitts would say he hadn't heard much news that day.

"I didn't want to get into what people were saying," Pitts said. "I'm not going to give him anything unpleasant. He was my boss."

One afternoon, Alexander Butterfield, who would later reveal the existence of the Nixon tapes, came in for a haircut just before Nixon did. Motioning to the television set, Butterfield said to Pitts, "Leave that on. I want him [Nixon] to see what they are doing to us."

But as soon as Nixon walked into the barbershop, "He pushed the button, and the TV went off," Pitts says. "He said, 'Well, what are they saying about us today?' I said, 'Mr. President, I haven't heard much news today, sir.'"

As the Watergate scandal progressed, "Nixon got very paranoid," a Secret Service agent says. "He didn't know what to believe or whom to trust. He did think people were lying to him. He thought at the end everyone was lying."

While Nixon rarely drank before the Watergate scandal, he began drinking more heavily as the pressure took its toll. He would down a martini or a manhattan.

"All he could handle was one or two," a Secret Service agent says. "He wouldn't be flying high, but you could tell he wasn't in total control of himself. He would loosen up, start talking more, and smile. It was completely out of character. But he had two, and that was that. He had them every other night. But always at the end of business and in the residence. You never saw him drunk in public."

In contrast to the blustering in his taped conversations, Nixon in private seemed passive and often out of it, although he did have a sense of humor. After spending a weekend at Camp David, Nixon stepped out of his cabin with Pat to get into a Secret Service limousine that would take them to Marine One, the president's helicopter.

"Secret Service agents were at the ready to move," says one of Nixon's agents. "The agent who was driving was checking everything out, making sure the heater was properly adjusted. Nixon paused to talk to Pat. The driver accidentally honked his horn, and Nixon, thinking he was being impatient, said, 'I'll be right there.'"

At his San Clemente home, Nixon was watching television one afternoon while feeding dog biscuits to one of his dogs.

"Nixon took a dog biscuit and was looking at it and then takes a bite out of it," says Richard Repasky, who was on his detail.

Nixon would walk on the beach wearing a suit—all his suits were navy blue—and dress shoes. Even in summer, he would insist on having a fire burning in the fireplace. One evening, Nixon built a fire in the fireplace at San Clemente and forgot to open the flue damper.

"The smoke backed up in the house, and two agents came running," says a former agent who was on the Nixon detail.

"Can you find him?" one of the agents asked the other.

"No, I can't find the son of a bitch," the other agent said.

From the bedroom, a voice piped up.

"Son of a bitch is here trying to find a matching pair of socks," Nixon said, poking fun at himself.

One agent will never forget a reunion for Vietnam prisoners of war held outside Nixon's San Clemente home.

"This POW did a series of paintings of Hanoi camp scenes," the former agent says. "He was quite good. He presented Nixon with a big painting of POWs. Later that evening, after everyone had left, Nixon was going back to his home. It was a warm night. His assistant turned to Nixon and said, 'What do you want me to do with the picture? Should I bring it in the house?'"

"Put that goddamned thing in the garage," Nixon said. "I don't want to see that."

The former agent says he shook his head and thought, "You smiled and shook hands with these guys, and you couldn't care less. It was all show."

"Monday through Friday, Nixon would leave his home at twelve-fifty-five P.M. to play golf," Dale Wunderlich, a former agent on his detail, says. "He would insist on golfing even in pouring rain."

Occasionally, Nixon's son-in-law David Eisenhower, grandson of former president Dwight Eisenhower, went with him. Agents considered the younger Eisenhower the most clueless person they had ever protected. One day, the Nixons gave him a barbecue grill as a Christmas present. With the Nixons inside his house, Eisenhower tried to start the grill to char some steaks. After a short time, he told Wunderlich it would not light.

"He had poured most of a bag of briquets into the pit of the grill and lit matches on top of them, but he had not used fire starter," Wunderlich says.

"Do you know anything about garage door openers?" Eisenhower asked another Secret Service agent. "I need a little help. I've had it two years, and I don't get a light. Shouldn't the light come on?"

"Maybe the lightbulb is burnt out," the agent said.

"Really?" David said.

The agent looked up. There was no bulb in the socket.

"We did a loose surveillance, or tail, on David Eisenhower when there were a lot of threats on the president, and he was going to George Washington University Law School in Washington," a former agent says. "He was in a red Pinto. He comes out of classes and goes to a Safeway in Georgetown. He parks and buys some groceries. A woman parks in a red Pinto nearby. He comes out in forty-five minutes and puts the groceries in the other Pinto. He spent a minute and a half to two minutes trying to start it. Meanwhile, she comes out, screams, and says, 'What are you doing in my car?'"

"This is my car," he insisted. "I just can't get it started right now."

The woman threatened to call the police. He finally got out, and she drove off.

"He was still dumbfounded," the former agent says. "He looked at us. We pointed at his car. He got in and drove off like nothing had happened."

Subsequently, Eisenhower bought a new Oldsmobile and planned to drive it from California to Pennsylvania to see his grandmother Mamie Eisenhower, who was code-named Springtime. In Phoenix, the car gave out. Eisenhower called a local dealership, which said it would fix the car the next morning. After staying overnight in a motel, Eisenhower went to the dealership where the car had been towed. The dealership told him the problem had been fixed: The car had run out of gas and needed a fill-up.

Near the end of Nixon's presidency, his vice president Spiro Agnew was charged with accepting one hundred thousand dollars in cash bribes. Agnew had taken the payoffs when he was a Maryland state official and later when he was vice president. Agnew pleaded nolo contendere and agreed to resign, leaving office on October 10, 1973.

What never came out was that the married Agnew, a champion of family values who made no secret of his disdain for the liberal press, was having affairs while in office. One morning in late 1969, Agnew asked his Secret Service detail of five agents to take him to what is now Washington's elegant St. Regis hotel at 923 Sixteenth Street NW.

"We took him in the back door and brought him to a room on the fourth floor," says one of the agents. "He asked us to leave him alone for three hours. The detail leader understood he was having an affair with a woman."

The agents waited in Lafayette Park, two blocks from the hotel and across the street from the entrance to the White House. They then returned to the hotel to pick up the vice president.

"He looked embarrassed," the former agent says. "Leaving him in an unsecured location was a breach of security. As agents, it was embarrassing because we were facilitating his adultery. We felt like pimps. We couldn't look her [his wife] in the eye after that."

In addition to that incident, Agnew was having an affair with a dark-haired, well-endowed female member of his staff. Agnew would not stay in hotels overnight unless the Secret Service arranged for her to be given an adjoining room, a former agent says. The woman was the age of one of Agnew's daughters.

Ironically, Agnew—who had a good relationship with his agents—expressed concern to them early on about whether they would be telling stories about him to others. In fact, while agents love to exchange stories about protectees among themselves, as a rule, Secret Service agents are more tight-lipped with outsiders than CIA officers or FBI agents. The reason the Secret Service insists that agents not reveal information about personal lives of protectees is that those under protection may not let agents close if they think their privacy will be violated.

While that is a legitimate concern, those who run for high office should expect a high degree of scrutiny and to be held accountable for personal indiscretions that conflict with their public image and that shed light on their character. Rather than expecting the Secret Service to cover up for them, they should not enter public life if they want to lead double lives. That is particularly true when one considers that a president or vice president having an affair opens himself to possible blackmail. If a lower-level federal employee was having an affair, he would be denied a security clearance.

"If you want the job, then you need to lead the kind of life and be the kind of person that can stand up to the scrutiny that comes with that job," says former Secret Service agent Clark Larsen.

"You just shake your head when you think of all the things you've heard and seen and the faith that people have in these celebrity-type people," a former Secret Service agent says. "They are probably worse than most average individuals." He adds, "Americans have such an idealized notion of the presidency and the virtues that go with it, honesty and so forth. In most cases, that's the furthest thing from the truth. . . . If we would pay attention to their track records, it's all there. We seem to put blinders on ourselves and overlook these frailties."

The poor personal character of presidents like Nixon and Johnson translated into the kind of flawed judgment that led to the Watergate scandal and the continuing fruitless prosecution of the Vietnam War when American security interests were not at stake. Voters tend to forget that presidents are, first and foremost, people. If they are unbalanced, nasty, and hypocritical, that will be reflected in their judgment and job performance.

If a friend, an electrician, a plumber, or a job applicant had a track record of acting unethically, lying, or displaying the kind of unbalanced personality of a Johnson or a Nixon, few would want to deal with him. Yet in the case of presidents and other politicians, voters often overlook the signs of poor character and focus instead on their acting ability on TV.

No one can imagine the kind of pressure that being president of the United States imposes on an individual and how easily power corrupts. To be in command of the most powerful country on earth, to be able to fly anywhere at a moment's notice on Air Force One, to be able to grant almost any wish, to take action that affects the lives of millions, is such a heady, intoxicating experience that only people with the most stable personalities and well-developed values can handle it. Simply inviting a friend to a White House party or having a secretary place a call and announce that "the White House is calling" has such a profound effect on people that presidents and White House aides must constantly remind themselves that they are mortal.

Of all the perks, none is more seductive than living in the one-hundred-thirty-two-room White House. Servants are always on call to take care of the slightest whim. Laundry, cleaning, and shopping are provided for. From three kitchens, White House chefs prepare meals that are exquisitely presented and of the quality of the finest restaurants.

If members of the first family want breakfast in bed every day—as Lyndon Johnson did—they can have it. A pastry chef makes everything from Christmas cookies to chocolate éclairs. If the first family wants, it can entertain every night. Invitations—hand-lettered by five calligraphers—are rarely turned down. In choosing what chinaware to eat from, the first family has its choice of nineteen-piece place settings ordered by other first families. They may choose, for example, the Reagans' pattern of a gold band around a red border, or the Johnsons' pattern, which features delicate wildflowers and the presidential seal.

Fresh flowers decorate every room, and lovely landscaping—including the Rose Garden and the Jacqueline Kennedy Garden—adorns the grounds.

"The White House is a character crucible," says Bertram S. Brown, M.D., a psychiatrist who formerly headed the National Institute of Mental Health and was an aide to President John F. Kennedy. "It either creates or distorts character. Few decent people want to subject themselves to the kind of grueling abuse candidates take when they run in the first place," says Dr. Brown, who has seen in his practice many top Washington politicians and White House aides. "Many of those who run crave superficial celebrity. They are hollow people who have no principles and simply want to be elected. Even if an individual is balanced, once someone becomes president, how does one solve the conundrum of staying real and somewhat humble when one is surrounded by the most powerful office in the land, and from becoming overwhelmed by an at times pathological environment that treats you every day as an emperor? Here is where the true strength of the character of the person, not his past accomplishments, will determine whether his presidency ends in accomplishment or failure."

Thus, unless a president comes to the office with good character, the crushing force of the office and the adulation the chief executive receives will inevitably lead to disaster. For those reasons, the electorate has a right to know about the true character of its leaders.

6

Daro

ALMOST DAILY, SOMEONE comes to the White House gates and demands to see the president or causes a disturbance requiring the Secret Service's Uniformed Division to intervene. Each year, twenty-five to thirty people try to ram the White House gates in cars, scale the eight-foot-high reinforced steel fence, shoot their way in, set themselves on fire at the gates, or cause other disruptions. Most of the people who cause disturbances around the White House are mentally ill.

"For the same reason that people stalk the president, the White House is a magnet for the psychotic," says former agent Pete Dowling. "The president is an authority figure, and many people who have psychoses or have paranoid schizophrenia think that the government is transmitting rays at them or interrupting their thought processes. And what is the ultimate symbol of the government? It's the White House. So, many of these people come to the gate at the White House and say they want to have an appointment to see the president or they want to see the president."

"The White House is a mecca for what we call M.O.s—mental observation nuts," says a former Uniformed Division officer. "Sometimes almost every day there was what we call a White House collar. You'd have people that show up and say, 'Listen, I demand to talk to the president now. My son's in Iraq, and it's his fault.'"

Unlike Secret Service agents, uniformed officers are required to have only high school diplomas. Nor do they have the background and training of Secret Service agents. To apply, they must be U.S. citizens. At the time of their appointment, they must be at least twenty-one years of age and younger than forty. They also must have excellent health, be in excellent physical condition, and have uncorrected vision no worse than 20/60. Besides a background check, they are given drug and polygraph tests before being hired. In addition to their White House duties, the Uniformed Division protects foreign embassies.

In protecting the White House and providing security at events, the Uniformed Division employs canine units. Mainly Belgian Malinois, most of the dogs are cross-trained to sniff out explosives and to attack an intruder. Much like German shepherds in appearance, the breed is believed to be higher energy and more agile. The dogs are prey driven, and ball play is their reward after they locate their "prey." The Secret Service pays forty-five hundred dollars for each trained canine unit. In all, the agency has seventy-five of them.

While waiting to check cleared vehicles that arrive at the White House's southwest gate, the dogs stand on a white concrete pad that is refrigerated in summer so their paws don't get hot. Each dog eagerly checks about a hundred cars a day.

Demonstrating how a canine unit operates, a technician in the underground garage at Secret Service headquarters proudly introduces Daro, a brawny eighty-seven-pound Czech shepherd. The dog is presented with a real-world scenario: Hidden from view, a metal canister holding real dynamite has been planted behind a dryer, which is used in laundering the rags that polish the president's limos. Because the dynamite is not connected to a blasting cap or fuse, it is considered safe to bring it into headquarters.

Daro races around the parked cars, sniffing. Then he walks up to the dryer, stops, and sits. At this point, some explosives-sniffing dogs are trained to bark, but Daro sits down, as he has been trained to do. After his success, his reward is not the usual doggie treat but a hard red rubber ball, which he ravages, chewing off bits of red rubber.

The dogs are certified once a month. For new recruits, there's a seventeen-week canine school at the Secret Service training facility in Laurel, Maryland, where the dogs are paired up with their handlers. The dogs come with a lot of training already, but the Secret Service gives them more—in explosives detection and in emergency response to incidents such as a fence jumper at the White House.

"You know right away if there's a fence jumper," a Secret Service agent says. "There are electronic eyes and ground sensors six feet back [from the sidewalk] that are monitored twenty-four hours a day. They sense movement and weight. Infrared detectors are installed closer to the house. You have audio detectors. Every angle is covered by cameras and recorded."

Uniformed Division officers and the Uniformed Division's Emergency Response Team, armed with P90 submachine guns, are the first line of defense.

"If somebody jumps that fence, ERT is going to get them right away, either with a dog or just themselves," an agent says. "They'll give the dog a command, and that dog will knock over a two-hundred-fifty-pound man. It will hit him dead center and take him down. The countersniper guys within the Uniformed Division are always watching their backs."

A suspect who is armed and has jumped the fence may get a warning to drop the weapon. If he does not immediately obey the command, the Secret Service is under orders to take the person out quickly rather than risk any kind of hostage-taking situation.

As part of their work in developing criminal profiling, FBI agents under the direction of Dr. Roger Depue interviewed assassins and would-be assassins in prison, including Sirhan B. Sirhan, who killed Bobby Kennedy, and Sara Jane Moore and Lynette "Squeaky" Fromme, both of whom tried to kill President Ford.

The FBI profilers found that in recent years, assassins generally have been unstable individuals looking for attention and notoriety. In many cases, assassins keep diaries as a way of enhancing the importance of their acts. Like most celebrity stalkers, assassins tend to be paranoid and lack trust in other people.

"Usually loners, they are not relaxed in the presence of others and not practiced or skilled in social interaction," John Douglas, one of the profilers who did the interviews, wrote in his book *Obsession*. Often detailing their thoughts and fantasies in a diary, assassins "keep a running dialogue with themselves," Douglas said. Before an assassination attempt, the perpetrator fantasizes that "this one big event will prove once and for all that he has worth, that he can do and be something. It provides an identity and purpose," Douglas said. As a result, assassins rarely have an escape plan. Often, they want to be arrested.

When interviewed in prison, Sirhan told profiler Robert Ressler that he had heard voices telling him to assassinate Senator Kennedy. Once, when looking in a mirror, he said he felt his face cracking and falling in pieces to the floor. Both are manifestations of paranoid schizophrenia, Ressler wrote in his book *Whoever Fights Monsters*.

Sirhan would refer to himself in the third person. An Arab born in Jerusalem of Christian parents, Sirhan asked Ressler if FBI official Mark Felt—later identified as Deep Throat—was a Jew. He said he had heard that Kennedy supported the sale of more fighter jets to

Israel. By assassinating him, he believed he would snuff out a potential president who would be a friend of Israel, Sirhan told Ressler.

When John Hinckley tried to assassinate President Reagan, the FBI's Washington field office called on the FBI profilers for help. While the Secret Service is in charge of protecting the president, the FBI is in charge of investigating assassinations and assassination attempts.

Douglas and Ressler had identified typical characteristics of the assassin. Based on that research, Ressler told the FBI that Hinckley would have had a fantasy about being an important assassin and would have photographs of himself for the history books, records of his activities kept in a journal or a scrapbook, materials about assassinations, and audio tapes of his exploits. The agents were able to use the tips in drawing up search warrants for Hinckley's home. They found all of the items Ressler had described.

Sometimes if would-be assassins decide security at the White House looks too tight, they try the Capitol instead. That was the path taken by Russell E. Weston, who shot up the Capitol on July 24, 1998. Weston walked into the Capitol through a doorway on the east side and shot and killed Capitol Police Officer Jacob J. Chestnut, who manned a security post there. Then Weston burst through a side door leading into the offices of Republican Representative Tom DeLay of Texas, the majority whip. Weston then shot Capitol Police Detective John M. Gibson, who returned fire and wounded the assailant.

The two Capitol Police officers died. Republican Senator Bill Frist of Tennessee, a medical doctor, raced across the Capitol and helped save Weston's life.

Weeks earlier, Weston had called the Secret Service in Montana, where he lived. He spoke with agent Norm Jarvis, claiming he was John F. Kennedy's illegitimate son and was entitled to share in the Kennedy family trusts. Jarvis let him ramble on.

"I asked if he was being threatened by anybody in the government," Jarvis recalls. "Did he have any feelings towards the president? What was getting him upset at this time? Because psychotics have these episodes. Suddenly something sparks them, and they get wound up."

Weston did not express any anger toward the president, who at the time was Bill Clinton. But years earlier, he had penned a non-threatening but disturbing letter to the president, and as a result, Jarvis's predecessor in Montana interviewed him. While that agent, Leroy Scott, concluded then that Weston did not represent a threat to the president, he established a relationship with the man, as good agents do.

"Weston would call and speak to Leroy now and then whenever he was upset about something," Jarvis says. "He was an on-call counselor, if you will. We acquire pet psychos along the way during a career. You'd get a call from another agent from somewhere in the country once in a while looking for background information. It was not uncommon for repeat psych cases to carry an agent's business card with them. They would usually produce those cards at some point during an interview if they had a repeat episode."

After the shooting at the Capitol, Secret Service agents discovered a tape Weston had made of his conversation with Jarvis, and the agent eerily got to review his own performance. In retrospect, he wouldn't have done anything differently. After the shooting, Weston was committed to a federal mental health facility near Raleigh, North Carolina.

If an individual causes a disruption at the White House, Secret Service agents detain the person and interview him at the field office at Thirteenth and L Streets NW in Washington or at a Metropolitan Police station. Agents would never bring them anywhere near the White House. Yet in his book, *The Way of the World: A Story of Truth and Hope in an Age of Extremism,* Ron Suskind relates a story about Usman Khosa, a Pakistani national who graduated from Connecticut College.

As Suskind tells it, on July 27, 2006, Khosa was leisurely strolling by the White House as he was "fiddling" with his iPod, which was playing tunes in Arabic. Suddenly, Khosa found himself confronted by a "large uniformed officer" who lunged at him.

"The backpack!" the officer yelled as he pushed Khosa against the gates in front of the nearby treasury building and ripped off the man's backpack. Other Secret Service uniformed officers swarmed him. "Another officer on a bicycle arrives from somewhere and tears the backpack open, dumping its contents on the sidewalk," Suskind writes breathlessly in his first chapter.

The Secret Service then allegedly escorted Khosa, who now works for the International Monetary Fund, through one of the perimeter gates and onto the grounds of the White House.

"No one speaks as the agents walk him behind the gate's security station, down a stairwell, along an underground passage, and into a room—cement-walled box with a table, two chairs, a hanging light with a bare bulb, and a mounted video camera," Suskind writes. "Even after all the astonishing turns of the past hour, Khosa can't quite believe there's actually an interrogation room beneath the White House, dark and dank and horrific."

There, the frightened Khosa is asked if he is in league with "Mr. Zawahiri and his types," referring to Ayman al-Zawahiri, Osama bin Laden's deputy. Meanwhile, Suskind claims, President George W. Bush is receiving an intelligence briefing one floor above.

It was, Suskind said in interviews, a "day literally in hell," but Khosa apparently never noted the names of the officers, which were displayed on tags pinned to their shirts.

As anyone familiar with security and law enforcement knows, if a person is acting suspiciously in front of the White House, the last place the Secret Service would want to take him is inside the tightly guarded White House grounds. Such individuals may have explosive devices strapped to their bodies. Even if they were thoroughly searched, they could have deadly pathogens in their clothing. If Khosa's tale was not implausible enough, Suskind claims that Khosa agreed to go with the Secret Service officers initially only if he could make a few calls.

"Then, I promise, I'll go with you," Suskind quotes him as saying.

Khosa then called the Pakistani embassy and friends and family, according to Suskind. No doubt the Secret Service trusted Khosa not to call possible co-conspirators or remotely controlled bombs to detonate them.

Rather than being "dark and dank" and illuminated with a bare lightbulb, the room under the Oval Office—W-16—is brightly lit with fluorescent lights. It's where Secret Service agents spend their downtime. Agents use computers in the room to fill out reports. In the room, they also store formal wear they may need for an event that evening. So they can check their appearance, the room is outfitted with full-length mirrors.

Khosa declined to comment. Suskind told me that in researching the book, he spoke with a Secret Service spokeswoman, who searched records but found nothing on Khosa. Suskind quoted her as saying it is not uncommon if the individual was "in and out that we don't find a permanent record."

As for the question of whether the Secret Service would ever take a suspicious person into the White House, Suskind told me, "It seems like that was just a matter of convenience. It was a block from where they were questioning him for a half hour on the street." What about explosives and pathogens? "They patted him down," Suskind said.

When asked why he did not include in the book the fact that the Secret Service has no record of questioning and detaining Khosa, Suskind said he did not consider it "pertinent."

Asked for comment on Suskind's account, Edwin Donovan, assistant special agent in charge of government and public affairs at the Secret Service, told me, "We have no record of the incident or the individual referenced [Khosa]." He added, "Bringing an individual inside the White House for questioning defies standard security and protocols and safety procedures. We would not bring a 'suspicious person,' potential prisoner, prisoner, or any person who has not been properly vetted, onto the White House grounds."

7

Passkey

IN CONTRAST TO Richard Nixon, Secret Service agents found Gerald Ford—code-named Passkey—to be a decent man who valued their service. But agents were amazed at how cheap Ford was. After he left the White House, "He would want his newspaper in the morning at hotels, and he'd walk to the counter," says an agent on his detail. "Lo and behold, he would not have any money on him. If his staff wasn't with him, he would ask agents for money."

The agent remembers Ford checking in at the chic Pierre hotel in New York. A bellboy loaded his cart with the Fords' bags and took them into their room.

"After the bellboy was through, he came out holding this one-dollar bill in front of him, swearing in Spanish," the former agent says.

At Rancho Mirage, where Ford lived after leaving the White House, "You'd go to a golf course, and it's an exclusive country club, and the normal tip for a caddy is twenty-five dollars to fifty dollars," another agent says. "Ford tipped a dollar, if at all."

On September 5, 1975, Lynette "Squeaky" Fromme, twenty-six, drew a Colt .45 automatic pistol and squeezed the trigger as President

Ford shook hands with a smiling crowd outside the Senator Hotel in Sacramento, California. Bystanders said Ford was shaking hands with everyone and smiling when suddenly he turned ashen and froze as he saw a gun being raised only a few feet away.

"I saw a hand coming up behind several others in the front row, and obviously there was a pistol in that hand," Ford said later.

Secret Service Agent Larry Buendorf had already noticed the woman moving along with the president. As Fromme pulled the trigger, Buendorf jumped in front of Ford to shield him. He then grabbed the gun and wrestled her to the ground. It was later determined that she had cocked the hammer of the gun. Fortunately, there was no bullet in the firing chamber. There were four in the gun's magazine. Fromme later claimed she had deliberately ejected the cartridge from the weapon's chamber, and she showed agents the cartridge at her home.

Fromme was a disciple of Charles M. Manson, who had been convicted of the ritualistic murders of actress Sharon Tate and six others. Two months before the assassination attempt, Fromme had issued a statement saying she had received letters from Manson blaming Nixon for his imprisonment.

Just seventeen days after this incident, Ford was leaving the St. Francis Hotel in San Francisco when Sara Jane Moore, a forty-five-year-old political activist, fired a .38 revolver at him from forty feet away. At the report of the shot, Ford looked stunned. Color drained from his face, and his knees appeared to buckle.

Oliver Sipple, a disabled former U.S. Marine and Vietnam veteran, was standing next to the assailant. He pushed up her arm as the gun discharged. Although Ford doubled over, the bullet flew several feet over the president's head. It ricocheted off the side of the hotel and slightly wounded a cab driver in the crowd.

Secret Service agents Ron Pontius and Jack Merchant quickly pushed Moore to the sidewalk and arrested her. As bystanders screamed, the agents pushed the uninjured Ford into his limousine and onto the floor, covering his body with theirs.

For more than three hours, Moore had waited for Ford outside the hotel. Wearing baggy pants and a blue raincoat, she had stood with her hands in her pockets the entire time. Agents will sometimes ask people to remove their hands from their pockets, but this time, as people milled around her, agents did not notice her.

Moore is the only presidential assailant who was listed as a possible threat in the Secret Service data bank before the assassination attempt. Two days before the attempt, Moore had called the San Francisco police and said she had a gun and was considering a "test" of the presidential security system. The next morning, police interviewed her and confiscated her gun.

The police reported her to the Secret Service, and the night before Ford's visit, Secret Service agents interviewed her. They concluded she did not pose a threat that would justify surveillance during Ford's visit. By definition, evaluating anyone's intentions is an inexact science. Indeed, the next morning, she purchased another weapon.

Agents ask themselves, "Did that interview trigger it?" a Secret Service agent says. "By giving them a feeling of importance, we may prompt them to think, 'I better follow through.' The rational person would say, 'Holy s—. I almost got arrested.'"

The following month, another incident convinced Ford he was jinxed. His motorcade was returning to the airport on October 14, 1975, after he gave a speech at a GOP fund-raiser in Hartford, Connecticut. Motorcycle policemen were supposed to block side streets, the teams leapfrogging each other from block to block. By the time the motorcade passed a narrow street, the police officers had left. James Salamites, nineteen, barreled through the intersection on a green light in a Buick sedan and crashed into the president's limousine.

Andrew Hutch, the Secret Service driver, swerved sharply left. The maneuver blunted the impact of the collision, but Ford was still knocked to the floor. When Ford's car halted with a dented right front fender, Secret Service agents with guns drawn surrounded the Buick and hauled out its shaken driver.

"I looked at the other car, and looking at me is President Ford. I recognized him right away. I just couldn't believe it," Salamites recalls.

At first, agents were sure the crash was an attempt on Ford's life. But after Salamites was questioned for a few hours, he was released, and Hartford police said he was not to blame for the accident.

The press portrayed Ford as a dullard and a klutz, but agents say he was neither. A University of Michigan football player who was voted most valuable player, Ford was an expert skier who taunted agents who could not keep up with him. Finally, the Secret Service assigned a world-class skier to his detail. The agent would ski backward and wave as the president tried to catch up with him.

"Ford was a very athletic guy," says Dennis Chomicki, who was on his detail. "He used to swim every day, he was a good golfer, and he was an outstanding skier."

But one day after he left office, Ford was driving an electric golf cart in Palm Springs, California, when he accidentally crashed into an electric panel hanging on the wall of a shack for golf carts.

"The whole panel came off its fasteners and fell down on top of the carts," Chomicki says. "He was mad as hell, and he looked at me and said, 'You know, after all those years, they were all right. All the reporters used to say I was awkward. Well, they're right. I'm just one big clumsy sonofabitch.' And he walked away."

Unlike many other presidents, Ford never engaged in any dalliances. Until *The Miami Herald* revealed Gary Hart's fling with Donna Rice in May 1987, the media had not exposed extramarital affairs of presidents and presidential candidates. Indeed, throughout American history, the press had been aware of presidential affairs and covered up for occupants of the White House. Yet the hypocrisy and lack of judgment exhibited by a politician engaging in extramarital relations is a clue to character that the electorate needs to consider.

Ironically, the press's record was broken only because *The Miami Herald*'s political editor Tom Fiedler wrote a column defending Hart, the Democratic Party's leading contender, against unsubstantiated rumors of being a womanizer. A woman who refused to identify herself called Fiedler to say she disagreed with his column. In fact, she said a friend of hers who was a part-time model in Miami was flying to Washington that Friday evening to spend the weekend with Hart. The caller described the woman as quite attractive and blond.

Fiedler, reporter Jim McGee, and investigations editor Jim Savage looked at airline schedules and picked out the most likely nonstop flight to Washington that Friday evening, May 1. McGee took the flight and spotted several women who matched the description. One was carrying a distinctive shiny purse. When they touched down in Washington, she disappeared into the crowd.

After taking a cab to Hart's townhouse, McGee saw the same young woman with the shiny purse walking arm in arm with Hart out the front door of his Washington home. Joined by Savage and Fiedler on Saturday, McGee watched their comings and goings at the townhouse for the next twenty-four hours. When Hart came outside and seemed to have spotted them, they confronted him and asked about the beautiful young woman sitting inside his home.

Hart denied that anyone was staying with him.

"I have no personal relationship with the individual you are following," Hart said. He described the woman as "a friend of a friend of mine" who had come to Washington to visit her friends.

That night, after the story had been filed with Rice still unidentified,

Savage, Fiedler, and McGee met with a Washington friend of Hart's who had introduced the candidate to Rice. Savage pointed out that the effort to identify the woman would create a media feeding frenzy, and it would be in Hart's interest to name her. The story ran in *The Miami Herald* on Sunday, May 3. That morning, a spokesman for Hart told the Associated Press that the unidentified woman was Donna Rice.

On the same Sunday, *The New York Times* ran a story quoting Hart as denying the allegations of affairs. He challenged the reporters to "follow me around . . . it will be boring." Hart continued to deny he had been having an affair with Rice, but CBS ran an amateur video of them together aboard the luxury yacht *Monkey Business* in Bimini. CBS noted that Rice, who was not identified, later disembarked from the yacht to compete in a "Hot Bod" contest at a local bar. The *National Enquirer* followed with a photo of Rice sitting on Hart's knee on the boat. Hart was forced to withdraw as a presidential contender, a victim of his own arrogance and deceit.

In fact, there was more to the story. According to a former Secret Service agent who was on Hart's detail, well before his encounter with Rice, Hart routinely cavorted with stunning models and actresses in Los Angeles, courtesy of one of his political advisers, actor Warren Beatty.

"Warren Beatty gave him a key to his house on Mulholland Drive," the agent says. "It was near Jack Nicholson's house." Beatty would arrange to have twenty-year-old women—"tens," as the agent described them—meet Hart at Beatty's house.

"Hart would say, 'We're expecting a guest,'" the former agent says. "When it was warm, they would wear bikinis and jump in the hot tub in the back. Once in the tub, their tops would often come off. Then they would go into the house. The 'guests' stayed well into the night and often left just before sunrise. Beatty was a bachelor, but Hart was a senator running for president and was married."

Sometimes, the agent says, "There were two or three girls with him at a time. We would say, 'There goes a ten. There's a nine. Did you see that? Can you believe that?' Hart did not care. He was like a kid in a candy store."

Asked for comment, Gayle Samek, his spokesperson, said, "Senator Hart tends to focus on the present rather than the past, so there's no comment."

8

Crown

TO ENTER THE West Wing, a visitor presses a white button on an intercom mounted at the northwest gate and announces himself. If the visitor appears legitimate, a uniformed Secret Service officer electronically unlocks the gate, allowing the visitor to enter. He then passes his driver's license or other government photo identification through a slot in a bulletproof booth to one of four uniformed Secret Service officers.

Before being allowed into the White House, a visitor with an appointment must provide his Social Security number and birth date in advance. The Uniformed Division checks to see if the individual is listed by the National Crime Information Center (NCIC) maintained by the FBI or by the National Law Enforcement Telecommunications Systems (NLETS) as having been arrested or as having violated laws.

Besides the threat list compiled by the Secret Service, the Uniformed Division maintains a Do Not Admit list of about a hundred people who are barred from the White House because they have caused embarrassment. For example, the White House press office may place a journalist on the list because he or she made it a practice of disobeying rules about where reporters may wander in the White House.

If a visitor is on the appointment list and has been cleared, he is given a pass and allowed into the security booth. The visitor swipes the pass and goes through a metal detector before being allowed to walk outside again toward the West Wing. For years, when most people thought of the White House, they thought of the main building at 1600 Pennsylvania Avenue NW, which serves as the president's home and once served as his office. Abraham Lincoln had his office in what is now known as the Lincoln bedroom on the second floor of the White House. Only with the recent TV series has the public come to understand that the West Wing now houses the presidential offices.

The West Wing was added onto the White House in 1902. In 1909, the president's Oval Office was constructed in the center of the south side of the West Wing. In 1934, it was moved to its current location on the southeast corner, overlooking the Rose Garden. Finally, in 1942, the East Wing was built to house the offices of the first lady as well as the White House military office.

A visitor to the West Wing passes more than a dozen TV cameras on tripods sprouting along the driveway that leads to the entrance to the West Wing lobby. This strip, where correspondents broadcast from the White House, was once known as Pebble Beach. Now, because flagstone has replaced the pebbles, wags in the press corps call it Stonehenge. A separate entrance to the left of the lobby entrance goes directly to the James S. Brady press briefing room. White House correspondents must pass a Secret Service background check before being issued press credentials that let them go through the security booth when the pass is swiped.

Even with appointments, the Secret Service will not admit visitors if they have violations involving assaults or fraud. If an individual had a conviction for marijuana use ten years earlier, for example, officers will inform the White House employee who is expecting the guest.

Then the decision to admit the person falls to the aide, who may invent an excuse to cancel the appointment.

Occasionally, a wanted fugitive makes the mistake of setting up an appointment at the White House, which is code-named Crown. During the administration of George H. W. Bush, a man who was wanted for grand larceny planned to enter the White House with a friend of Bush's. He submitted his Social Security number in advance of the appointment. The Secret Service arrested him on arrival.

"If there is a warrant, the [computer] screen says, 'There is a warrant for this man's arrest. Call an agent,'" a Secret Service agent says.

Richard C. Weaver, a self-proclaimed Christian minister, made it through all the security layers and walked right up to President George W. Bush during his inauguration in 2001. He proceeded to shake his hand and hand him an inaugural coin and a message from God. Known to the Secret Service as the Handshake Man, Weaver had pulled the same stunt when Bill Clinton was inaugurated. Apparently, he was on the inaugural committee's access list. After the Bush inaugural, he tried a few other times to gain access to presidents and senators.

"His picture is plastered in every security booth we have," a Secret Service agent says.

As with the question of how much protection a president should have, the amount of security around the White House has always been an issue of contention. For decades, the District of Columbia government resisted closing off Pennsylvania Avenue in front of the White House. When a threat arose or a demonstration took place, the Secret Service would close off the street or encircle the White House with buses. During the Reagan administration, Jersey barriers were installed around the perimeter of the White House complex. In 1990, they were replaced with bollards. The gates were reinforced with steel beams that rise from the ground after the gates are closed. After 9/11, the Bush administration turned Pennsylvania Avenue into a pedestrian plaza.

"One reason we reinforced the gates is people have tried to drive their cars through the gates to see the president," a longtime agent says. "An iron beam comes out of the ground behind those gates when the gates close. A two-ton truck could slam them at forty miles per hour, and they will withstand it."

The Secret Service's Technical Security Division (TSD) installs devices at White House entrances to detect radiation and explosives. Populated with real-life versions of Q, James Bond's fictional gadget master, TSD sweeps the White House and hotel rooms for electronic bugs. While electronic bugs have never been found in the White House, they are occasionally found in hotel rooms because they were planted to pick up conversations of previous guests. When Ronald Reagan was to stay at a hotel in Los Angeles, for example, the Technical Security Division found a bug in the suite he was to occupy. It turned out the previous occupant was Elton John.

TSD samples the air and water in the White House for contaminants, radioactivity, and deadly bacteria. It keeps air in the White House at high pressure to expel possible contaminants. It provides agents with special hoods called expedient hoods to be placed over the president's head in the event of a chemical attack. Each year, TSD screens nearly a million pieces of mail sent to the White House for pathogens and other biological threats. In conjunction with Los Alamos National Laboratory or Sandia National Laboratories, it runs top secret risk assessments to find any holes in physical or cyber security measures.

In case an assassin manages to penetrate all the security to see the president, TSD installs panic buttons and alarms in the Oval Office and the residence part of the White House. They can be used if there is a medical emergency or physical threat. Many of the alarm triggers are small presidential seals that sit on tables or desks and are activated if knocked over.

The panic alarms bring Secret Service agents running, guns drawn. Besides agents and uniformed officers stationed around the Oval Office, the agents deployed to W-16 under the Oval Office can leap up the stairway in a few seconds.

As a last resort, the White House has emergency escape routes, including a tunnel that is ten feet wide and seven feet high. It extends from a subbasement of the White House under the East Wing to the basement of the Treasury Department adjacent to the White House grounds.

One of the more dramatic attacks took place on October 29, 1994, at two fifty-five P.M., when Francisco Martin Duran stood on the south sidewalk of Pennsylvania Avenue and began firing at the White House with a Chinese SKS semiautomatic rifle. As he ran toward Fifteenth Street, he paused to reload, and a tourist tackled him. Uniformed officers drew their weapons but held fire as more tourists grappled with Duran.

"I wish you had shot me," Duran said as the officers arrested him.

Since a white-haired man was coming out of the White House when Duran began firing, Secret Service agents concluded that Duran likely thought he was firing at President Clinton. He was convicted of attempting to assassinate the president and sentenced to forty years in prison. He was also ordered to pay the government thirty-two hundred dollars to repair damage to the White House, including replacing pressroom windows riddled with bullets.

In December 1994, four more such attacks—perhaps inspired by previous ones—occurred within a few days of one another. On December 20, Marcelino Corniel dashed across Pennsylvania Avenue toward the White House brandishing a knife. Uniformed Division officers and Park Police ordered him to drop it. When he refused and lunged toward a Park Police officer, another Park Police officer shot and killed him.

What was not included in news reports was that the man had a "seven-inch knife taped to his arm, so when the officer told him to drop the knife, he couldn't," says former Secret Service agent Pete Dowling. "This was what they call 'suicide by cop.' The guy wanted to be killed. And unfortunately the police officer felt that his life was being threatened, and he shot and killed the man."

A day after that incident, Uniformed Division officers opened the southwest gate to admit an authorized vehicle. Just then, a man burst past them and ran toward the mansion. The officers tackled and arrested him. The man was a disturbed individual who had an obsession with the White House.

Two days later, a man fired at the mansion with a nine-millimeter pistol from the perimeter of the south lawn. While two shots fell short of the White House, one landed on the State Floor balcony, and another penetrated a window of the State Floor dining room. After a Uniformed Division officer scanning the south Executive Avenue sidewalk noticed a fidgety man, a Park Police officer ran after him, searched him, and confiscated the pistol.

A previous incident on September 11, 1994, demonstrated the White House's vulnerability. That evening, after drinking and smoking crack cocaine, Frank E. Corder found the keys to a Cessna P150 airplane that had been rented and returned to the Aldino Airport in Churchville, Maryland. Although the thirty-eight-year-old truck driver was not a licensed pilot, he had taken some lessons and had flown that particular aircraft several times.

Corder stole the plane and flew to the White House. He then dove directly toward it at a steep angle. While aircraft are not supposed to fly over the White House, airplanes periodically do so by mistake. As a result, the military must exercise judgment when deciding whether to shoot down aircraft that stray into White House airspace. Given that after 9/11, cockpits of commercial airliners were hardened, air marshals were added to most flights, and many pilots are now armed, it is unlikely that such a plane would again be commandeered. But after 9/11, any general aviation aircraft that violated restrictions on flights near the White House and did not respond to military commands would be shot down by missiles or fighter aircraft. Each year, about four hundred general aviation aircraft are intercepted across the country and forced to land on threat of being shot down.

The Joint Operations Center at Secret Service headquarters now interfaces twenty-four hours a day with the Federal Aviation Administration and the control tower at Ronald Reagan Washington National Airport. Headquarters also views on radar any planes flying in the area.

Corder's plane crashed onto the White House lawn just south of the Executive Mansion at one forty-nine A.M. and skidded across the ground. What Corder did not plan for was the Sony JumboTron that had been set up on the south lawn in front of the White House for an event. It was a giant television screen measuring thirty-three feet by one hundred ten feet.

"There's no way he could have flown the plane into the White House," says Pete Dowling, who was on the president's protective detail at the time. "He couldn't have navigated the plane without hitting the JumboTron. So he had to land a little bit early, and what he did was, he just came to rest against one of the magnolias that was right in front of the south part of the White House."

Corder died of multiple, massive blunt-force injuries from the crash. At the time, the White House was undergoing renovations, and President Clinton and his family were staying at Blair House.

While Corder had expressed dissatisfaction with Clinton's policies, and his third marriage had just gone on the rocks, the Secret Service concluded that—like most assassins—his purpose had been to gain notoriety. He had told friends he wanted to "kill himself in a big way" by flying into the White House or the Capitol.

Corder's brother John said the pilot had expressed interest in Mathias Rust, a German teenager who flew a Cessna plane through five hundred fifty miles of heavily guarded Soviet airspace and landed in Red Square in 1987. John Corder quoted his brother as saying of the German: "The guy made a name for himself."

The greatest embarrassment to the Uniformed Division took place on February 17, 1974, when U.S. Army Private First Class Robert K. Preston stole an army helicopter from Fort Meade, Maryland, and landed on the south lawn at nine-thirty P.M.

Instead of firing at the helicopter, uniformed officers called a Secret Service official at home, asking him what they should do. He told them to shoot at the helicopter. By then, the helicopter had flown away. It returned fifty minutes later. This time, Uniformed Division officers and Secret Service agents fired at it with shotguns and submachine guns.

"They riddled it with bullets," a Secret Service agent says. "When he landed [the second time], he opened the door and rolled under the helicopter. It probably saved his life. They put seventy rounds through that. There were twenty rounds in the seat. He would have been shot to death [if he had not rolled under the chopper]. It was not going to take off this time."

Preston, twenty, had flunked out of flight school and perhaps wanted to show them all that he did have some flying skills. He was treated for a superficial gunshot wound. He was sentenced to a year at hard labor and fined twenty-four hundred dollars.

Neither President Nixon nor his wife, Pat, was at the White House at the time.

9

Jackal

IN THEIR IN-HOUSE jargon, agents refer to any possible assassin as "the jackal." Were a jackal to strike, it would most likely be when the president has left the cocoon of the White House. Every assassin has pounced when a president is most vulnerable—outside the White House, usually when arriving or departing from an event. That window of vulnerability opens several times a week when the president leaves the White House for an event in Washington or goes on a domestic or overseas trip.

Even a visit to a friend's home requires elaborate preparation. When George W. Bush was president, he and Laura had dinner at the home of Anne and Clay Johnson, a close friend from high school. Guests included Bush's Yale friend Roland W. Betts and FBI director Robert S. Mueller III, and his wife, Ann. Checking out the Spring Valley home in Washington beforehand, the Secret Service set up a command post in the basement.

"They asked that drapes be put up in the dining room and suggested a chair in which the president should be seated," Anne Johnson recalls. "Agents were posted around the yard, and no-parking cones were put up in front of the house."

The Secret Service asked the Johnsons to clear a closet that was big enough for at least two people.

"In case of an emergency, an agent was going to grab the president, and the two of them were going to dive in," Anne Johnson says. "That would have been an interesting dive, because GWB would have had Laura by the hair, at the very least."

Anne Johnson asked an agent, "What should everyone else do in case of an emergency?"

"I only have one client: the president," the agent replied.

Ten days before a presidential trip, at least eight to twelve agents fly to the intended destination. That is in contrast to the two-man advance team sent for President Kennedy's trip to Dallas. Back then, the Secret Service had about 300 special agents, compared with 3,404 today.

Now an advance team includes a lead agent, a transportation agent, airport agent, agents assigned to each event site, a hotel advance agent, one or two logistics agents, a technical security agent, and an intelligence agent. As part of advance preparations, a team of military communications personnel from the White House Communications Agency is sent to handle radios, phones, and faxes. They ship their equipment and additional personnel on Air Force C-130 cargo planes. The Uniformed Division's countersniper team and the counterassault team from the Secret Service's Special Operations division may also send agents on an advance.

The counterassault team, or CAT, as it is referred to, is critical to providing protection outside the White House. A heavily armed tactical unit, it is assigned to the president, vice president, foreign heads of state, or any other protectee, such as a presidential candidate, deemed to require extra coverage. In the event of an attack, CAT's mission is to divert the attack away from a protectee, allowing the working shift of agents to shield and evacuate the individual. Once the "problem," as

Secret Service agents put it, is dealt with, CAT members regroup, and the shift leader directs them to their next position.

The Secret Service first started using the teams on a limited basis in 1979. They were formed after several agents involved in training were having lunch and began asking themselves how the Secret Service would deal with a terrorist attack, according to Taylor Rudd, one of the agents. After President Reagan was shot in 1981, the teams were expanded and eventually centralized at headquarters in 1983. CAT differs from a special weapons and tactics team (SWAT), which the police or Secret Service may deploy once an attack occurs. Code-named Hawkeye, CAT takes action as the attack occurs.

"Depending on the circumstances, before 1979, besides agents riding with the president, we had five or six agents in a muscle car with Uzi submachine guns," says William Albracht, a founding member of the counterassault teams. "If something happened, they were supposed to lay down a base of fire or have firepower available. They added another layer of protection to the principal. If they came under attack, they would have returned fire. The job of the agents with the protectee is always to cover and evacuate. Get him the hell out of there. So they would try to cover a withdrawal, or if they're in a kill zone, try in some way to get him out with extra firepower."

The muscle car concept was "very loose, and the criteria for engaging hostile fire was somewhat unclear," Albracht says. "The CAT program, which replaced it, was designed to codify and standardize the Secret Service's response to terrorist-type attacks."

Clad in black battle-dress uniform, known as BDU, CAT members travel with the president. They are trained in close-quarter battle— when small units engage the enemy with weapons at very close range. They are also trained in motorcade ambush tactics and building defense tactics.

Each CAT team member is equipped with a fully automatic SR-16 rifle, a SIG Sauer P229 pistol, flash bang grenades for diversionary tactics, and smoke grenades. CAT agents also may be armed with Remington breaching shotguns, a weapon that has been modified with a short barrel. The shotgun may be loaded with nonlethal Hatton rounds to blow the lock off a door.

One time a CAT team had to deploy was January 12, 1992, when a protest rally got out of hand during a visit by President George H. W. Bush to Panama City, Panama. Agents rushed Bush and his wife back into their limousine, and they sped away unharmed. No shots were fired by the Secret Service.

In August 1995, CAT deployed again when President Clinton was playing golf at the Jackson Hole Golf & Tennis Club in Wyoming. Secret Service agents spotted a worker aiming a rifle at Clinton from the rooftop of a home under construction on the edge of the golf course. It turned out that the man was using the rifle's telescopic site to watch the presidential party up close. Agents held him for questioning and then released him.

In contrast to the CAT team, the countersniper team, also dressed in BDUs, does not travel in the motorcade. Instead, the counter-snipers—code-named Hercules and long used by the Secret Service—take positions at key exit and entrance points. For instance, when the president is leaving or entering the White House, they position themselves on the roof and on balconies across the street.

Thus, the countersnipers are observers and can respond to a distant threat with their .300 Winchester Magnum—known as Win Mag—rifles. The rifle is customized for the shooter who is assigned the weapon. Each team is also equipped with one Stoner SR-25 rifle. Counter-snipers are required to qualify shooting out to a thousand yards each month. If they don't qualify, they don't travel or work.

The countersnipers work hand in hand with the counterassault team. If CAT is in a building and wants to leave for the motorcade, the

CAT team leader calls out to the countersniper unit to ask if the area is clear.

In contrast to the cursory look given to Kennedy's planned Dallas parade route, the Secret Service's Forensic Services Division now creates virtual three-dimensional models of buildings along a motorcade route so that agents will know what to expect and can plan what to do at spots where the motorcade may be more vulnerable to attack. The division also produces slide shows of the floor plans of buildings where the president will speak.

As part of advance work, the Secret Service designates safe houses, such as fire stations, to be used in case of a threat. It also plots the best routes to local hospitals and alerts them to an impending presidential visit.

If the president plans to stay in a hotel, the Secret Service takes over the entire floor where his room will be, as well as the floors above and below. Agents examine carpeting to check for concealed objects. They check picture frames that might be hollow and conceal explosives. They plan escape routes from every room that the president will enter.

"In the hotel, if the president will stay overnight, we secure the suite and floor he will stay on and make it as safe as the White House," an agent says. "We seal it off. No other guests can be on the floor. If the floor is huge, we will separate it. But no outside people will be on the floor, guaranteed."

Before the president walks into a hotel room, a Secret Service countermeasures team sweeps it for radioactivity and electronic bugging and video devices. Permanent hotel residents pose a special problem. Agents ask them to move temporarily to other rooms in the same hotel. Hotels usually offer their residents better accommodations free of charge. But some refuse to take them.

"If they say, 'We are absolutely not going,' then we will not bring the president," an agent says.

Like the rest of us, presidents hate the thought of getting stuck in elevators, so the Secret Service pays a local elevator repair company a daily fee to station a service person in a hotel where the president is staying.

The Secret Service checks on the backgrounds of employees preparing food for the president. If they have been convicted of an assault or drug violation, agents will ask the establishment to give the employees a day off. To ensure that no one slips any poison into food served the president at a hotel or restaurant, an agent watches the preparation, randomly selects a prepared dish, and watches as the dish is served. Employees who have been cleared are given color-coded pins to wear. On overseas trips, navy stewards might prepare dishes for the president. With food prepared at the White House, the Secret Service does not get directly involved.

"You can't watch everything," a Secret Service agent says. "But the majority of stuff is checked. We have lists of the suppliers. We check the employees once and go back randomly and check them again to see if anyone has been added."

10

Deacon

IF THE SECRET Service considered Richard Nixon the strangest modern president, Jimmy Carter was known as the least likeable. If the true measure of a man is how he treats the little people, Carter flunked the test. Inside the White House, Carter treated with contempt the little people who helped and protected him.

"When Carter first came there, he didn't want the police officers and agents looking at him or speaking to him when he went to the office," says Nelson Pierce, an assistant White House usher. "He didn't want them to pay attention to him going by. I never could understand why. He was not going to the Oval Office without shoes or a robe."

"We never spoke unless spoken to," says Fred Walzel, who was chief of the White House branch of the Secret Service Uniformed Division. "Carter complained that he didn't want them [the officers] to say hello."

For three and a half years, agent John Piasecky was on Carter's detail—including seven months of driving him in the presidential limousine—and Carter never spoke to him, he says. At the same time, Carter tried to project an image of himself as man of the people by carrying his own luggage when traveling. But that was often for show. When he was a candidate in 1976, Carter would carry his own bags when the press was around but ask the Secret Service to carry them the rest of the time.

"Carter would have us carry his luggage from the trunk to the airport," says former Secret Service agent John F. Collins. "But that is not our job, and we finally stopped doing it." On one occasion, says Collins, "We opened the trunk and shut it, leaving his luggage in the trunk. He was without clothes for two days."

As president, Carter engaged in more ruses involving his luggage.

"When he was traveling, he would get on the helicopter and fly to Air Force One at Andrews Air Force Base," says former Secret Service agent Clifford R. Baranowski. "He would roll up his sleeves and carry his bag over his shoulder, but it was empty. He wanted people to think he was carrying his own bag."

"Carter made a big show about taking a hang-up carry-on out of the trunk of the limo when he'd go someplace, and there was nothing in it," says another agent who was on his detail. "It was empty; it was just all show."

On the first Christmas morning after his election, Carter strode out of the front door of his home in Plains, Georgia, to get the newspaper. Instead of saying "Merry Christmas" to the Secret Service agent standing post, he ignored him. After church and a Christmas brunch, Carter's wife, Rosalynn, put some leftovers out for their Siamese cat. According to agent John Collins, the detail had befriended a stray Jack Russell terrier and given him the code name Dolphin. "Dolphin" conformed with the Secret Service code names beginning with *D* assigned to the Carters.

Seeing the food, Dolphin began gobbling it up, pushing away the cat. According to another agent who was there, Carter got a bow saw—the kind that is used to saw down trees—and actually tried to attack the dog with the saw.

"Carter got the bow saw off a woodpile near the family room patio and in full view of his family—including his mother, Miss Lillian— tried to kill the dog," says the agent who was there. "Dolphin, who was much faster than Carter, playfully dodged the president-elect's efforts. Carter then called the detail leader and demanded that the dog be removed from Plains. The Secret Service gave the dog to the press corps covering Carter."

Incredibly, Carter refused to carry out the biggest responsibility a president has—to be available to take action in case of nuclear attack. When he went on vacation, "Carter did not want the nuclear football at Plains," a Secret Service agent says. "There was no place to stay in Plains. The military wanted a trailer there. He didn't want that. So the military aide who carries the football had to stay in Americus," a fifteen minute drive from Carter's home.

Because of the agreed-upon protocols, in the event of a nuclear attack, Carter could not have launched a counterattack by calling the aide in Americus. By the time the military aide drove to Carter's home, the United States would have been within five minutes of being wiped out by nuclear-tipped missiles.

"He would have had to drive ten miles," an agent says. "Carter didn't want anyone bothering him on his property. He wanted his privacy. He was really different."

Through his lawyer, Terrence B. Adamson, Carter denied that he refused to keep the nuclear football near him in Plains and that he instructed uniformed officers not to say hello to him in the White House. But Bill Gulley, who, as director of the White House Military Office, was in charge of the operation, confirmed that Carter refused to let the military aide stay near his residence. "We tried to put a trailer in Plains near the residence for the doctor [who travels with the president] and the aide with the football," Gulley says. "But Carter wouldn't permit that. Carter didn't care at all."

Carter—code-named Deacon—was moody and mistrustful.

"When he was in a bad mood, you didn't want to bring him anything," a former Secret Service agent says. "It was this hunkered-down attitude: 'I'm running the show.' It was as if he didn't trust anyone around him. He had that big smile, but when he was in the White House, it was a different story."

"The only time I saw a smile on Carter's face was when the cameras were going," says former agent George Schmalhofer, who was periodically on his detail.

"Carter said, 'I'm in charge,'" a former Secret Service agent says. "'Everything is my way.' He tried to micromanage everything. You had to go to him about playing on the tennis court. It was ridiculous."

One day, Carter noticed water gushing out of a grate outside the White House.

"It was the emergency generating system," says William Cuff, the assistant chief of the White House Military Office. "Carter got interested in that and micromanaged it. He would zoom in on an area and manage the hell out of it. He asked questions of the chief usher every day: 'How much does this cost? Which part is needed? When is it coming? Which bolt ties to which flange?'"

At a press conference, Carter denied reports that White House aides had to ask him for permission to use the tennis courts. But that was more dissembling. In fact, even when he was traveling on Air Force One, Carter insisted that aides ask him for permission to play on the courts.

"It is a true story about the tennis courts," says Charles Palmer, who was chief of the Air Force One stewards. Because other aides were afraid to give Carter the messages asking for permission, Palmer often wound up doing it.

"He [Carter] approved who played from on the plane," Palmer says. "Mostly people used them when he was out of town. If the president was in a bad mood, the aides said, 'You carry the message in.' On the bad days when we were having problems, no one wanted to talk to the president. It was always, 'I have a note to deliver to the president. I don't want him hollering at me.'"

Palmer says Carter seemed to relish the power. At times, Carter would delay his response, smugly saying, "I'll let them know," Palmer says. "Other times, he would look at me and smile and say, 'Tell them yes.' I felt he felt it was a big deal. I didn't understand why that had to happen."

Early in his presidency, Carter proclaimed that the White House would be "dry." Each time a state dinner was held, the White House made a point of telling reporters that no liquor—only wine—would be served.

"The Carters were the biggest liars in the world," Gulley says. "The word was passed to get rid of all the booze. There can't be any on Air Force One, in Camp David, or in the White House. This was coming from close associates of the Carter family."

Gulley told White House military aides, "Hide the booze, and let's find out what happens."

According to Gulley, "The first Sunday they are in the White House, I get a call from the mess saying, 'They want Bloody Marys before going to church. What should I do?' I said, 'Find some booze and take it up to them.'"

"We never cut out liquor under Carter," Palmer says. "Occasionally Carter had a martini," Palmer adds. He also had a Michelob Light. Rosalynn—code-named Dancer—would have a screwdriver.

Lillian Carter, Carter's own mother, contradicted her son's claim. In a 1977 interview with *The New York Times*, she said that, even though the White House was officially "dry," she managed to have a nip of bourbon every afternoon when she stayed there.

"She said one evening to one of the butlers, 'I'm kind of used to having a little nip before going to bed. Do you think you could arrange to give me a little brandy each night?'" says Shirley Bender, the White House executive housekeeper.

When Vice President Walter "Fritz" Mondale visited Carter at Plains for the first time, Miss Lillian knocked on the door of a Winnebago the Secret Service was using as a command post.

"I opened the door, and there's Miss Lillian standing there with a paper bag with two six-packs of beer in it," says David Curtis, an agent on the Mondale detail.

"I've got something for the boys," Lillian Carter said. "Don't tell Jimmy."

"I appreciate that, Miss Lillian, but we can't accept that," Curtis said.

When he was in the White House, Carter would regularly make a show of going to the Oval Office at five A.M. or six A.M. to call attention to how hard he was working for the American people.

"He would walk into the Oval Office at six A.M., do a little work for half an hour, then close the curtains and take a nap," says Robert B. Sulliman, Jr., who was on Carter's detail. "His staff would tell the press he was working."

Another agent says that at other times, he could see Carter through the Oval Office windows dozing off in his desk chair while pretending he was working.

Carter claimed to the press that he was saving energy by having solar panels installed on the roof of the White House to heat hot water. "It would not generate enough hot water to run the dishwasher in the staff mess," Cuff says. "It was a fiasco. The staff mess had to go out and buy new equipment to keep the water hot enough. That blew any savings."

Carter even tried to cut back the crew on Air Force One.

"Air Force One is an airplane, and you need a minimum number of people to fly it," Cuff notes. "You have to have a pilot, copilot, and others. They never understood that. The presidential pilot and the vice chief of staff of the air force had to argue with them."

Carter found out that after a catering company put on parties at Blair House for foreign dignitaries, instead of throwing away any leftovers as it normally would, the company would offer the food to Secret Service agents standing post.

"The guys were working shifts of twelve to fourteen hours a day," a former agent says. "Sometimes you could not break away to get food."

Carter insisted that the catering firm figure out the cost of the extra food and charge agents for the leftovers they ate in the future, the former agent says.

Gulley, the head of the military office, says Carter became so involved in micromanaging the White House that he would veto the replacement of carpets.

"He wouldn't allow them to change the carpeting where the public went through the White House," Gulley says. "The White House looked like a peanut warehouse when I left," referring to Carter's business enterprise. "Thousands of people pass through there, and it requires a high degree of maintenance. Carter himself got involved in that. It [the carpeting] was worn and dirty."

Carter thought of himself as a better runner than his Secret Service agents and would challenge them to races. The Secret Service began assigning its best runners to his detail. One day at Camp David, Carter collapsed into the arms of an agent as he was trying to outrun them.

"He wasn't in bad shape, but he never warmed up," agent Dennis Chomicki says. "It was an exceptionally hot day, and he took off real fast and kind of burned himself out. He basically lost it."

On another occasion, agents warned Carter that cross-country skiing at Camp David would be dangerous because there was not enough snow on the ground and there were a lot of bare spots. Carter ignored the advice.

"Yeah, okay, I'll decide on that," Carter said, according to agent Chomicki.

"He went out, and sure enough, he fell on his face and broke his collarbone," Chomicki says.

In Washington, the Secret Service tried to find secluded routes so Carter could run. One beautiful fall morning, Carter went running on the towpath along the C&O Canal. He planned to run from Key Bridge to Chain Bridge, then back to Fletcher's Boat House, where Secret Service agents had been instructed to wait in their vehicles to pick him up. Because of a miscommunication, when Carter and his detail got to the boathouse, agents were nowhere to be seen.

Stephen Garmon, the detail leader, and other agents had been following Carter on bicycles. Garmon, who later became deputy director of the Secret Service, tried to radio to the Secret Service vehicles, but his transmission was not getting through.

"The president said he was getting cold," Garmon recalls. "I asked if he would mind running back to Key Bridge, and we could flag a cab if necessary. Then I saw a pay phone, but I didn't have any change." Garmon decided to try calling the 911 emergency number. Identifying himself as a Secret Service agent, he asked to be connected to the White House Communications Agency switchboard.

"The 911 operator connected me, and I was able to communicate to the vehicles so agents would pick us up," Garmon says.

Besides seeing what presidents and first families are really like,

Secret Service agents get to see the real face of the White House political staff. When Carter was meeting with Israeli Prime Minister Menachem Begin and Egyptian President Anwar el-Sādāt at Camp David, former agent Cliff Baranowski heard a strange noise in the woods around midnight.

"Then Hamilton Jordan, Carter's chief of staff, came out of the woods with a pretty intern," Baranowski says. "They were parked in the woods, and his car got stuck. The noise was the spinning of wheels."

As a micromanager, Carter gave his vice president, Walter Mondale, few duties. So Mondale was able to spend much of his time playing tennis and traveling.

Toward the end of his term, Carter became suspicious that people were stealing things and eavesdropping on his conversations in the Oval Office.

Carter and his staff were becoming "very paranoid," says a General Services Administration (GSA) building manager in charge of maintenance of the West Wing. "They thought GSA or the Secret Service were listening in."

One afternoon, Susan Clough, Carter's secretary, insisted that someone had stolen a vial of crude oil from the Oval Office. The vial was a gift to Carter from an Arab leader.

"Susan Clough swore up and down that someone poured some of it out," a GSA manager says. Even though the vial was sealed, "There was a big fuss over it. The Secret Service photographs everything in the president's suite. They photographed it [again], and it hadn't been touched. It shows the paranoia."

Before going on a fishing trip in Georgia one morning, Carter accused a Secret Service agent of stealing fried chicken that stewards had prepared. In fact, White House aides Jody Powell and Hamilton Jordan had eaten it.

After Reagan was inaugurated, GSA discovered that the Carter staff had left garbage in the White House and had trashed furniture in the Eisenhower Executive Office Building.

GSA saw "furniture, desks, and file cabinets turned over," a GSA building manager says. "They shoved over desks. We had to straighten it out. It was fifteen or twenty desks in one area. It was enough to look like a cyclone had hit."

After he was voted out of office, Carter occasionally stayed in the townhouse GSA maintains for former presidents at 1716 Jackson Place. On the walls of the townhouse are photos of former presidents.

Checking the premises, GSA managers found that when Carter was visiting, he would take down the photos of Republican presidents Ford and Nixon and decorate the townhouse with another half dozen sixteen-inch by twenty-four-inch photos of himself. Each time, Charles B. "Buddy" Respass, then the GSA manager in charge of the White House, became irate because GSA had to find the old photos and hang them again.

Through his lawyer Adamson, Carter denied this. He also denied that he thought people were listening to his conversations in the Oval Office.

But Lucille Price, the GSA manager who then reported to Respass, says, "Carter changed the photos. . . . He didn't like them [Ford and Nixon] looking down at him. We would find out he would put photos of himself up." Then, she says, Carter "would take the photos of himself back with him."

For all his bizarre behavior and shams, Carter was genuinely religious, did not swear, and had a loving relationship with his wife, Rosalynn, who acted as an adviser.

Says Richard Repasky, who was on Carter's detail, "Rosalynn really was the brains of the outfit."

11

Stagecoach

AS PART OF an advance, the Secret Service reviews reports from the intelligence community about possible threats. In 1996, former president George H. W. Bush was planning to fly to Beirut, Lebanon. The itinerary called for him to land on Cyprus, then helicopter over to Lebanon.

"The CIA informed us there was a threat on the former president's life," says Lou Morales, an agent who was with Bush 41, as he is called, on the trip. "The informant knew the itinerary of the helicopter flight and the time it was to take off. In fact, he was part of the plot, which had been hatched by Hezbollah. They were going to shoot missiles to take the helicopter down."

The Secret Service informed Bush, who insisted he wanted to go to Beirut regardless of the risk. The Secret Service scrubbed the helicopter flight and instead drove him in a motorcade at ninety miles per hour from Damascus to Beirut. As with most thwarted plots against protectees, this one never appeared in the press.

Once agents have completed an advance, they recommend how many additional agents will be needed to cover the president. The normal working shift consists of a shift leader or whip and four shift agents. These are the "body men" around the protectee. Other agents include three to four transportation agents, along with counter-surveillance agents and a complete counterassault team of five to six agents.

Besides agents from the local field office, the additional agents for a presidential visit come from the rest of the Secret Service's 139 domestic offices. They include forty-two field offices in cities such as New York, Los Angeles, and Chicago; fifty-eight resident offices; six-teen resident agency offices; and twenty-three one-agent domiciles. These offices are in addition to twenty overseas offices.

Prior to a presidential visit, agents are flown to the location on air force transports, along with the president's limo—code-named Stage-coach—and Secret Service vehicles. The countersniper and counter-assault teams and bomb techs fly in the same aircraft. These agents are in addition to shift agents who accompany the president on Air Force One. Canada prohibits agents from carrying arms, but they sneak in their weapons in presidential limousines.

In contrast to the open car President Kennedy used, the presidential limousine now is a closed vehicle. Known affectionately as "the Beast," the 2009 Cadillac now in use was put into service for Barack Obama's inauguration. The Beast lives up to its moniker. Built on top of a GMC truck chassis, the vehicle is armor-plated, with bulletproof glass and its own supply of oxygen. It is equipped with state-of-the-art encrypted communications gear. It has a remote starting mechanism and a self-sealing gas tank. The vehicle can keep going even when the tires are shot out. It can take a direct hit from a bazooka or grenade. The car's doors are eighteen inches thick, and its windows are five inches thick. The latest model has larger windows and greater visibility than the Cadillac first used by President Bush for his January 2005 inauguration.

Often the first limousine in the motorcade is a decoy. The second limousine is a backup. The president could actually be in a third limousine or in any vehicle in the motorcade. The number of cars in the motorcade depends on the purpose of the trip. For an unannounced visit to a restaurant, seven or eight Secret Service cars, known as the informal package, make the trip. For an announced visit, the formal package of up to forty vehicles, including cars for White House personnel and the press, goes out. Agents refer to their Secret Service vehicles as G-rides.

Including the White House doctor and other administration personnel, a domestic trip entails two hundred to three hundred people. An overseas trip could involve as many as six hundred people, including military personnel. In 2008 alone, the Secret Service provided protection on 135 overseas trips. On such trips, the Secret Service relies on local police even more than it does in the United States. But when Richard Nixon was vice president, local police disappeared as an angry mob descended on Nixon and his wife, Pat, at the Caracas, Venezuela, airport on May 13, 1958.

"The police were supposed to provide protection at the airport," recalls Chuck Taylor, one of the Secret Service agents on the detail. "We noticed the police started to leave the motorcade. They were afraid of the mob, and so the police deserted their security arrangements."

As stones and bottles were being thrown at the couple, agents formed a tight ring around them and quickly escorted them into the president's bulletproof limousine. Along the route to the American embassy, protestors had erected a roadblock. Wielding clubs and pipes, a crowd swarmed the car.

"They had firebombs, and they were bent on killing everybody in the party," Taylor says. "In some cases they put small kids out in front of the car, so we'd run over the kids. We appraised that situation and decided to walk the car through."

The crowd tried to pry open the doors and then began to rock the limo and try to set it on fire. But as long as the agents were facing down the insurgents, they seemed afraid to approach too closely. The agents managed to get Nixon safely to the American embassy, where more angry insurgents confronted them.

"They wanted to burn down the embassy," Taylor says. "We went ahead and put these sandbags around, and we jerry-rigged a radio system so that we were able to talk to Washington. I understand they had cut the transatlantic cable, and we weren't able to communicate normally. We were able to radio the president and tell him what the story was. The president sent the Sixth Fleet out to evacuate everybody."

Now on domestic trips, each motorcade includes a car for the Secret Service counterassault team armed with submachine guns. Another Secret Service car, known as the intelligence car, keeps track of people who have been assessed as threats and picks up local transmissions to evaluate them. If necessary, it jams the communications of anyone who presents a threat. Normally, a helicopter supplied by the Park Police or local law enforcement hovers overhead.

For a motorcade, local police on motorcycles block access from side streets and leapfrog from intersection to intersection. Agents check out offices along the route. Before President Ford visited Conroe, Texas, Agent Dave Saleeba was told that one office in a building along the motorcade route could not be opened. Checking further, he learned that the building was owned by the heirs of a local lawyer.

Back in 1915, the lawyer had become heartbroken when his son, who'd been riding to see him, fell off his horse, hit his head on a well, and died. The lawyer never entered his office again and directed that his heirs never open it. However, at Saleeba's request, the lawyer's granddaughter agreed to open the office. Saleeba found the man's desk covered with dust. A brown bag on top of the desk looked as if it had contained his lunch, now disintegrated.

Secret Service agents believe that simply being there, scanning crowds with a ferocious look, often wearing sunglasses, deters would-be assassins. Agents are looking for signs of danger—people who don't seem to fit in, have their hands in their pockets, are sweating or look nervous, or appear as if they have mental problems. Agents lock in on movements, objects, or situations that are out of place.

"We look for a guy wearing an overcoat on a warm day," says former agent William Albracht, who was a senior instructor at the Secret Service's James J. Rowley Training Center. "A guy not wearing an overcoat on a cold day. A guy with hands in his pockets. A guy carrying a bag. Anybody that is overenthusiastic, or not enthusiastic. Anybody that stands out, or is constantly looking around. You're looking at the eyes and most importantly the hands. Because where those hands go is the key."

If an agent sees a bystander at a rope line with his hands in his pockets, he will say, "Sir, take your hands out of your pockets, take your hands out of your pockets NOW."

"If he doesn't, you literally reach out and grab the individual's hands and hold them there," Albracht says. "You have agents in the crowd who will then see you're having problems. They'll come up to the crowd, and they'll grab the guy and toss him. They will take him out of there, frisk him, pat him down, and see what his problem is. You are allowed to do that in exigent circumstances in protection because it's so immediate. You don't have time to say, 'Hey, would you mind removing your hands?' I mean if this guy's got a weapon, you need to know right then."

An agent who sees a weapon screams to fellow agents: "Gun! Gun!"

To identify themselves to other agents and to police helping during events, Secret Service agents wear color-coded pins on their left lapels. The pins, which bear the five-pointed star of the Secret Service, come in four colors. Each week, agents change to one of the four prescribed colors so they can recognize one another in crowds. On the back of the pin is a four-digit number. If the pin is stolen, the number can be entered on the FBI's National Crime Information Center (NCIC), the computerized database that police use when they stop cars to see if they are stolen or if the occupants are fugitives. If the pin is found, police return it to the Secret Service.

When on protection duty, Secret Service agents wear trademark radio earpieces tuned to one of the encrypted channels the Secret Service uses. Known as a surveillance kit, the device includes a radio transmitter and receiver that agents keep in their pockets.

As for the sunglasses, "In training, they would give us clear Ray-Ban glasses," former agent Pete Dowling says. "The reason they did that was eye protection, in case somebody threw something at the protectee. Most of the guys had them shaded. But the stereotype is the Secret Service guy always has sunglasses on, even when he is indoors."

In practice, some agents wear sunglasses so people do not see where they are looking. Others prefer not to wear them.

Agents wearing plain clothes and no earpieces infiltrate crowds and patrol around the White House. If they spot a problem or vulnerability, they use a cell phone to notify the Joint Ops Center at Secret Service headquarters.

"They're the guys in the crowd," an agent says. "You wouldn't know they were there, and they're on the outside looking in during an event and during an advance."

These agents try to think like assassins: How can they breach the security?

"It's their job to take apart our plan prior to game day," the agent says. "It's their job to basically say, here are the holes, here are your vulnerabilities, tell us how you're going to plug these holes."

Technicians take photos of the crowds at presidential events. The images are compared with photos taken at other events—sometimes using facial recognition software—to see if a particular individual keeps showing up.

Since the attempts on Ford's life, presidents have generally worn bulletproof vests at public events. They are currently Kevlar Type Three vests that will stop rounds from most handguns and rifles but not from more powerful weapons. Agents on the president's and vice president's details are now supposed to wear them at public events, but some agents prefer not to wear them. While the vests have been improved, they are uncomfortable and can make life unbearable on a hot day.

"You have to be hypervigilant," says former agent Jerry Parr, who headed President Reagan's detail when he was shot. In the twenty years before the attempt on Reagan's life, "You had one president murdered, one shot and wounded, a governor shot and wounded and paralyzed, two attempts on Ford, and you had Martin Luther King killed. You know it's out there. You just don't know where."

12

Rawhide

IN CONTRAST TO Jimmy Carter, Ronald Reagan treated Secret Service agents, the Air Force One crew, and the maids and butlers in the White House with respect.

"Carter came into the cockpit once in the two years I was on with him," says James A. Buzzelli, an Air Force One flight engineer. "But [Ronald] Reagan never got on or off without sticking his head in the cockpit and saying, 'Thanks, fellas,' or 'Have a nice day.' He [Reagan] was just as personable in person as he came across to the public."

"One Christmas when we were at the ranch, he came up to me and apologized to me for having to be away from my family on a holiday," former agent Cliff Baranowski says. "A lot of times they would give us food from a party. I certainly did not expect it, but sometimes they insisted."

Former agent Thomas Blecha remembers that when Reagan was running for president the first time, he came out of his home in Bel Air to drive to Rancho del Cielo, the seven-hundred-acre Reagan ranch north of Santa Barbara. Another agent noticed that he was wearing a pistol and asked what that was for.

"Well, just in case you guys can't do the job, I can help out," Reagan—code-named Rawhide—replied. Reagan confided to one agent that on his first presidential trip to the Soviet Union in May 1988, he had carried a gun in his briefcase.

For a time, East Executive Avenue was closed, and when Reagan's motorcade left the White House, it would go along E Street onto Fifteenth Street instead of using Pennsylvania Avenue in front of the White House. As a result, unless he looked out a window of the White House, Reagan did not see demonstrators opposed to nuclear arms who camped out across Pennsylvania Avenue in Lafayette Park. After East Executive Avenue reopened, Agent Patrick Sullivan was driving when Reagan looked out the window of his limo. Reagan saw a perennial demonstrator in Lafayette Park give him a "Heil Hitler" salute as the vehicle passed him.

"This one gentleman was there all the time, and he had posters," Sullivan recalls. "He was a nonviolent protester. We pulled the president's motorcade up East Exec and made the left turn on Pennsylvania. The demonstrator was so shocked, because he had been there for a year and had never seen the motorcade go that way."

The demonstrator jumped up.

"He starts giving President Reagan the Nazi salute," Sullivan says. "He starts yelling 'Heil Reagan! Heil Reagan!' The president sees him standing up giving him the Nazi salute. The president was so shocked and hurt, he said to us, 'Did you see that man giving me the Nazi salute? Why would he do that?'"

While it seemed to be a rhetorical question, Reagan clearly wanted a response.

"Mr. President, he's out there all the time. He's a nut," Sullivan said to Reagan. "That's all he does. He camps out there; he's there every day."

"Oh, okay," Reagan said.

"That's just the way he was," Sullivan says. "Once he realized he was a nut, he was okay with him. He just didn't want this guy to be a regular citizen. Reagan was just a sincere, down-to-earth gentleman. And I think it hurt his feelings that this guy was giving him the Nazi salute."

Quite often, Reagan quietly wrote personal checks to people who had written him with hard-luck stories.

"Reagan was famous for firing up air force jets on behalf of children who needed transport for kidney operations," says Frank J. Kelly, who drafted presidential messages. "These are things you never knew about. He never bragged about it. I hand-carried checks for four thousand or five thousand dollars to people who had written him. He would say, 'Don't tell people. I was poor myself.'"

While Reagan liked to look for the best in people, he was not a Boy Scout. On one occasion, Reagan gave a speech at Georgetown University. As the motorcade drove down M Street toward the White House, Reagan noticed a man in a crowd.

"Fellows, look," Reagan said to his agents. "A guy over there's giving me the finger, can you believe that?"

Reagan started waving back, smiling.

"We're going by, and he's still waving and smiling, and he goes, 'Hi there, you son of a bitch,'" agent Dennis Chomicki remembers, imitating Reagan's buttery-smooth delivery.

One late Friday afternoon, Reagan had left the White House for Camp David. Agent Sullivan was working W-16, the Secret Service's office under the Oval Office.

"A guy came up to the northwest gate carrying a live chicken, demanding to see the president," Sullivan says. "He said he wanted to do a sacrifice for President Reagan. And he impaled the chicken on the fence of the White House. He took the chicken and stuck him on a point on top."

Uniformed officers arrested the man, and he was sent to St. Elizabeth's Hospital for observation.

When Reagan was to go to Spokane, Washington, in 1986, Pete Dowling was part of the advance team sent to scope things out. Besides reviewing all known threats, he met with the Spokane police department, the FBI, and other agencies that might have intelligence on possible threats.

One night, the police department called Dowling to report that an older couple staying at a Best Western downtown had found a large paper dinner napkin on the floor of an elevator. The napkin appeared to have writing on it, so they looked closer. The napkin apparently had a diagram of the Spokane Coliseum, where Reagan was going to speak in four days.

"I went to the police department, I got the napkin, and sure enough, it was a diagram of the coliseum," Dowling recalls. "And it had a legend; it had Xs around the exterior of the coliseum, and then in the legend it said X equals security post. Then it had all of our license plates of the cars we were using. Clearly somebody was conducting surveillance of us."

At the time, a neo-Nazi group called the Aryan Nations was headquartered at Coeur d'Alene, Idaho, a drive of about forty-five minutes from Spokane. Among other things, the group objected to the tax system and was threatening to assassinate public officials. Dowling thought the napkin could have originated from the group. He drove to the Best Western and asked the clerk to show him all the sign-in cards.

"He gave me a little wooden box that contained index cards," Dowling says. "There were four hundred rooms in the hotel, so I started thumbing through the index cards, and when I got to the sixtieth one, bingo. It was the exact handwriting and hand printing that I saw on the napkin."

Dowling noted the license plate listed on the card. He walked into the parking lot and saw a four-door sedan with the same license plate number. Looking inside, he saw blankets neatly piled in the back and two pillows on top of the blankets. Some books were piled on the floor. Obviously, someone was living in the car. Dowling thought it odd that someone living in a car would be so tidy. He called the police and asked for two backup cars.

"We went up to the room, and I knocked on the door, and the guy said, 'Who is it?'" Dowling says.

"It's me, open up," Dowling replied.

"The idiot opened the door. He was just in his underpants. I grabbed him by his hair, and I pulled him out into the hallway," Dowling says. "One of the officers grabbed him, and we all went in and did what we call a protective sweep of the room, just to ensure that nobody else was in there armed."

Dowling noticed a bullet on top of the dresser. Attached to the bullet was a string, and attached to the string was a little white piece of paper.

"Reagan will die," the paper said.

The suspect gave Dowling permission to search the room but not his car.

"I'm going to be up all night anyway, so to do an application for a search warrant and to bring it to a judge at his home at three o'clock in the morning, that's no sweat for me," Dowling said to the man. "Either way, it doesn't matter."

"You can search my car," the man said. "The gun's in the car."

It turned out the man had just gotten out of prison after being convicted of bank robbery. While he was in jail, he had had a romantic relationship with another male inmate. The other inmate had just been transferred to another prison, and the suspect heard that his former lover was romantically involved with somebody else.

"He wanted to do something spectacular in the Spokane area so he could go back to jail and be reunited with the other man," Dowling says.

As Reagan was running for reelection in 1984, a New York state trooper spotted an old Buick sedan going twenty-five miles an hour on the New York State Thruway, where the speed limit was sixty-five. The trooper pulled the man over and immediately noticed an array of guns and hundreds of rounds of ammunition on the floor and front passenger seat.

"What do you think you're doing?" the officer asked.

"I'm going to kill the people running against Reagan," the man replied.

The officer arrested the man, who was committed to a mental hospital north of New York City for observation. Because the man had threatened to kill presidential candidates, two Secret Service agents, at the direction of the Secret Service Intelligence Division, were dispatched to interview him. At first, the patient's psychiatric manager balked at the idea of a law enforcement interview. He then relented as long as the agents removed their guns and handcuffs and did not bring radios or briefcases.

"The man said he was glad to see us," one of the agents says. "He said he loves the Secret Service and was willing to tell us everything."

But first, the man asked the agents to pray with him.

"We folded our hands and bowed our heads at the interview table and prayed with the man," the agent says. "At that moment, the psychiatrist walked in. It's a wonder he didn't have us committed."

When the news broke that Democratic presidential candidate Gary Hart was having an affair with Donna Rice, Reagan was returning to the White House from an evening event.

"We were in the elevator going up to the residence on the second floor of the White House," says former agent Ted Hresko. "The door of the elevator was about to close, and one of the staffers blocked it. The staffer told Reagan the news about Donna Rice and Gary Hart."

Reagan nodded his head and looked at the agent.

"Boys will be boys," he said.

When the door of the elevator shut, Reagan said to Hresko, "But boys will not be president."

13

Rainbow

IF NANCY REAGAN'S wealthy California friends reported getting their copies of *Vogue* and *Mademoiselle* before she did, she took it out on the White House staff. For that reason, Nelson Pierce, an assistant usher in the White House, always dreaded bringing Nancy her mail.

"She would get mad at me," Pierce says. "If her subscription was late or one of her friends in California had gotten the magazine and she hadn't, she would ask why she hadn't gotten hers."

White House ushers would then have to search for the errant magazine at Washington newsstands, which invariably had not received their copies.

One sunny afternoon Pierce brought some mail to Nancy in the first family's west sitting room on the second floor of the White House. Nancy's dog Rex, a King Charles spaniel, was lying on the floor at her feet.

Pierce was old friends with Rex, Ronald Reagan's Christmas gift to his wife, or so he thought. During the day, the usher's office—just inside the front entrance on the first floor of the mansion—is often a napping place for White House pets. But for some reason, Rex was not happy to see Pierce this time. As Pierce turned to leave, Rex bit his ankle and held on. Pierce pointed his finger at the dog, a gesture to tell the dog to let go.

Nancy turned on Pierce.

"Don't you ever point a finger at my dog," she said.

From the start of his political life, Reagan was stage-managed by Nancy.

"Did I ever give Ronnie advice? You bet I did," Nancy Reagan wrote in *My Turn: The Memoirs of Nancy Reagan*. "I'm the one who knows him best, and I was the only person in the White House who had absolutely no agenda of her own—except helping him."

"Mrs. Reagan was a precise and demanding woman," recalls John F. W. Rogers, the Reagan aide over administration of the White House. "Her sole interest was the advancement of her husband's agenda."

It turned out that most of Nancy's advice was sound. As she explained it, "As much as I love Ronnie, I'll admit he does have at least one fault: He can be naive about the people around him. Ronnie only tends to think well of people. While that's a fine quality in a friend, it can get you into trouble in politics."

Code-named Rainbow, Nancy was "very cold," a Secret Service agent in the Reagan White House says. "She had her circle of four friends in Los Angeles, and that was it. Nothing changed when she was with her kids. She made it clear to her kids that if they wanted to see their father, they had to check with her first. It was a standing rule. Not that they could not see him. 'I will let you know if it is advisable and when you can see him.' She was something else."

Like Nancy, the Reagans' daughter Patti Davis was difficult. When agents were with her in New York, she would attempt to ditch them by jumping out of the official vehicle while it was stopped in traffic. She viewed her detail as a nuisance.

"On one visit to New York City, she was with movie actor Peter Strauss, whom she was dating at the time," Albracht says. "Ms. Davis started to engage in the same tricks as on her previous visits and in general treated the assigned agent with disrespect. Strauss became incensed at her actions and told her, 'You'd better start treating these agents with respect or I'm going back to L.A.'"

"Guess what," Albracht says. "She started treating us better."

Another agent says Nancy Reagan was so controlling that she objected when her husband kibitzed with Secret Service agents.

"Reagan was such a down-to-earth individual, easy to talk to," the agent says. "He was the great communicator. He wanted to be on friendly terms. He accepted people for what they were. His wife was just the opposite. If she saw that he was having a conversation with the agents, and it looked like they were good ol' boys, and he was laughing, she would call him away. She called the shots."

"There was a dog out at the ranch, and the agents used to play with the dog, and the dog barked," says Albracht, relaying what an agent on the scene told him. "One night the dog was barking and Nancy got mad, and she told the president, 'You go out there and you tell the agents to leave that dog alone.'"

Apparently, the barking was interrupting her sleep. Nancy was as persistent as the dog's barking, so Reagan said he would take care of it and left the bedroom.

"He went to the kitchen, and he just stood there," Albracht says. "He got a glass of water, went back to bedroom, and said, 'All right, I took care of it.' He just didn't want to bother the agents. He was a true gentleman."

On the day Reagan left office, he flew to Los Angeles on Air Force One. Bleachers had been set up near a hangar, and a cheering crowd welcomed him while the University of Southern California band played.

"As he was standing there, one of the USC guys took his Trojan helmet off," a Secret Service agent says. "He said, 'Mr. President!' and threw his helmet to him. He saw it and caught it and put it on. The crowd went wild."

But Nancy Reagan leaned over to him and said, "Take that helmet off right now. You look like a fool."

"You saw a mood change," the agent says. "And he took it off. That went on all the time."

While Reagan and Nancy had a loving relationship, like any married couple, they had occasional fights.

"They were very affectionate and would kiss," Air Force One steward Palmer says of the Reagans. But they also got mad at each other over what to eat and other small issues. Moreover, Palmer says Nancy could only push the president so far.

"We were going into Alaska. She had put on everything she could put on," Palmer says. "She turned around and said, 'Where are your gloves?' He said, 'I'm not wearing my gloves.' She said, 'Oh, yes, you are.' He said he was not."

Palmer says Reagan finally took the gloves, but he said he could not shake hands while he was wearing them. He said he would not put them on, and he didn't.

Nancy tried to restrict her husband's diet to healthy foods, but he reverted to his favorites when Nancy was not around.

"She was protective about what he ate," Palmer says. "When she was not there, he ate differently. One of his favorite foods was macaroni and cheese. That was a no-no for her. If it was on the menu, she said, 'You're not eating that.'"

For all the spin from the Carter White House about not drinking, it was the Reagans who drank the least.

"I may have served the Reagans four drinks, maybe, with the exception of a glass of wine," Palmer says.

When they were at the ranch, the Reagans would ride horseback together every day after lunch. Despite his cinematic roles in Westerns, he rode English, in breeches and boots. He usually rode El Alamein, a gray Anglo-Arab given to Reagan by former president José López Portillo of Mexico. Reagan had a routine he would follow.

"He would go up to the barn just outside the house. He would saddle up the horses, get them all ready, then he had one of those triangle bells," former agent Chomicki says. "He would always bang on that iron triangle, and that was Nancy Reagan's sign that the horses are ready, come on out, let's go."

One afternoon, Reagan was banging away on the bell, but Nancy did not appear. Finally he went into the house to get her. He came out with her looking unhappy. At that point, a technician from the White House Communications Agency told Chomicki that he had detected a problem with the ranch's phone system. A telephone set must have been off the hook, and the technician wanted to check. Chomicki allowed the technician to enter the home. The technician soon came out holding a phone that had been smashed to pieces.

"She was on the phone," Chomicki says. "That's why she didn't come up to the barn. Nancy never really liked the ranch. She would go up there because the president liked it. Other than the ride, she used to stay in the house almost all the time, and a good portion of the time she'd be talking to her friends down in L.A. For the president, the highlight of his day was to go riding with Nancy. And when she didn't come out because she was talking on the phone, he threw the phone on the floor."

Besides riding at the ranch, Reagan rode at the Marine Corps Base Quantico southwest of Washington, at Camp David, and in Washington's Rock Creek Park. Agents assigned to his detail were trained in horseback riding by the U.S. Park Police. One of the agents, Barbara Riggs, was a skilled equestrian and required no training. Sworn in in

1975, Riggs was the tenth female to become a Secret Service agent. The first female agents—five in all—joined the agency in 1971.

Riggs was on a first-name basis with Reagan. When she fell off one of her own horses and suffered a concussion, he called her upstairs to the living room of the White House after she returned to work. Reagan handed her a book called *The Principles of Horsemanship and Training Horses*. With a wink, he suggested she reread it.

"Yes, I encountered sexual harassment, barriers, and attitudes that women should not be law enforcement agents," Riggs says. "There were some who did not believe women were capable, either physically or mentally, of doing the job. But I also encountered many individuals who acted as my mentors and gave me great opportunities."

In 2004, Riggs became the first female deputy director of the Secret Service. The Secret Service now has three hundred eighty female agents.

"You are always going to find a dinosaur in the bunch," says Patricia Beckford, the eighth female agent hired. "You did have to prove yourself. But at a certain point, they realized that our .357 Magnum shot just as well as theirs."

14

Hogan's Alley

IT GOES WITH the territory that an agent may have to take a bullet for the president. But the actual instruction to trainees is a little more complicated.

"What we are trained to do as shift agents is to cover and evacuate if there is an attack," an agent says. "We form a human shield around the protectee and get him out of the danger area to a safer location. If an agent is shot during the evacuation, then that is something that is expected. We rely on our layers of security to handle the attacker, while the inside shift's main function is to get the heck out of Dodge."

"People always say to me, 'Hey, would you really take a bullet for the president?'" says former agent Dowling. "I say, 'What do you think, I'm stupid?' But what we'll do is we'll do everything in our power to keep the bullet out of the event. And that's what the Secret Service is all about. It's about being prepared, it's about meticulous advance preparation, and it's about training properly so that when you do your job, you don't have to bumble around for the steps that you take."

The key to that is the James J. Rowley Training Center in Laurel,

Maryland. The training facility is nestled between a wildlife refuge and a soil conservation area. The forest muffles the gunfire, the squealing wheels, and the explosions that are the sounds of training Secret Service agents and Uniformed Division officers. Like many of the buildings on this 440-acre spread, the center itself is named for a former director. Rowley headed the Secret Service when Kennedy was assassinated, and he spearheaded many changes after the tragedy.

The main classroom building, made of stone with a green roof, looks like it was lifted from a community college and dropped there. The building was named for Lewis C. Merletti, another former Secret Service director, who now heads security for the Cleveland Browns.

While most of the photos on the walls at headquarters downtown tell of sunny days, triumphant moments, and protectees well protected, the photos here in the Merletti building tell of the underside, the hard work of processing evidence; and the dark side, the failures and poignant reminders. There are photos from the JFK assassination and an overhead of President McKinley's funeral procession in 1901. That's the year Congress informally asked the Secret Service to protect presidents, a little late.

Along one wall, every graduating class has its class photo, going back to the start of formalized special agent training in the fifties. Back then, they wore fedoras. The photos proceed to the sixties, when agents had preppie hair, through the big-hair days of the seventies, to the "normal"-looking agents of today.

Here, new agents receive a total of sixteen weeks of training, combined with another twelve and a half weeks of training at the Federal Law Enforcement Training Center (FLETC) at Glynco, Georgia. To apply to be a Secret Service agent, an individual must be a U.S. citizen. At the time of appointment, he or she must be at least twenty-one years of age but younger than thirty-seven.

Agents need a bachelor's degree from an accredited college or university or three years of work experience in the criminal investigative or law enforcement fields that require knowledge and application of laws relating to criminal violations. Agents' uncorrected vision can be no worse than 20/60, correctable to 20/20 in each eye. Besides passing a background examination, potential agents must take drug tests and pass a polygraph before they are hired and given a top secret security clearance.

Each year, the training center graduates seven to eleven classes of twenty-four Secret Service and Uniformed Division recruits. Even though the training center is in Laurel, agents refer to it as Beltsville, which is actually the town next door. Most of the training center's roads have names appropriate to the task at hand—Firearms Road, Range Road, Action Road, and Perimeter Road. Nothing called Ambush Road, but there is always an ambush in the works.

At what the Secret Service calls Hogan's Alley—not to be confused with the FBI's Hogan's Alley at its Quantico, Virginia, training academy—a body is lying in the middle of the road. Members of the Uniformed Division (UD) sit in a small grandstand watching down the street as four UD officers in BDUs—battle-dress uniforms—clear the buildings and sort out how to take the bad guys down. Except for a real two-story house and soft drink machine, the block-long village is like a Hollywood set, with the façades of a hardware store, hotel, restaurant, bar, and bank, and real cars parked in front. Suddenly the body comes to life, gets up, and walks away, signaling the end of the scenario.

Instructors play the roles of hostage, baddies, and bodies. The retired head of the Prince George's County SWAT team runs the training here along with other special ops experts. They talk about the big picture, what agents have encountered in assassination attempts, as well as the details, such as how to get small behind a trash can. Most important, when agents hear gunshots, they are trained to respond rather than flinch—to cover a protectee and relocate him. However, at the training center, a sign says this is a simulated attack area and warns, "No live weapons beyond this point."

Narrating one of the scenarios, Bobbie McDonald, assistant to the special agent in charge of training, explains to me, "What we're viewing is how they come upon the problem, how they alert about the problem, how they alert their partner, how they react to the situation. Did they take cover? Did they draw their weapon in an appropriate fashion and at an appropriate time? Did they shoot when they should have? Was it what we would call a good shoot, versus a bad shoot?"

In another section of the tactical village, a black van slowly drives past, packed with counterassault team (CAT) members doing in-service training. Wearing black "unis," rifles at the ready, they watch out the van's windows, scowling behind their sunglasses.

Down the road, a smoke bomb goes off near a motorcade. The CAT team jumps out to deal with whatever its members find—a motorcade ambush, a suicide bomber, a shooter. Perhaps the explosion is a distraction from the real threat. The team leader sees something in the woods, a sniper hiding behind a tree. Sniper subdued, the instructor says "the problem" has been dealt with. The team hustles back into the van. The motorcade reassembles and drives off to continue around campus, where more scenarios are waiting.

Near another part of the tactical village is a White House gate with a kiosk where the occasional trapped bird can be found fluttering in exhaustion at all the windows. Replicas of the Uniformed Division's White House kiosks, those familiar white houses with pointed roofs, dot the Secret Service campus.

A scenario staged at one of these guardhouses could be dealing with a "gate caller" about to jump the fence. This part of the tactical town is two blocks long with the same lettered and numbered streets as downtown Washington near the White House. The buildings here are not back-lot façades but heavier duty, including an eight-story repelling tower for countersnipers' practice shots.

Here, trainees work rope line scenarios where they take turns playing the protectee. When trainees interview a "subject" in the lockup room, the person is usually a contracted role player—an actor or a retired police officer. Agents learn to use pressure points to unlock the grip of an assailant or an overeager fan. Outside there are "instant action drills" where motorcades are ambushed, people fire guns from windows, and things blow up.

Many of the practical exercises begin at the "airport," where air traffic is always grounded. Permanently stuck on the tarmac is Air Force One-Half, a mock-up of the front half of the presidential plane, including the presidential seal and gangway. Next to it in similar unflyable condition is Marine One-Half, the center's version of the president's Marine One helicopter.

At the protective operations driving course, the regular students get about twenty-four hours of training in driving techniques. If they are assigned to drive in a detail, they receive an additional forty hours of training.

The giant parking lot is like a driver obstacle course from TV commercials or reality shows. Here they use Chargers—high-powered, high-energy vehicles—to speed out of the kill zone. As a countermeasure, they learn to do the J-turn, making a perfect one-hundred-eighty-degree turn at high speed by going into reverse, jerking the wheel to right or left, and shifting into drive.

Trainees learn to negotiate serpentine courses, weaving around road objects and crashing through barriers, roadblocks, and other cars. If a protectee's car is disabled, they learn to push it through turns and obstacles with their own vehicle. When backing up their vehicle, to give them more control, agents are trained not to turn around to look out the rear window but to use their side-view mirrors.

Besides physical training, agents get eight to twelve hours of swimming instruction, including escaping from a submerged helicopter. For this, the training center uses the dunker, which is meant to simulate what would happen if a helicopter went down and an agent—strapped into his seat—was on it.

In fact, that happened back in May 1973, when Agent J. Clifford Dietrich died while on assignment with Nixon. Dietrich drowned when a U.S. Army helicopter crashed into the Atlantic Ocean about two hundred yards from Grand Cay Island in the Bahamas. The helicopter flipped upside down, and Dietrich was unable to extricate himself. The pilot and the other six agents with him survived.

At several indoor and outdoor firing ranges, trainees and Secret Service agents doing periodic requalification shoot handguns, shotguns, and automatic weapons. Out of view, from behind bulletproof glass, a voice issues commands over a PA. "Hot reload all the remaining slug rounds from the stock and one from your pocket. . . . Shooter will continue one line of rifle slug in four seconds. . . ."

A barrage of bullets flies from six stations. As they are riddled with bullets, the targets spin in place.

"Everything we teach out here, we hope we never have to do," Bobbie McDonald says.

If it comes down to taking a bullet, "You did something wrong," says an agent. "And if that happens, I don't think it's something you're going to think about before you do it. It's just basically you're going to try to get the man out of the way, and if you take some rounds, so be it. But the whole goal is for both of you to get out of there without a scratch."

15

"I Forgot to Duck"

COMING BACK FROM the ranch one day, President Reagan chatted with his agents about how tough it was being president, always surrounded by security.

"I would love to be able to walk into a store like any person, just go down a magazine rack and browse through the magazines like I used to. Walk here, walk there," Reagan said.

His agents suggested he go into a store spontaneously to lessen the risk. While he was in the store, they would block the entrance.

"Valentine's Day was coming up, and he said he wanted to go to a card store in Washington and get a card for Nancy," says former agent Dennis Chomicki. "So we pull up in a small motorcade, the president gets out of the car and goes into the store. He was just browsing around, having a great time."

Meanwhile, a man was looking at cards.

"Reagan picks a card up, and he looks over to this guy and shows it to him and he says, 'Hey, do you think Nancy would like this?'" Chomicki says.

At first, the customer said, "Oh, yeah, your wife would like that." Then he looked up.

"Oh, my God, the president!" he said.

Not long after that, Reagan would be reminded of why presidents need protection. At two thirty-five P.M. on March 30, 1981, John W. Hinckley, Jr., twenty-five, fired a .22 Röhm RG-14 revolver at Reagan as he left the Washington Hilton Hotel after giving a speech.

Members of the public had been allowed to greet Reagan as he left the hotel. Magnetometers were then used at stationary locations such as the White House but not when the president traveled outside the White House. As a result, no one had been screened. By inserting himself into that crowd, which included the press, Hinckley managed to get within twenty feet of the president.

Instinctively, Agent Timothy McCarthy hurled himself in front of Reagan and took a bullet in the right chest. It passed through his right lung and lacerated his liver. While Secret Service agents and Uniformed Division officers have been wounded or killed during protection duty, McCarthy is the only agent to have actually taken a bullet for the president by stepping into the line of fire. In a second and a half, Hinckley fired six rounds. Besides McCarthy, Metropolitan Police Officer Thomas Delahanty and Press Secretary Jim Brady were wounded. Brady suffered extensive brain damage.

Agent Dennis McCarthy—no relation to Timothy—would be the first to pounce on Hinckley. At first, McCarthy thought he was hearing firecrackers go off.

"After the second shot, I knew it was a gun," McCarthy says. "At that point, I had a feeling of panic. I knew I had to stop it."

By the third shot, McCarthy spotted a pair of hands gripping a pistol in between the television cameras just eight feet away. McCarthy lunged for the gun and hurled himself on Hinckley as he was still firing.

"As I was going through the air, I remember the desperate feeling: 'I've got to get to him! I've got to get to him! I've got to stop him!'" McCarthy says.

Crouched in a combat position, Hinckley collapsed as McCarthy landed on his back. While the assailant offered no resistance, McCarthy remembers hearing the fast click, click, click as Hinckley continued squeezing the trigger, even after the .22 caliber revolver's six shots had been expended. McCarthy had always wondered how he would react when gunfire actually started. Now he knew.

Like McCarthy, President Reagan at first thought he was hearing the sound of firecrackers.

"I was almost to the car when I heard what sounded like two or three firecrackers over to my left—just a small fluttering sound, pop, pop, pop," Reagan said later. "I turned and said, 'What the hell's that?' Just then, Jerry Parr, the head of our Secret Service unit, grabbed me by the waist and literally hurled me into the back of the limousine. I landed on my face atop the armrest across the backseat, and Jerry jumped on top of me."

"I remember three quick shots and four more," Parr tells me. "With Agent Ray Shaddick, I pushed the president down behind another agent who was holding the car door open. Agent McCarthy got hold of Hinckley by leaping through the air. I got the president in the car, and the other agent slammed the door, and we drove off."

The limo began speeding toward the White House.

"I checked him over and found no blood," Parr says. "After fifteen or twenty seconds, we were under Dupont Circle moving fast. President Reagan had a napkin from the speech and dabbed his mouth with it. He said, 'I think I cut the inside of my mouth.'"

Parr noticed that the blood was bright red and frothy. Knowing that to be a danger sign, he ordered the driver to head toward George Washington University Hospital. It was the hospital that had been preselected in the event medical assistance was needed.

It turned out that the president may have been within minutes of death when he arrived at the hospital. Going straight there probably saved his life.

Reagan remembered how, as they neared the hospital, he suddenly found he could barely breathe. "No matter how hard I tried, I couldn't get enough air," he said. "I was frightened and started to panic a little. I just was not able to inhale enough air."

In fact, Parr says, "I didn't know he was shot until we got to the hospital. He collapsed as we walked in."

As he was placed on a gurney, Reagan felt excruciating pain near his ribs.

"What worried me most was that I still could not get enough air, even after the doctors placed a breathing tube in my throat," Reagan said. "Every time I tried to inhale, I seemed to get less air. I remember looking up from the gurney, trying to focus my eyes on the square ceiling tiles, and praying. Then I guess I passed out for a few minutes."

When Reagan regained consciousness, he became aware of someone holding his hand.

"It was a soft, feminine hand," he said. "I felt it come up and touch mine and then hold on tight to it. It gave me a wonderful feeling. Even now I find it difficult to explain how reassuring, how wonderful, it felt. It must have been the hand of a nurse kneeling very close to the gurney, but I couldn't see her. I started asking, 'Who's holding my hand? Who's holding my hand?'"

At one point, Reagan opened his eyes to see his wife, Nancy.

"Honey, I forgot to duck," he joked.

As luck would have it, that afternoon most of the doctors who practiced at the hospital were attending a meeting only an elevator ride away from the emergency room.

"Within a few minutes after I arrived, the room was full of specialists in virtually every medical field," Reagan said. "When one of the doctors said they were going to operate on me, I said, 'I hope you're a Republican.' He looked at me and said, 'Today, Mr. President, we're all Republicans.' I also remember saying, after one of the nurses asked me how I felt, 'All in all, I'd rather be in Philadelphia.'" It was the epitaph of fellow actor W. C. Fields.

Surgeons found a bullet that had punctured and collapsed a lung. It was lodged an inch from Reagan's heart. If he had been wearing a bulletproof vest, the bullet likely would not have penetrated Reagan's body.

"On several previous occasions when I'd been out in public as president, the Secret Service had made me wear a bulletproof vest under my suit," Reagan explained later. "That day, even though I was going to speak to some die-hard Democrats who didn't think much of my economic recovery program, no one had thought my iron underwear would be necessary because my only exposure was to be a thirty-foot walk to the car."

"Some of my colleagues have said, 'Well, I would have taken him to the White House because it's the safest place,'" Parr says. "You take a chance when you take the president to the hospital. If he's not hurt, then you frighten the nation. But in this case, we were right. And there was a trauma team there that gets a lot of gunshot wounds."

For Parr, it was a decision he had never wanted to make. He joined the Secret Service in 1962, a year before John F. Kennedy was assassinated.

"We never forgot it," Parr says. "We never wanted it to happen on our watch. Unfortunately, it almost happened on mine."

"The agents who got him [Reagan] out of there did everything right," says former agent William Albracht, who, as a senior instructor at the training center, taught new agents about lessons learned from previous assassination attempts. "The other agents went to the assassin and helped subdue him."

In retrospect, he says, "Maybe they should have jumped in the follow-up [car] and gone with the protectee instead of staying there and trying to subdue Hinckley. Because you have police there to do that job. All agents are always thinking diversion: Is this the primary attack, or are the bad guys trying to get us to commit all our assets and then hit us on the withdrawal? So whether more agents should have gone with Reagan is twenty-twenty hindsight. We teach agents to go with the protectee to make sure there is a successful escape."

At the hospital, the FBI confiscated Reagan's authentication card for launching nuclear weapons, saying that all of Reagan's effects were needed as evidence. Because no guidelines had been worked out for a situation where a president undergoes emergency surgery, it was not clear who could launch a nuclear strike.

The Twenty-fifth Amendment to the Constitution allows the vice president to act for the president only if the president has declared in writing to the Senate and the House that he is disabled and cannot discharge his duties. If the vice president and a majority of the Cabinet agree that the president is unable to discharge his duties, they may make the vice president the acting president. But that would require time.

Vice President George H. W. Bush could have taken it upon himself to launch a strike by communicating with the defense secretary over a secure line. But it was questionable whether he had the legal authority to do so. When Bush became president, his administration drafted a highly detailed, classified plan for immediate transfer of power in the case of serious presidential illness.

Before he shot Reagan, Hinckley had been obsessed with movie star Jodie Foster after seeing her in *Taxi Driver*. In the 1976 film, a disturbed man plots to assassinate a presidential candidate. The main character, played by Robert DeNiro, was based on Arthur Bremer, who shot Governor George Wallace. After viewing the movie many times,

Hinckley began stalking Foster. Just before his attack on Reagan, he wrote to her, "You'll be proud of me, Jodie. Millions of Americans will love me—us."

On October 9, 1980, about six months before his assault on Reagan, Hinckley had been arrested as he attempted to board a plane at the Nashville, Tennessee, airport while carrying three pistols. President Carter was in Nashville at the time. Reagan, then running for the presidency, had just canceled a trip to Nashville.

As a result of the Reagan incident, the Secret Service began using magnetometers to screen crowds at events. "We started to look at acceptable standoff distances to keep crowds away," says Danny Spriggs, who took Hinckley into custody at the shooting and became a deputy director of the Secret Service. "The distances would vary with the environment."

The Secret Service also learned to segregate the press from onlookers and keep better tabs on them to make sure no one infiltrates the press contingent, pretending to be a reporter. An agent is assigned to watch the press, and members of the press themselves report those who try to infiltrate.

Similarly, the Secret Service learned lessons from the John F. Kennedy assassination. It doubled its complement of agents, computerized and increased its intelligence data, increased the number of agents assigned to advance and intelligence work, created countersniper teams, expanded its training functions, and improved liaison with other law enforcement and federal agencies.

"Before the Kennedy assassination, training often consisted of agents telling war stories," says Taylor Rudd, an agent assigned to revamp training. "Many agents on duty had never had any training."

Now the Secret Service shares intelligence and techniques with a range of foreign security services. After the assassination of Israeli prime minister Yitzhak Rabin, the Secret Service and Israel's Shin Bet spent a week together comparing notes.

"The Rabin assassination was much like the Hinckley attempt on Reagan," says former agent Dowling, who was in charge of foreign liaison when the meetings with Shin Bet took place. "It happened at a motorcade departure site."

Shin Bet officials laid bare their own shortcomings.

"It was a very emotional, sad thing for them to do," Dowling says. "This particular guy loitered for some time around the motorcade, and he should have been noticed. And we kind of experienced something similar with Hinckley. We had somebody who was clearly stalking the president, somebody who had stalked presidents before. It's not because this guy thinks Reagan's a bad guy, or he thinks Jimmy Carter's a bad guy. It's the office that interests them. It's the authority."

About a year after the Reagan assassination attempt, the Secret Service's Washington field office began receiving calls from a man threatening to kill Reagan. The man would say, "I'm going to shoot him." Then he would hang up.

Agent Dennis Chomicki was assigned to protective intelligence and was aware that the calls were coming in because he'd been reading what the Secret Service calls "squeal sheets," which recount incidents over the previous twenty-four hours. One morning, Chomicki was reading about the caller when someone called the main line of the field office, which at the time was at Nineteenth Street and Pennsylvania Avenue. Since Chomicki was one of the first agents in that morning, he picked up the call.

"Hi, it's me again," the caller said. "You know me."

"No, I don't know you," Chomicki responded.

"Well, I'm the guy that's going to kill the president," the man said.

"Look, do me a favor," Chomicki said. "I'm standing here on a wall phone because I just opened up the door. Why don't you call back on my desk so I can sit and talk with you?"

The man agreed, and Chomicki gave him his direct dial number.

Back then, the Secret Service had an arrangement with what is now Verizon that the phone company would immediately trace calls even from unlisted numbers when an agent called a telephone company supervisor. Chomicki called a supervisor and gave him the number at his desk so that all incoming calls would be traced. He was sure the man would not be stupid enough to call the number.

"I walked over to my desk, and sure enough, he called back," Chomicki says. "So we started talking, and I was able to record that conversation."

The man said he had a rifle with a scope.

"I'm going to aim in, squeeze the trigger off, and blow his head apart like a pumpkin," the man said.

"Hey, this is pretty serious stuff. Why don't we meet?" Chomicki said.

"What do you think, I'm crazy?" the caller said, and hung up.

The phone company called and said the man had called from a pay phone on New York Avenue. With the location of the pay phone in his pocket, Chomicki dashed out the door. Just then, another agent was walking in.

"Bob, come on, we got to go," Chomicki said. "I'll tell you all about it on the way down."

They ran to the Secret Service garage and jumped into their respective Secret Service cars. They drove to New York Avenue and Eleventh Street, where the Greyhound bus terminal was located at the time.

"We were looking around, and we didn't see anybody," Chomicki says. "There was a coffee-to-go truck sitting nearby. We went up and asked the guy, 'Did you see anybody on the phone a short while ago?'"

Secret Service agent Norm Jarvis, shown on the South Lawn of the White House, interviewed a psychic as part of advance preparations for a trip President George H. W. Bush
took to Oklahoma. Based on the psychic's vision that a sniper would assassinate Bush, the
Secret Service changed his motorcade route. *(Photo courtesy of the U.S. Secret Service)*

Secret Service agents knew that Vice President Spiro Agnew, right, who was married
and a champion of family values, had affairs while in office. *(AP)*

Barbara Bush, left, and Jenna Bush Hager often gave Secret Service agents a hard time. Jenna would try to elude her Secret Service detail to the point that agents had to conduct surveillance of her car to find out when she was leaving the White House. *(AP)*

President Barack Obama—code-named Renegade—treats agents with consideration and respect. Agents report that contrary to his claims, he has continued to smoke regularly. *(AP)*

Secret Service agents carry SIG Sauer P229 pistols. Counterassault teams are armed with fully automatic Stoner SR-16 rifles as well. *(Photo courtesy of the U.S. Secret Service)*

Teams of countersnipers from the Secret Service's Uniformed Division cover the president when he enters or leaves the White House. *(Photo courtesy of the U.S. Secret Service)*

The first female agents joined the Secret Service in 1971. The agency now has three hundred eighty female agents. *(Photo courtesy of the U.S. Secret Service)*

At the Rowley Training Center in Laurel, Maryland, new agents learn to respond to attacks. *(Photo courtesy of the U.S. Secret Service)*

Unknown to members of Congress or other VIPs who visit the Rowley Training Center, agents secretly rehearse the "impromptu" scenarios. *(Photo courtesy of the U.S. Secret Service)*

When John Hinckley began firing at President Reagan as he was leaving the Washington Hilton on March 30, 1981, Secret Service Agent Timothy McCarthy hurled himself in front of Reagan and took a bullet in his chest. *(AP)*

In recent years, the Secret Service—under pressure from presidential candidates or the White House—has shut down magnetometer screening at major events when the president or candidate is about to start speaking and stragglers are still arriving, risking an assassination. *(Photo courtesy of the U.S. Secret Service)*

"Requests were made by staff to expedite or stop magnetometer screening," says Danny Spriggs, who headed protection and retired as deputy director of the Secret Service in 2004. "I would never have acquiesced to that," says Spriggs, shown at right, running with then president Clinton. *(Photo courtesy of the U.S. Secret Service)*

The Secret Service's canine units are mainly Belgian Malinois, most of them cross-trained to sniff out explosives and attack an intruder. *(Photo courtesy of the U.S. Secret Service)*

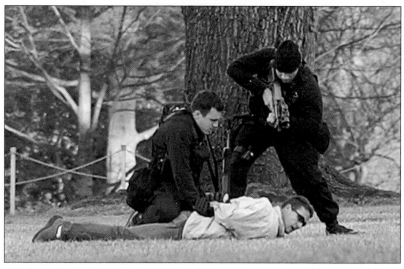

When individuals jump the fence at the White House, as in this February 2004 incident, the Emergency Response Team from the Secret Service's Uniformed Division is the first line of defense. *(AP)*

The Secret Service provides protection at so-called special events of national significance, including the Olympics, presidential inaugurations, national nominating conventions, and visits from the pope. *(Photo courtesy of the U.S. Secret Service)*

The Secret Service scripted when President Barack Obama and Michelle Obama would alight from "the Beast" after his inauguration. Since Obama took office, threats against the president are up 400 percent. *(AP)*

"Yeah, about quarter to eight there was a guy," the man said.

He gave the man's estimated height and weight and described him as wearing blue pants and a blue shirt. The time cited by the coffee man coincided with the call Chomicki had received at the field office. Chomicki asked the coffee man why he had noticed the individual using the public pay phone.

"Usually I show up on the corner at eight," the man explained. "I just happened to get here early today, and my customers don't expect me here until eight, so business was slow. I was just sitting here staring at the phone booth and saw this guy on the phone, and I just happened to remember what he looked like."

The agents jumped into their cars. Chomicki drove east on New York Avenue; the other agent drove west. Just then, Chomicki spotted a man who matched the description given to him by the coffee man. He was using a pay phone on the outer wall of the bus terminal building.

Chomicki made a U-turn and parked his car across the street. He walked up behind the man and heard him talking in a Midwestern accent. It was the voice of the man who had called him at the field office.

"I grabbed him by the scruff of his neck, and I pushed him between the phone and the side panel, and I grabbed the phone," Chomicki says.

"This is agent Chomicki of the Secret Service," he said into the receiver. "To whom am I speaking?"

"Wow! How'd you get him?" a voice on the other end of the line said. It was another agent back at the field office. He said the man had just called, threatening to kill Reagan.

The suspect claimed he was just trying to call a taxi. As he tried to get away, Chomicki dragged him to his car, placed him against the trunk, and handcuffed him. After he was given a psychiatric examination, a judge committed him to a mental institution.

Secret Service agents often deal with what is called White

House–itis, a malady of arrogance that grips some White House aides. Near the end of Reagan's term, that affliction almost got one of his aides shot. Agent Glenn Smith was guarding Reagan at the Waldorf-Astoria in New York for the U.N. General Assembly. Smith heard a man shout, "Stop or I'll shoot!" Smith took out his .357 Smith & Wesson Magnum and placed his finger on the trigger. Just then, a man came bolting through a door with a New York City police officer in hot pursuit.

The man turned out to be a White House staffer who was so full of himself that when a Secret Service agent asked him to identify himself at an inner checkpoint, he refused. When the agent tried to block his way, he pushed the agent away. The police officer then chased after him.

"If I had gotten a clear shot at the man, I would have shot him," Smith says.

As with all presidents, some people totally lost it when meeting Reagan. One woman in a crowd threw her baby into the air. Agent Glenn Smith had to catch the little girl. An eighty-year-old woman held on to Reagan's hand so tightly that Smith had to pry it loose. Hoping to get an autograph, a sheriff approached Air Force One at high speed in his cruiser with lights flashing. The sheriff brought his car to a halt just in time.

"In a few more seconds, we would have opened fire on the car," Smith says.

While in office, Reagan never showed the effects of Alzheimer's disease, which ultimately led to his death. "We had a hundred twenty agents on his detail, and he seemed to remember everyone's name," Smith says.

But in March 1993, a year before he announced that he was suffering from Alzheimer's, former president Reagan honored Canadian prime minister Brian Mulroney at his library and invited him to his ranch. As Mulroney was leaving, the prime minister asked Agent Chomicki, "Do you notice something with the president?"

Chomicki said he did but did not know what the problem was.

"He would just stop midsentence and forget what he was saying," Chomicki recalls. "Then he would just start a whole new story."

After Reagan had been out of office for three years, he was to speak at an event in Akron, Ohio. In contrast to the retinue he'd had as president, Reagan traveled with just one staffer and his Secret Service contingent. The agent in charge of the former president's protective detail came into the command post and said to agent Dowling, "You know, the president's been sitting in his room alone all morning. And he'd really like for some folks to talk to. Would you guys mind if he came over and sat in the command post and just chatted with you guys for a while?"

"That'd be terrific. Bring him over," Dowling said.

For two hours, Reagan chatted with the agents, telling stories and jokes.

"He told us he and Mikhail Gorbachev had private conversations," Dowling says. "They agreed that their talks were not about today and are not about us. They're about our grandchildren and the life that they're going to live."

16

The Big Show

TO SIGN UP to take a bullet for the president requires extraordinary commitment. Besides the glamour and the travel, "I see being in the Secret Service as a calling for me to serve my country and do good at a higher level," one agent says.

"Agents do not protect any individual but rather the integrity of the office, so the bullet we may take is for the office—not the person," another agent says.

The job requires not only protecting the president but safeguarding the lives of other agents.

"When I walked into an event with the president as part of the protective detail, I knew and trusted that everybody would do their job," former agent Norm Jarvis says. "The formation has shift agents, and each has responsibilities unique to each position. So if everybody takes care of their position, then you don't have to worry about your back, or who's looking out over your shoulder. Somebody is. You just have to focus on what your job is at the time. Agents build up an awful lot of trust and appreciation for each other."

The reverse is true as well.

"If you detect that somebody's lazy or not thorough or not doing the job, it means more than just 'Hey, this guy's a bum and I've got to spend my time with him,'" Jarvis says. "You feel like your life could possibly be in danger. Certainly the president's life would be in danger. So there's a lot of us within the detail policing ourselves and using positive and negative sanctions to get people to do the right thing all the time."

Agents recognize that the job entails long hours and extensive travel. In describing job opportunities, the Secret Service's website makes a point of that.

"Agents have a certain drive," a Secret Service agent says. "They're all kind of wired the same; they all want to see the job get done, and they want to get it done the right way."

But many say that the agency's management needlessly makes the job tougher. In particular, the Secret Service's senseless transfer policies drive agents to quit before retirement, adding to the government's costs. This comes at a time when, because of threats from terrorists, the need for the Secret Service has never been greater.

Agents cite numerous situations where fellow agents are denied transfers to cities where their spouses work, while others are forced to transfer to those same cities. Often, the agents who want to transfer have offered to pay their own moving costs. Instead, the Secret Service pays fifty thousand to one hundred thousand dollars each to move agents who do not want to be transferred to those cities.

"We sign up to take a bullet, but that's not the hardest part of the job," Jessica Johnson, a former Secret Service agent, says. "It's not anything that we normally face. The risk is there. But what makes the job very difficult is the mismanagement. If the Secret Service were better managed, you'd have a lot better workforce, a lot more people who don't quit."

Since 9/11, the private sector has been offering hefty salaries to anyone with a federal law enforcement background. Typically, former

Secret Service agents sign up as vice president for security of a major corporation or start their own security firms. For those who want to remain vested to earn full government pensions, opportunities have expanded as well at other federal law enforcement agencies.

Until 1984, under a previous retirement system, Secret Service agents could not keep their pensions if they transferred to another government agency. Now they can. Agents can retire at any age after twenty-five years with the agency. They can retire at age fifty if they have served twenty years. For both government agencies and private companies, a Secret Service or FBI agent is a prize catch.

The FBI has taken steps to retain agents, while the Secret Service has not. In contrast to the Secret Service, after three years with the bureau, unless he or she chooses to go into management, an FBI agent can stay in the same city for the rest of his or her career. An agent going into management can remain in the same city for five years.

The Secret Service, on the other hand, typically transfers agents three to four times during a twenty-five-year career. An agent who enters management may move five to six times. The rationale is that agents need to acquire experience in different offices. But experience in one office does not translate into another. Decades ago, the FBI had the same policy. The bureau scrapped it because the constant moves were not necessary and resulted in many agents leaving the bureau. In turn, that led to high costs both for moving families and for training new agents to replace those who left.

Not having to transfer as often, FBI agents can better work out living arrangements with spouses. The FBI at least tries to take into account situations where a spouse must work in a particular city, sometimes addressing these as hardship cases.

Essentially, according to agents, the Secret Service moves agents around like checkers on a board without regard to their wishes. Rather than explaining the reasoning behind transfers or other policies that impinge on the agents' personal lives, the Secret Service will typically give the high-handed response that the change is necessary because of the "needs of the service." The exception is when an agent has "juice," meaning connections to higher-ups, a situation that contributes to poor morale.

After two years on the Clinton detail based at the Clintons' home in Chappaqua, New York, Johnson wanted to transfer back to California, where she grew up.

"All of a sudden, they said they can't transfer anyone out of New York," she says. "They said they have no one to replace me. At the same time, they're sending out an email that says anyone, regardless of where you are in your career track, if you would like to go to Los Angeles, New York, or San Francisco, raise your hand and you're there. So I write the little memo and I raise my hand. I jump up and down, and they tell me, 'Oh, well, we can't replace you. So you can't go.'"

At the same time, Johnson says, friends in the Los Angeles office were sending her copies of emails they were receiving from management saying they had to leave Los Angeles to go to protective details.

"A year later when I went to my management, they said, 'Oh, well, L.A.'s full. How about the New York field office?'" she says.

When the Secret Service finally agreed to transfer her to Los Angeles after three years in New York, "I find out that we were eleven bodies short in L.A. So how did we go from being full to being eleven bodies short in four months?"

In other cases, the Secret Service disregards situations where a spouse has a job in another city. Johnson and others describe one situation where an agent based in Los Angeles began dating a doctor in Hawaii. Eventually, they married, and the agent put in for a transfer to Hawaii, where his wife had an established medical practice.

"We have an office in Hawaii, so it's easier for him to transfer than it is for her," Johnson says. "But the management we had in L.A. at the time had no juice. He was told he couldn't be transferred to Hawaii. He quit because he said his marriage was more important."

About a month later, after he moved to Hawaii, he applied to return to the Secret Service. The head of the Hawaii office, who had juice, rehired him.

"Here you're being told you can't transfer, and the bottom line was, it was all about who your boss is," Johnson says.

In another case, agent Dan Klish was issued orders to transfer to Los Angeles. His wife's career as a radiation oncologist made it difficult for her to find a position there. Finally, she obtained a job near Denver. Klish asked for a transfer to Denver or Cheyenne and offered to pay for the move himself. That would have saved the government about seventy-five thousand dollars in moving costs. The transfer was denied. For more than two years, they lived apart, and the agent flew to Denver once or twice a month to see his wife and young daughter.

During that time, the service asked for volunteers to transfer to Denver. Approximately ten other agents were transferred to Denver, some with less seniority, at a cost to the government of seventy-five to one hundred thousand dollars for each move.

"If the opening isn't available at that moment, then the service can say, 'Oh, sorry, that office is overstaffed. Here are your only options,'" Klish says. "Then, sure enough, while you're still on orders to move somewhere else but haven't moved yet, an opening in a city that would work for you comes out, and you can't even put in for it because you're already on orders to go elsewhere. Later, after you've moved, they transfer several others to that city. There is a strong bond among agents, but unless you have the right connection, the Secret Service doesn't care about the agents."

After eight years with the Secret Service, Klish finally quit to join another federal agency in Colorado.

Joel Mullen, an agent who was based in Washington, D.C., is married to a navy lawyer. When the navy gave her orders to transfer to San Diego, Mullen asked to transfer to the Secret Service field office there, saying the navy would pay the cost. After initially approving the transfer, headquarters blocked it, even though San Diego had openings. Mullen and his wife had started building a home near San Diego. The Secret Service told Mullen to transfer to the Los Angeles office instead.

"I commuted ninety-six miles one way from my door to the office," Mullen says. "I did that for fourteen months. Then I left and went with the Naval Criminal Investigative Service."

Besides losing an agent with ten years' experience, the Secret Service wound up paying out $240,000 for the transfer to cover Mullen's costs, including the decline in the value of his house in the Washington area.

Nor does the agency have an open process for listing anticipated vacancies and agents' preferences for transfers. All are kept secret. If an agent has "juice," he or she is bumped ahead of others.

In contrast, the FBI, which has 12,500 agents, maintains online lists of requested transfers to each field office so that agents can see who is ahead of them. FBI agents say connections play no role in transfers. Because of the open lists, if the FBI did engage in such under-the-table preferential treatment, the agents would know it.

That the Secret Service's computer program for listing transfer preferences and bidding on promotions is an antiquated DOS-based program symbolizes how much the Secret Service cares about agents' wishes.

Resignations before retirement have increased substantially in recent years. In all, the Secret Service has 3,404 special agents. More than half their man-hours are devoted to protection of the president and other national leaders, as well as visiting foreign dignitaries.

Attrition rates are increasing. As the trend accelerated, the Secret Service declined to provide full yearly figures, but the rate is roughly 5 percent a year. Turnover rates are as high as 12 percent a year in the Uniformed Division, which has 1,288 officers. More alarming, agents who have been in the service ten years say a third to half of the agents who were in their initial training class have left.

"These people who are leaving are very qualified agents who are doing a really good job and are held in high esteem," an agent says. "That's what really hurts us."

The Secret Service asked an analyst then based in Washington to study the problem of retention and the costs associated with agent turnover. She found it was an increasingly serious problem. The incremental cost to the government of training a new agent is eighty thousand dollars for the agent's salary and the cost of equipment and travel. That excludes the fixed costs of the training facilities and the salaries of instructors.

"The higher-ups basically dismissed her findings, saying, 'Oh, we don't have any kind of retention problem,'" says a current agent. "They didn't want to hear it."

Johnson, who is now a real estate investor, describes trying to raise the issue during her exit interview.

"The supervisor who was giving me the exit interview was literally saying, 'Tell me if there are any problems we should know about' as he was starting to escort me out the door," Johnson says. "I said, 'Well, yes, I'm sure you hear this a lot,' and I began to lay out examples of unnecessary burdens imposed on agents."

The supervisor became defensive.

"He started going on about how the military does more, and there are civilians who sacrifice more than we do in the service," she says. "He couldn't even listen to what I had to say."

In a rare move, an agent raised the issue at a meeting of Secret Service officials at the agency's Washington field office.

"You've got a bunch of Generation X agents," he said. "We're concerned about our families; we're concerned about our wives and our kids. Something has to change."

Shortly after that, the agent resigned.

In recent years, agents say a dismissive, insular culture and a disregard for the need to retain agents have remained constant.

"Our leadership is in absolute denial that there's a problem," an agent says. "They don't want to do anything to fix it."

Agents say the Secret Service promotes those who have a similar mind-set and that agency directors stay for two or three years, then leave without changing the culture. As one example of poor management practices, they cite a statement made by a special agent in charge of the vice president's protective detail. The supervisor said that no agents on the detail would ever be promoted because of the number of agents who are seeking promotions.

"The best you can hope for is to get to an office you can make the most of, because the next move will probably be your last," the official told his own agents.

"Needless to say, morale went from low to rock bottom with that," says an agent who was at the meeting. "Several agents left saying they were done, time to move on."

Johnson says she accepts that by its very nature, a Secret Service agent's job is demanding. While she was assigned to protect former president Clinton, he was constantly traveling all over the world. She could hardly ever plan anything in her personal life, because her schedule was his schedule.

What Johnson and others resented was that the Secret Service ignored simple opportunities to lessen the necessary burdens of the job. For example, the Secret Service lets agents know their schedules for the coming week late Friday afternoon, just before the weekend starts. As a result, agents are prevented from planning social and family events.

On trips, agents are expected to work virtually around the clock. In the past several years, the Secret Service imposed limits on overtime pay, offering compensatory time instead. But the agency often denies agents the opportunity to use compensatory or flextime they have earned in lieu of overtime pay. When flextime is taken, it usually must be taken within a week. If an agent has other duties already scheduled, the agent may be forced to forfeit the flextime. After seven years, an agent based in a major city might make upward of $110,000 a year without overtime.

"When you're doing foreign advances, you're working eighteen- and twenty-hour days, seven days a week, yet the schedule says you are working nine to five," says an agent.

What this means is that the Secret Service pays overtime for weekends worked but not for additional hours during the week. In another twist, the agency, as a matter of practice delays paying out overtime earned for two or three years. In the fall of 2008, supervisors on the president's protective detail even began refusing to record agents' overtime pay. When agents began complaining to the financial management division, they were told by supervisors not to make further inquiries.

Paid or not, agents end up working eighteen-hour days.

"How tired do you get? Just imagine sleeping three or four hours a night for a week," says an agent.

"Pilots have mandatory rest periods," says a former agent. "But you've got a guy standing next to the president with a loaded gun who hasn't had sleep in three days and has traveled through four different time zones."

One night, the agent and his wife had an argument.

"You have no right to discipline your children, because you're not their father," his wife said to him. "You don't act like their father; you're never around."

She was right, the former agent says.

"I was never around," he says. "I was missing everything. I was missing Christmas, I was missing Thanksgiving."

The agent quit.

The agency's rigidity extends to administrative personnel. An investigative assistant who was a crackerjack at her job of providing agents with the data they needed asked for a schedule change. She wanted to come to work a half hour earlier than her current schedule called for and leave a half hour earlier so she could pick up her child at day care.

The Secret Service refused, so she left for the Department of Housing and Urban Development. There, she got the schedule she wanted. She even got to work at home on Fridays.

After being a Secret Service agent for almost ten years, Johnson finally quit. She says the agency is mostly run by agents who are "old-school" and think everyone wants to join the Secret Service at any cost.

"In the old days, the Secret Service was a great gig," Johnson says. "People lined up to join. They had applications on the shelves for years. People would drop everything at the drop of a hat to get a Secret Service job. It was great pay and offered stability. Well, times have changed, but their mentality hasn't. People can go out and make a lot more money in the private sector, a lot more money on their own, for much less risk. Management's attitude is almost as though we should literally be thanking them every day we wake up and have a job."

The Secret Service has trouble finding qualified applicants to replace those who are driven away.

"Getting a number of applicants is not a problem. Getting quali-fied applicants is always a problem," Johnson says. "Because of the [service's] high standard, a large portion of the population wouldn't qualify to be an agent. They've done various things trying to recruit good people, but the bottom line is that their policies are driving away the good people they already have."

"They chew their people up," says a former agent. "They treat agents like the Apache Indians treated their horses: They would take their best horse and ride it and ride it, and when it dies, they finally eat it."

17

Timberwolf

THE VICE PRESIDENT'S residence is a handsome 9,150-square-foot three-story mansion overlooking Massa-chusetts Avenue NW. Complete with pool, pool house, and indoor gym, the white brick house was built in 1893 as the home of the superintendent of the U.S. Naval Observatory. Congress turned it into the official residence of the vice president in 1974 and gave it the address One Observatory Circle.

Vice President Mondale was the first to live at the residence. While Mondale's predecessor Nelson Rockefeller could have moved there, he chose to remain in his Foxhall Road estate in Washington and use the vice president's residence for entertaining.

During the day, at least five navy stewards attend to every personal need of the second family, including cooking, shopping for food, cleaning, and doing the laundry. At night, the stewards—known as navy enlisted aides—bake chocolate chip cookies and other goodies for the second family. They also stash leftovers from parties in the refrigerator.

The Secret Service has a separate building—code-named

Tower—on the grounds. The vice president's residence itself is referred to by agents simply as "the res."

Back when George H. W. Bush was vice president, Agent William Albracht was on the midnight shift at the vice president's residence. Agents refer to the president's protective detail as "the big show" and to the vice president's protective detail as "the little show with free parking," because unlike the White House, the vice president's residence provides parking for agents.

New to the post, Albracht was told by Secret Service Agent Pete Dowling, "Well, Bill, every day the stewards bake the cookies, and that is their job, and that is their responsibility. And then our responsibility on midnights is to find those cookies or those left from the previous day and eat as many of them as possible."

At three A.M., Albracht, assigned to the basement post, was getting hungry.

"We never had permission to take food from the kitchen, but sometimes you get very hungry on midnights," Albracht says. "I walked into the kitchen that was located in the basement and opened up the refrigerator. I'm hoping that there are some leftover snacks from that day's reception," the former agent says. "It was slim pickin's. All of a sudden, there's a voice over my shoulder."

"Hey, anything good in there to eat?" the man asked.

"No. Looks like they cleaned it out," Albracht said.

"I turned around to see George Bush off my right shoulder," Albracht says. "After I get over the shock of who it was, Bush says, 'Hey, I was really hoping there would be something to eat.' And I said, 'Well, sir, every day the stewards bake cookies, but every night they hide them from us.' With a wink of his eye he says, 'Let's find 'em.' So we tore the kitchen apart, and sure enough we did find them. He took a stack of chocolate chip cookies and a glass of milk and went back up to bed, and I took a stack and a glass of milk and went back to the basement post."

When Albracht returned to the post, Dowling asked, "Who the hell were you in there talking to?"

"Oh, yeah, sure, right," Dowling said when Albracht told him.

Bush's regular vice presidential detail played a prank on an agent who was on temporary assignment, telling him that it was okay to wash his clothes in the vice president's laundry room.

"He went down and used the vice president's washing machine and dryer," former agent Patrick Sullivan recalls. "Mrs. Bush came down and said to the other agents, 'He's doing his laundry!'"

A supervisor heard about the incident. Mortified, he told Barbara Bush that it had all been a practical joke.

"Oh, don't worry about it," she said.

In fact, at the Bush home in Kennebunkport, Maine, Barbara Bush once strode to the Secret Service post and asked if agents had any laundry they would like her to do, since she was about to do a load anyway. She was so close to the agents that when Pete Dowling's wife, Lindy, was expecting a baby, the first lady instructed him to call her when the baby arrived, day or night.

As vice president, Bush flew to a fund-raiser in Boise, Idaho, during the 1982 election campaign. He was to have dinner at the Chart House seafood restaurant on North Garden Street on the banks of the Boise River.

"The way we protected him, we had some agents inside, but typically what we'd do was situate ourselves at dining tables near him," says former agent Dowling.

Dowling had been seated a few minutes when he heard a radio transmission that two white males in camouflage outfits with long weapons were low-crawling around the back toward their location.

They had their weapons in their hands and were crawling on their bellies, moving themselves along with their elbows.

Just then, Dowling looked up and saw the two bad guys. He recalled intelligence reports that Libya had sent a hit squad to the United States to kill American officials. The agent instinctively jumped out of his chair and tackled Bush to protect him. As food flew everywhere, Dowling threw the vice president onto the ground and flopped on top of him.

"What's going on here?" Bush asked.

"I don't know, but just keep your head down," Dowling replied.

Dowling looked up. He saw about a hundred law enforcement officers with their guns drawn—Secret Service agents, sheriff's department deputies, and state troopers. They were on the scene as part of routine protection for a visit by the vice president. The two bad guys were kneeling with their hands clasped behind their heads.

"We evacuated the VP out of the restaurant to get him away from whatever danger may have still been there," Dowling says. "You would think I had just thwarted an assassination attempt."

As it turned out, the restaurant was near an apartment complex where the girlfriend of one of the two men lived.

"The guy had gone to see his girlfriend, and she was there with another guy," Dowling says. "So the boyfriend got very angry. The other guy who was there with his girlfriend pulled out a knife, kind of slashed him, didn't hurt him badly. So this fellow who had been cut decided that he and another guy were going to go back and kill the guy that night."

Not knowing that the vice president was coming, they parked in the lot at the Chart House and decided to sneak through the woods to get to the apartment complex. They were tried and convicted on illegal weapons and attempted assault charges.

In contrast to many other presidents, Bush—code-named Timberwolf—treated Secret Service agents and everyone else around him with respect and consideration, as did his wife, Barbara. After Bush 41 became president, his twelve-year-old grandson, George Prescott Bush, was hitting tennis balls off the back of the White House tennis court. J. Bonnie Newman, assistant to the president for management and administration, and Joseph W. Hagin, deputy assistant to the president for scheduling, approached the court to play. The two White House aides had earlier reserved the court, but when they saw the president's grandson playing, they turned away and began walking back toward the White House.

Just then, Barbara Bush—code named Tranquility—came along and told George, son of Jeb Bush, to get off the court.

"When we went down and saw the president's grandson, there was no question he should be the one playing on the court," Newman says. "But Mrs. Bush saw it and just plucked him off. She really sent the message not only to staff but to family as well that you remember your manners."

"Bush 41 is a great man, just an all-around nice person," an agent says. "Both he and Mrs. Bush are very thoughtful, and they think outside their own little world. They think of other people."

Bush "made it clear to all his staff that none of them was a security expert, and if the Secret Service made a decision, he was the one to sign off on it, and they were never to question our decisions or make life difficult," Dowling says. "So consequently it was kind of a moment in time, because all the entities really worked well together to make his protection and the activities that he participated in successful."

Bush was so considerate of the agents who protected him that he would stay in town on Christmas Eve so agents could spend it with their families. Then he would fly to Texas the day after Christmas. The Secret Service's only complaint about Bush is that, to this day, he is hyperactive.

"He can't sit still," an agent says. "He is in perpetual motion."

In every hotel, the Secret Service had to make sure Bush had an exercise bike in his suite. If the hotel did not have one, the agency rented one.

"He can't read a book," the agent says. "He has to be on a treadmill or StairMaster. It's go, go, go. For the Secret Service, that meant more work. The tennis court, horseshoes, the golf course, the boat. Always something."

Early on, Bush chafed at protection.

"Most people have difficulty adjusting to having protection," says former Secret Service deputy director Danny Spriggs. "These folks do it because it goes with the job. However, it's nothing they embrace initially. You infringe on their private lives. Even though I did it for twenty-eight years, I can't imagine what it would be like to be told I can't go to a movie or amusement park whenever I want, or to be told that friends I have known for years must submit their name, Social Security number, and date of birth before they can visit me."

One week, with motorcycle sirens screaming, the motorcade twice took him to events just a few blocks from the White House. Bush fussed about the precautions and wanted to know why he couldn't simply walk to the events. His protective detail decided to play a joke on him. While the president's limousine and backup are driven by agents, other Secret Service vehicles in the motorcade are driven by what are called physical support technicians. Billy Ingram, one of these drivers, was a grizzled Korean War veteran.

"He always had a cigarette dangling from his lips with ashes dropping all over," says Joe Funk, an agent who was on Bush's detail. "His personal car was twenty years old and dented. It reeked of cigarette smoke."

Agents affixed the presidential seal and American flag to Ingram's car. When the president came out for the next motorcade ride, his limousine was nowhere in sight. Instead, Ingram's car was at the head of the procession.

"He looked at it," Funk says. "He turned to Barbara and said, 'What's going on?'"

"Well, you're always complaining about the limos. Let's go," the first lady said.

Bush got into Ingram's beat-up car and said to the agents, "You win."

"They drove him to the gate, and that's where the presidential limo was," Funk says.

Despite warnings from his detail, Bush had a habit of leaving the Oval Office through the door to the Rose Garden and greeting tourists lined up along the fence on Pennsylvania Avenue. The detail assigned agents to rush to the fence as soon as an alarm notified them that Bush had opened the door to the outside. Soon, *The Washington Post* ran a story reporting that onlookers were delighted at their unexpected greetings from the president. Right after that, when Bush again greeted fans at the fence, agents spotted what agent Glenn Smith calls a "textbook" possible assassin.

"The man had on a coat in the summer, he looked disheveled, and his eyes were darting in all directions," Smith says. "We patted him down, and it turned out he had a nine-millimeter pistol on him and probably intended to use it on the president."

The head of the detail pointed out to Bush that by greeting people spontaneously, he was not only endangering himself but his agents. After that, "Bush would give us time to set up a secure zone at the fence."

As a courtesy, Secret Service agents try to preset the radio in the limousine to the stations the president or vice president likes. Bush is a country-western fan, so agents preset the radio to country-western stations in whatever town they happened to be in.

"One time, Bush 41 got into the limo and turned on the radio, and, of course, a country-western station came on immediately, and one of his favorite songs was playing," Albracht says. "He started singing along with it. The agent who was driving looked up in the rearview mirror and saw Bush."

"Larry, what do you think?" Bush asked the driver.

Without hesitation, Larry answered, "Don't give up the day job, boss."

Secret Service agents are instructed to ignore any conversations that take place in their presence, but of course they hear everything. At one point, the Secret Service was driving President Bush and Barbara Bush, along with two of their children, who were in the backseat of the limo.

"They were engaged in a deep conversation about something, and suddenly they were distracted," Albracht says. "When they asked each other what they had been talking about, they couldn't remember, and the agent who was driving said 'Y'all talkin' about Social Security.'"

That was a violation of Secret Service protocol, and the supervisor in the right-front seat later reprimanded the agent. The agent's tenure in the transportation section was about to end, but Bush liked him. When he hadn't seen him for a while, Bush asked the Secret Service to assign him as his driver. That did not sit well with supervisors.

When Bush was president, the Secret Service obtained intelligence that a Colombian drug cartel had put out a contract on his family. As a result, Secret Service agents began protecting future president George W. Bush, his children, and his sister and brothers.

"He [George W. Bush] had just bought a new Lincoln, and we were following him closely," former agent John Golden says. "He stopped quickly when a traffic light turned yellow. We plowed into his car, but it turned out there was no damage."

Because Bush's entire family would converge on his summer home in Kennebunkport, agents referred to it as Camp Timberwolf. Because the home is on the water, the Secret Service enlisted the military to search for underwater explosives and patrolled the ocean in boats.

"Our cigarette boat at Kennebunkport was faster than his boat, but if we told him that, he would go out and buy a faster boat," says Andrew Gruler, who was on the president's detail.

At one point, Bush and Barbara flew to their Kennebunkport home in the winter. It was freezing cold, and the president and his wife came out for a walk.

"I had a hat on, and two of the other agents had hats on, but the one agent assigned to the first lady didn't bring a hat with him," says former agent Sullivan, who was on the president's detail. "So the president came out with Mrs. Bush, and we started to walk."

"Where's your hat?" Mrs. Bush asked the hatless agent.

"Oh, Mrs. Bush, I didn't bring one. I didn't realize it was going to be so cold here," he said.

"George, we need to get this agent a hat," Barbara said.

"Okay, Bar," he replied.

She walked back into the house, got one of President Bush's furry hats, and gave it to the agent.

"No, Mrs. Bush, that's fine," the agent said.

"Hey, don't argue with Mrs. Bush," Bush said.

The agent put on the president's hat.

"That was Mrs. Bush," Sullivan says. "She was everyone's mother, and she didn't want this forty-year-old man walking around at Kennebunkport without a hat on. She was a sweetheart."

"Barbara and George Bush were genuinely in love," former agent Albracht says. "They share a special bond of being married and being each other's best friends that you don't really see a lot of. I know there was a woman on the staff that Bush was always rumored to be having an affair with, but I'm telling you, I never saw it, and I was with the guy for four years."

While Barbara "can be sweet and nice, you do anything to cross anybody in the family, and you are written off," says a former agent on Bush's detail. "I remember the Bushes had some friends that would come to visit them, and one of them had decided to vote for Ross Perot, and she wrote that person off. And President Bush would say, 'Aw, Barb, that's just politics.' And she'd say, 'No, that's just not right.' And if somebody divorced his wife and married a younger woman, she didn't like that at all."

18

A Psychic's Vision

RUNNING FOR REELECTION against Bill Clinton, Bush 41 was to give a speech on September 17, 1992, at the civic auditorium in Enid, Oklahoma. Agent Norm Jarvis was assigned to run intelligence investigations for the visit, and a detective from the Oklahoma State Bureau of Investigation called him.

"He said that a woman who was a psychic had told her police contact, whom she worked with on a homicide case in Texas, that she had had a vision that President Bush was going to be assassinated by a sniper," Jarvis says.

People call the Secret Service all the time reporting a vision they have just had about the president being shot. They are usually self-promoters. But in this case, the detective told Jarvis that this psychic's visions had actually helped police find buried bodies and had provided useful leads in criminal investigations. Another seasoned law enforcement homicide investigator from Texas also told Jarvis that he needed to pay attention to her.

"She's the real deal," the Oklahoma detective said.

Jarvis remembered seeing the psychic on television. Sporting a beehive hairdo, she would don what she called a special pair of cowboy boots and then tell police not only where bodies were buried but how the victims had been murdered. The evening before Bush's visit, Jarvis and his partner drove to the woman's home in Enid. She invited them in, and Jarvis told her why they were there. The psychic confirmed that she had had a vision that Bush 41 was about to be assassinated.

"About that time, her husband comes walking into the house, and he looks at me and he says, 'Has she had another one of them visions?'" Jarvis says.

"Yeah," Jarvis said.

The man shook his head and walked through the living room and into the kitchen.

"I gave my partner the nod to go in and talk to him," Jarvis says. "My impression was he was disgusted because he didn't believe her."

Jarvis asked the psychic what she had seen in her vision. The woman said the president was going to come to Oklahoma: He was going to get off the plane, and he was going to get in a limousine.

"I see him sitting behind the driver," she said. "As they start to drive by an overpass, the passenger window is shattered, and he is killed." The next thing she saw was Bush in front of the family home in Kennebunkport. At that point, he is no longer the president.

"How could he be killed, and then your vision down the line is that he's no longer the president and he's at Kennebunkport?" Jarvis asked her.

The woman wasn't sure, but as Jarvis questioned her, she offered more details of her premonition. When Bush gets into his limousine, he does not have a suit on, she said. Instead, he is wearing a light jacket and an open-collar shirt.

Jarvis knew that when the president flew in on Air Force One, he always came out in a suit and tie, and the dress code for the visit was suit and tie. Moreover, when the president is in the limousine, he is not behind the driver; he is on the right rear side, the position of honor.

Just then, Jarvis's partner came out of the kitchen.

"What did he say?" Jarvis asked.

"The husband said if she's seen a vision, it's going to happen," the other agent said.

As a chill went up Jarvis's spine, he asked the woman to describe the limo. She correctly said the car was already in Enid. The Secret Service always flies its vehicles to the sites of presidential visits on a cargo plane prior to the visit, storing them in fire stations or in hangars at the airport where Air Force One is to land. At that point, Jarvis himself did not know where the limo was being stored.

Jarvis asked her to pinpoint where the limo was. She said it was at the air force base near Enid. He asked if she could take him to it; she agreed.

As they drove to the base, Jarvis asked the woman a series of questions to see if she had learned the location of the vehicle through some other means besides her clairvoyance: Did she know anyone who worked at the base? Had anyone told her that they had seen a cargo plane unload a limousine at the base?

As they drove toward the five hangars on the base, the woman gave Jarvis directions.

"As we got close to this one hangar, she said to slow down," Jarvis says.

"Something is in that building right there," the woman said.

"What do you mean?" Jarvis asked.

"Something important is in that building there."

"Okay, but not the limo?"

"No," the woman said.

As they drove past another hangar, the woman said it contained the limo. She then identified another hangar as containing something important.

Jarvis's hunch was that the limo was in the firehouse bordering the runways. As it turned out, he was wrong and the psychic was right. Secret Service agents guard the president's limo until he steps into it. Jarvis checked with them and learned that the hangar identified by the psychic as housing the limo did indeed contain two presidential limousines.

Jarvis mentioned to the woman that the president usually sits on the right side. She insisted that he would be sitting behind the driver. As the woman walked back to Jarvis's car, he asked the special officer in charge of security for the limos what was in the other two hangars she had identified as containing something important.

"He said one contains Marine One, and the other contains other important assets for the president in case of emergencies," Jarvis says.

Jarvis immediately briefed supervisors at the Secret Service Intelligence Division duty desk in Washington.

"You guys are going to think I'm crazy," he said, and then related the information about the vision and how the woman had correctly led him to the president's limo.

As Jarvis saw it, "We deal in the bizarre all the time. Nothing's too wacky that hasn't come across the duty desk report sheet. You're just straight up and lay it out the way you see it. And together you examine and turn the thing over and make a determination."

At one A.M., Jarvis called the head of the advance team and briefed him. However, since the psychic seemed to have been wrong about what clothes Bush would be wearing and about where he would be sitting, they dismissed their concerns. Still, that morning before Bush left for Oklahoma, the head of the advance team informed detail leaders based in W-16 at the White House about the bizarre tale.

Jarvis then discussed the matter with the agent in charge of the motorcade. He asked if the motorcade route would take the president by an overpass. The agent said it would.

"Do you have an alternate motorcade route?"

"Sure. We always do," the agent replied.

That morning, Air Force One landed. Known by the Secret Service code name Angel, Air Force One got its name when Dwight D. Eisenhower—code-named Providence—was president. Prior to that, the aircraft used by Franklin D. Roosevelt and Harry S. Truman had been known by air force designations. Because a flight controller mistook the president's plane for a commercial one, the pilot suggested calling the plane the president was using Air Force One.

The current presidential plane is a Boeing 747-200B bubble top jumbo jet acquired in 1990 when George H. W. Bush was president. It has a range of 9,600 miles and a maximum cruising altitude of 45,100 feet. It cruises at six hundred miles per hour but can achieve speeds of seven hundred one miles per hour. In addition to two pilots, a navigator, and a flight engineer, the 231-foot-long plane carries Air Force One stewards and seventy-six passengers. The plane has eighty-seven telephones.

While the average 747 has 485,000 feet of electrical wire, the presidential plane has 1.2 million feet, all shielded from the electromagnetic pulses that would be emitted during a nuclear blast. Near the front of the six-story-high plane, the president has an executive suite with a stateroom, dressing room, and bathroom with shower. The president also has a private office near the stateroom and a combination dining room and conference room. Toward the back are areas for the staff, Secret Service, guests, and the press.

Under Federal Aviation Administration regulations, Air Force One takes precedence over all other aircraft. When approaching an airport, it bumps other planes that preceded it into the airspace. Before it lands, Secret Service agents on the ground check the runway for explosives or objects such as stray tires. Generally, other aircraft may not land on the same runway for fifteen or twenty minutes before Air Force One lands.

As Bush walked out to the ramp, Jarvis stared at him in amazement. Bush was not wearing a suit. He had on an outdoor jacket and an open-collar shirt, just as the psychic had said he would. Jarvis exchanged glances with the advance leader, who had a shocked look on his face. Then Bush walked down the steps and got into the limousine's right side, his usual position. Jarvis started to relax. But after giving a short speech in Enid, Bush invited some friends to sit with him in the limo for the drive back to the airport. They got in first—on the right side. So Bush walked around the limo and sat down on the left side behind the driver. Again, the psychic had been right.

The advance leader decided the psychic could not be ignored. Never mind if anyone thought they were crazy. Better safe than sorry, he and Jarvis thought.

The advance leader ordered the motorcade to take the alternate route, which did not go by the overpass. No harm befell Bush.

The president was never told what had happened. The psychic, Patsy Henigman, died in 1993 at the age of fifty-five.

19

Eagle

SECRET SERVICE AGENTS refer to what they call Clinton Standard Time. That is a reference to the fact that Bill Clinton—code-named Eagle—is often one to two hours late. To Clinton, an itinerary with scheduled appointments was merely a "suggestion," former agent William Albracht says.

Sometimes Clinton was late because he was playing a game of hearts with his staff. Other times he ignored his schedule because he wanted to chat with a janitor or hotel worker he happened to meet.

Back in May 1993, Clinton ordered Air Force One to wait on the tarmac at Los Angeles International Airport while he got a haircut from Christophe Schatteman, a Beverly Hills hairdresser whose clients have included Nicole Kidman, Goldie Hawn, and Steven Spielberg.

"We flew out of San Diego to L.A. to pick him up," recalls James Saddler, a steward on the fateful trip. "Some guy came out and said he was supposed to cut the president's hair. Christophe cut his hair, and we took off. We were on the ground for an hour."

While Clinton got his haircut on the plane, two LAX runways were closed. Because that meant all incoming and outgoing flights had to be halted, passengers were inconvenienced throughout the country.

The press reported that the haircut cost two hundred dollars, Christophe's fee at the time for a cut in his salon at 348 North Beverly Drive. But Howard Franklin, the chief Air Force One steward, tells me Schatteman told him on the plane that his charge for the cut was five hundred dollars, equal to seven hundred fifty dollars today, adjusted for inflation. Staffers informed Franklin that someone at a Democratic fund-raiser paid it.

When he learned of the flight delays, Clinton expressed anger at his staff for arranging the haircut. But it was his hair that was being cut, and he had given the orders to delay takeoff. As president, he was aware that if Air Force One sat on a runway, air traffic would be halted.

Clinton White House staffers ardently tried to turn the fiasco into a plus. "Is he still the president of the common man?" White House communications director George Stephanopoulos was asked at his daily White House briefing. "Absolutely," he responded. "I mean, the president has to get his hair cut. Everybody has to get their hair cut. . . . I think he does have the right to choose who he wants to cut his hair."

After Clinton's inauguration, Franklin told Clinton's advance people that "the key to being effective was planning." That idea brought a vigorous retort. "They said, 'We got here by being spontaneous, and we're not going to change,'" Franklin recalls. Besides an aversion to planning, Clinton and his people brought with them the attitude that "the military were people who couldn't get jobs," Franklin says.

If Clinton was often late, Hillary Clinton could make Richard Nixon look benign. Everyone on the residence staff recalled what happened when Christopher B. Emery, a White House usher, committed the sin of returning Barbara Bush's call after she had left the White House. Emery had helped Barbara learn to use her laptop. Now she was having computer trouble. Twice Emery helped her out. For that, Hillary Clinton fired him.

The father of four, Emery could not find another job for a year. According to W. David Watkins, a presidential assistant in charge of administration, Hillary was also behind the mass firings of White House travel office employees.

When Hillary found a hapless White House electrician changing a lightbulb in the residence, she began yelling at him because she had ordered that all repair work was to be done when the first family was out.

"She caught the guy on a ladder doing the lightbulb," says Franette McCulloch, the assistant White House pastry chef. "He was a basket case."

"When she's in front of the lights, she turns it on, and when the lights are off and she's away from the lights, she's a totally different person," says an agent who was on her detail. "She's very angry and sarcastic and is very hard on her staff. She yells at them and complains."

In her book *Living History*, Hillary Clinton wrote of her gratitude to the White House staff. The truth was, says a Secret Service agent, "Hillary did not speak to us. We spent years with her. She never said thank you."

Agents found that Clinton's vice president, Al Gore—code-named Sundance—was cut from the same cloth. Every agent has heard that when Gore was bawling out his son, Al Gore III, over poor performance at school, he warned him, "If you don't straighten up, you won't get into the right schools, and if you don't get into the right schools, you could end up like these guys."

Gore motioned toward the agents protecting him.

"Sometimes Gore would come out of the residence, get into the car, and he wouldn't even give the guys the coachman's nod. Nothing," former agent Albracht says. "It was like we didn't exist. We were only there to facilitate him to get from point A to point B." As professionals, Albracht says, "We do not have to like you to protect you, but it can make the long hours a bit more tolerable."

In contrast to Gore, his wife, Tipper, was so friendly with agents that she would play pranks, spraying them with water from a spritzer bottle she used after running. However, "She always insisted on male agents," says former agent Chomicki, who was on Gore's detail. "She didn't want any female agents on the protection squad."

Like Clinton, Gore was often late. One time he showed up an hour late for a dinner with the mayor of Beijing. Another time a Secret Service helicopter that was to shadow him in Las Vegas almost ran out of fuel because Gore was so late coming out of his hotel.

"The schedule would call for him to leave the vice president's residence at seven-fifteen A.M.," former agent Dave Saleeba says. "At seven-thirty A.M, we would check on him, and he would be eating a muffin at the pool."

Gore "wouldn't come out of the vice president's residence on time," Chomicki says. "He'd have an appointment at the White House, he'd get into the car and say, 'Could you speed it up, but don't use the lights and sirens? Get me there as fast as you can.'"

The Secret Service was not about to speed in traffic without lights and sirens. But agents quickly came up with a solution.

"The special agent in charge would come on the radio and say, 'Yeah, let's move as quick as we can but safely,'" Chomicki says. "He'd do it just for the entertainment of the vice president." Without pressing the button to transmit, another agent would pretend to say into the radio, "Hey, let's go, speed it up," Chomicki says. "That would satisfy Gore in the backseat."

Gore never carried money with him and would borrow from

Secret Service agents when he needed some. One of Gore's daughters was graduating from high school, and Gore attended a reception with a cash bar at Old Ebbitt Grill for the families of the graduates.

"So Gore goes up and tries to get a glass of wine, and they want money," recalls Chomicki.

"How much money you got?" Gore asked Chomicki.

Jokingly, Chomicki said, "I do real good. I'm a special agent. I make a lot of money."

Gore explained that he had to pay for drinks.

"What do you need, twenty dollars?" Chomicki asked.

"That'll work," Gore said.

Chomicki handed a twenty-dollar bill to Gore, who later paid him back.

"I think he always thought, 'I'm the vice president. I don't have to pay for anything,'" Chomicki says.

Gore would insist on low-calorie healthy food, but whenever he saw food, he would grab some. "We used to laugh at that," Chomicki says. "Usually, when they have a holding room, it's standard that wherever you go, the host is always going to put something out just to be courteous. Al Gore couldn't pass on a cookie. There wasn't a cookie he didn't like. He'd work hard at trying to keep his weight down. You saw after he got out of office how he bulked up."

As part of his health kick, Gore arranged to have bottled water delivery and a refrigerated dispenser at the residence. As part of routine security precautions, the Secret Service would test the water at the vice president's residence. "They've got this phenomenal water purification system in both the White House and the vice president's residence," says former agent Chomicki. "We would test the water once a month, and the technical security guys used to come up and take samples from all the sinks and taps."

But Chomicki, a Secret Service supervisor, noticed that the bottled water was not being tested. After he suggested that it be tested as well, the Secret Service sent samples of the water to the Environmental Protection Agency for testing. Two days later, EPA called Chomicki. A shocked technician told him the water at the vice president's residence was laced with bacteria.

"He said the EPA had to expand its graph to be able to count the number of bacteria," Chomicki recalls. "The water could cause headaches, diarrhea, and stomachaches."

As a result of the test findings, the EPA confiscated huge batches of water from the bottled water company.

Cutting Corners

FTER 9/11, THE Secret Service faced a double whammy. On the one hand, in a reflexive effort to show that the government was doing something to improve security, President George W. Bush and Congress created the Department of Homeland Security (DHS), an amalgam of twenty-two agencies with 180,000 employees. On March 1, 2003, the Secret Service was transferred from the Treasury Department to the new agency. After being a star at the treasury, the Secret Service became a stepchild competing for funds with other agencies, which were often dysfunctional.

On the other hand, demands on the Secret Service grew exponentially. As outlined in my book *The Terrorist Watch: Inside the Desperate Race to Stop the Next Attack*, al-Qaeda's goal is to deal a devastating blow to America, preferably with nuclear weapons. After 9/11, that threat meant that protection of the president and vice president needed to be much more extensive and robust.

In response to the attacks, President Bush roughly doubled the number of individuals given Secret Service protection to twenty-seven permanent protectees, plus ten family members. Another seven were protected when traveling abroad. By executive order, Bush provided protection to individuals such as his chief of staff and national security adviser. Others, such as the secretaries of the treasury and of homeland security, received protection because they are in the line of succession to the presidency. As such, they are authorized to receive protection as decided by the secretary of homeland security. Some officials received only partial protection, such as when traveling to and from work.

The Secret Service's expanded protective duties came in addition to protecting visiting heads of state and their spouses and other official guests, an enlargement of Secret Service duties authorized by Congress in 1971. Under the Presidential Threat Protection Act of 2000, the Secret Service was also charged with planning and implementing security arrangements at "special events of national significance."

The winter Olympics in Salt Lake City in 2002 was the first such event under the act. Prior to that, under a directive issued by President Clinton in 1998, some events such as the president's State of the Union address had a similar designation. Other so-called national special security events are the United Nations General Assembly, presidential inaugurals, the Democratic and Republican nominating conventions, the Super Bowl, G8 summits, and a major visit such as Pope Benedict XVI's trip to the United States in 2008. The state funerals of Presidents Ronald Reagan and Gerald Ford were also designated national special security events. At these events, the Secret Service is the lead law enforcement agency and coordinates all security arrangements.

While the vice president's protective detail now has a hundred fifty agents and the president's detail has three hundred agents, the details are stretched thin. These same agents undertake advance work for trips that often take place every day. With the 2008 presidential campaign being the longest in history, demands on the Secret Service went through the roof.

While the Secret Service receives modest budget increases, the annual appropriation is still a mere $1.4 billion—less than the cost of one stealth bomber. About a third of the budget goes to investigating crimes such as counterfeiting, check fraud, fraudulent use of ATM cards or credit cards, identity crimes, and computer-based attacks on the nation's financial, banking, and telecommunications infrastructure. Likewise, about a third of the Secret Service's agents are assigned to investigative work, but that figure is misleading because agents doing such work in field offices are routinely pulled off their assignments for protection work. In man-hours, slightly more than half of agents' time is devoted to protection. Because it can boast of arrests, the 6,489-employee Secret Service keeps expanding its jurisdiction in the investigative areas.

To be sure, the Secret Service's work on financial crimes is impressive.

Back in 1983, when Secret Service director Mark Sullivan started out as an agent, "When we picked up credit card fraud, a sophisticated credit card fraud back then would be somebody going to a dumpster behind some restaurant and diving in and getting somebody's credit card numbers out of the dumpster," Sullivan tells me.

Another scheme would be to steal an embossing machine from a hospital.

"They'd print a credit card number and somebody's name on there," Sullivan says. "And you know, you'd look at the credit card number, and it would be going like diagonally down the card. And that was a sophisticated credit card fraud."

Now the Secret Service is up against the most sophisticated cyber criminals. Learning about the investigative side of the agency is enough to scare anyone. Counterfeiters have become so devious that bank tellers who are trained to spot fake bills can't detect counterfeits even using a magnifying glass. Waiters with so-called skimmers swipe your credit card before they submit it for payment of your check. The encoded information on the magnetic strip is stored and then sold for twenty dollars per credit card.

On websites, criminals can buy the numbers imprinted on stolen credit cards. They can also fool banks into handing over all the money in your checking account, not to mention siphoning cash from ATMs. Phishing—fraudulently extracting money from people online—has been increasing at a rate of as much as 4,000 percent a year.

Then there are the Nigerian fraud artists who promise to make people rich, then wipe out their life savings. Some victims revictimize themselves: After losing most of their money, they fall for the scheme all over again. Nigeria prints and ships boxes of counterfeit treasury checks to the United States. Since the Nigerian government is often complicit, the Secret Service has closed its office in Lagos.

The North Korean government counterfeits U.S. currency using high-pressure intaglio presses that are about as good as those of the U.S. Bureau of Engraving and Printing. Other counterfeits are made with offset or flatbed presses or digital printers, which make the crudest counterfeits. About one in ten thousand bills in circulation is counterfeit. Most of them are hundred-dollar bills. Because counterfeit U.S. currency is so prevalent, banks and currency exchangers in many Asian countries refuse to accept U.S. bills.

Thefts of credit card numbers have become so widespread that "You have already been compromised; they just haven't gotten around to using your number," Tom Lascell of the criminal investigative division says reassuringly. "We used to think holograms on credit cards made them safe," he says. He then holds up a photo of dozens of credit cards for sale with holograms.

Investigations by the criminal side of the agency sometimes lead to strange findings. In 1986, Patrick Sullivan and other agents learned from an informant that Gregory Scarpa, Sr., a capo, or captain, in the

Colombo Mafia family, was involved in creating counterfeit credit cards. After Sullivan arrested him, he was driving him to the Secret Service field office in New York when Scarpa asked Sullivan to stop the car.

"We pull over, and he tells us he is the highest-level Mafia inform-ant in the FBI," Sullivan recalls. At the time, Sullivan was the Secret Service's representative to the Department of Justice's Organized Crime Strike Force in Brooklyn. He knew Scarpa was a prime target of the strike force.

"I was stunned," Sullivan says.

As later documented in court filings, Scarpa revealed that for at least twenty years, he had betrayed to the bureau secrets about the Mafia—including murders planned and committed. Moreover, Scarpa disclosed that at the behest of the FBI, he terrorized a Ku Klux Klan member into disclosing where the bodies of three civil rights workers who were murdered in 1964 were buried in Mississippi.

As important as the criminal side of the Secret Service is, with the exception of counterfeit currency investigations, the FBI investigates the same crimes. Each agency pursues leads it happens to receive. Yet the Secret Service seeks greater jurisdiction in these areas even as pro-tection demands increase.

From its early days, the Secret Service's culture dictated that the job got done, regardless of obstacles. While that ethic is admirable, taking on more duties without enough resources is not. Rather than taking a long-range view and making waves by demanding the neces-sary funding or shedding jurisdiction in some areas, Secret Service management makes do, boasting, "We do more for less."

The result, according to current and former agents, is that since it became part of DHS, the Secret Service has been cutting corners and covering up deficiencies to the point where the security of the presi-dent, vice president, and presidential candidates is compromised.

"They will cut a protective detail down to the bone to save on costs, but throw every agent into an operation that will result in arrests," an agent says. "The service either needs twice as many agents or half as much responsibility. The priorities are all messed up."

Some of those compromises are a result of the turnover rate that, in turn, stems from senseless transfer policies. Because so many agents are leaving before retirement, less experienced agents remain to do the job. On the vice president's detail alone, agents are being brought in from the counterassault team to stand protective duty.

"This acknowledges that we are losing people and now have to borrow from other divisions just for our daily activities," an agent on one of the major details points out. "I have never seen them have to resort to doing this."

Even more shocking, for presidential candidates and many protectees below the president and vice president, the counterassault teams themselves have been slashed in the past few years from the requisite five or six agents to only two agents.

"CAT is trained to operate as a full team of five to six men," a current agent who was formerly on CAT says. "Each member has a specific function based upon the direction of the attack. A two-man element responds to the problem, while another responds to the attack with a base of fire—providing cover fire and trying to suppress the attackers—while the other element moves on them to destroy them. The other two-man element—or solo member, if there are only five operators—provides coverage in the rear and assists the element that is moving to address the attack."

A team of only two men "cannot do all of those tasks, on top of communicating to the protective detail a status report detailing number of attackers, number of good guys or bad guys killed or captured, and then requesting direction from the detail leader about the next course of action," the agent says.

William Albracht, a founding member and four-year team leader of the counterassault teams, could not believe that the Secret Service now cuts corners by reducing the team in many cases to only two agents.

"CAT team members are comprised of highly trained and extremely motivated agents," Albracht says. "All are volunteers, and after an exhausting selection process, those that qualify are handpicked for the assignment. The counterassault team itself is organized as a coordinated unit."

Albracht, who taught new agents, says a counterassault team cannot operate with only two agents. "When an attack initiates, one team deploys immediately, tries to flank and go to the actual source of the attack," he says. "The other lays down a base of fire. Once the counterassault team achieves fire superiority, the second prong of the counterattack moves in."

If the team is cut to two members, "It's not a team," Albracht says. "Then it would be just two guys with submachine guns."

Similarly, Reginald Ball, who was on the counterassault team for three years, says, "The team is always at least five members. Otherwise, the concept does not work."

When first daughter Barbara Bush was in Africa in 2004 and 2005, a majority of the CAT team leaders and assistant team leaders signed a letter to the then assistant special agent in charge (ASAIC) of CAT, conveying their concerns over the fact that her CAT had been cut to two agents.

"The ASAIC responded by denying there was any problem and saying we should do the job we are tasked with, whether it is a full team or a two-man element," an agent who was on the trip says.

Besides cutting CAT teams, since its absorption by DHS, the Secret Service has cut back on protection of the U.N. General Assembly. When the General Assembly is in session, every spare agent is assigned to guard the more than one hundred thirty heads of state and the sixty-three spouses they bring to New York City. High-level protectees receive a full detail, with both counterassault and countersniper teams.

But the Secret Service now assigns lower-level protectees what is called a dot formation—only a detail leader and two agents working twelve-hour shifts. In many cases, agents are reassigned from protecting the president and vice president or from being on their CAT teams to go to New York. During this period, an agent is not allowed to take annual leave unless he has a death or major illness in his immediate family.

Before the Secret Service became part of DHS, it would make sure lower-level protectees had adequate protection by assigning officers from the Bureau of Alcohol, Tobacco, and Firearms; Customs and Border Protection; or the U.S. Marshals Service to supplement each detail.

"The dot formation is a joke and simply window dressing that allows us to accomplish our taxi service mission," an agent detailed to protect heads of state at the U.N. General Assembly says. "Any attempt on a protectee would in all likelihood be successful."

While U.N. coverage and CAT teams have been cut, in-service training, time for workouts, physical fitness and training, and firearms training and qualification also have been slashed.

"Every six weeks, you are supposed to cycle out to training for two weeks," says an agent. "For two solid weeks you should be training, shooting. These are the agents that are assigned to protect the vice president and the president. But I've been on the detail for nineteen months, and I've gone to Beltsville [the Secret Service training facility] once. Instead, you're told you have an assignment to go sit for the grandchildren of the vice president."

"Most law enforcement agencies require anywhere from forty to a hundred twenty hours per year of in-service training for its officers," says an agent on one of the top protective details. "Do you know how many days of protective training I've had in the last two years? Zero. No review of legal rulings, interview techniques, investigative trends, protective intelligence investigations, or advance protection work. No constant training in ambush response, emergency medicine scenarios, or emergency vehicle operation.

"Training is almost nonexistent, and it shows," says the agent. He cites one training scenario where a motorcade is ambushed. The shift leader is supposed to identify where the attack is coming from. Based on that, the agents know how to deploy and go after the attackers.

"What we saw was just an absolute embarrassment, people running around in circles, not knowing where to go, what to do, couldn't identify where the attack was coming from," the agent says. "They would have all been killed within a matter of seconds had that been an actual attack. We'd have lost everybody and the protectee."

According to Secret Service policy, "We are supposed to be given three hours a week just for physical training," another current agent says. "Well, that's never going to happen."

Secret Service rules require agents based in Washington to qualify with a pistol once a month and with long guns every three months. But, in contrast to years past, many agents find they are given time to take the qualifying test for long guns only once or twice a year.

"I've had conversations with special agents in charge who say they are not able to get the requalification training in they would like because of the operational demands they have," says Danny Spriggs, who retired from the Secret Service as deputy director in 2004. In previous years, "We never sacrificed training," he says.

Agents who have left the Secret Service to join other federal law enforcement agencies report that, in many cases, training in firearms and counterterrorism tactics in those agencies far exceeds the quality of what the Secret Service offers.

"They actually encourage training here rather than making up excuses for not training," one of those agents says.

Unlike the FBI, the Secret Service has no use for outside education.

"If you wanted to go out and get a master's degree or a doctoral degree, it's on your own, and they won't work around your schedule," a Secret Service agent says. "The FBI will give you sabbatical time." The bureau also will pay for outside education if it is related to an agent's field of work. "Management's mentality at the Secret Service is that the agent doesn't need to know that. The agent just needs to do his job and shut up."

Standards are so lax that agents are actually handed blank evaluations for possible promotions and fitness ratings and asked to fill them in themselves. According to agents, those who have "juice" or "hooks" with management because they play golf with someone receive good evaluations. Agents who don't have hooks are told, "You're getting a rating of forty-six out of fifty, no matter what."

"You are supposed to do your physical training test quarterly, but I haven't done one in two, three years," an agent says. "When you do, you enter your scores yourself on a form and hand it in." In fact, the agent says, "I'm one of the PT instructors. And because the service takes physical training so lightly, I don't take it seriously either. Just give me a sheet, and I trust that what the agent says he did is accurate."

A third agent estimates that 98 percent of the agents provide their own scores for the PT test. "You fill out a form, hand it to the guy, he enters it in, and he doesn't know if you did your PT test or not," he says. "You test yourself."

As a result, agents say, many of their colleagues are out of shape.

"Some of them, you just roll your eyes," an agent says. "One agent cannot even do a sit-up. I know for a fact he can't because his belly's already up to his chin. Just look at some of the details, and you can really see where the standards have gone—downhill."

"We had a post stander last weekend, a female agent, and I was in shock," says an agent, referring to agents assigned to guard a specific area or site on a temporary basis. "Overweight, out of shape, just disgusting. And you look at this person and say, 'If I'm going to go through a door with you to execute a search warrant, are you going to have my back? If I get shot, are you going to be able to carry me out? Or are you going to be able to get up four flights of stairs because I'm in a fight with somebody?' Probably not."

21

POTUS

THE CURRENT LOCATION of the president is displayed by an electronic box at key offices in the White House and at the Secret Service. He is listed as POTUS, for president of the United States. Called the protectee locator, the box also shows the location of the first lady (FLOTUS), the vice president (VPOTUS), and the president's and vice president's children. If they are not in Washington, the locator box displays their current city. In addition, Uniformed Division officers stationed at the White House update one another by radio on the location of the president and first lady within the Executive Mansion.

When the Clintons were in the White House, "It was funny, because on the radio you'd hear that she went somewhere, and then you'd hear that he went to the same location, and every time he went to her, she would go somewhere else," a former Uniformed Division officer says.

Like most other presidents, Clinton got a charge out of greeting his fans. One evening, he was to attend a high school reunion in Little Rock. The Secret Service had sealed off the floor of his hotel room and had checked out the hotel employees who would be given access to the floor. Two maids who had been cleared asked Agent Timothy Gobble if they could stay near the end of the hall to catch a glimpse of Clinton as he left for his motorcade. Already late, Clinton saw the two women waving at him and walked to the end of the hall to chat with them.

"You could see how thrilled they were," Gobble says. "Here was the leader of the free world who took three minutes to talk to them. They thanked me profusely for giving them that opportunity. There were no cameras around, so it was not for show."

Clinton not only loved greeting people but had a gift for remembering who they were. After a speech in New York at an AFL-CIO convention, Clinton was shaking hands. Agents noticed a busboy eyeing him and moving closer.

"Clinton saw him and called him by his name," says an agent on his detail at the time. "The president shook his hand and asked how his father was. The busboy got teary-eyed and said his father had died. Commiserating with him, Clinton turned to an aide and said the man's father had had cancer."

"When presidents get into a crowd, they just seem like they feed on the energy from the people they are shaking hands with," Albracht says. "They may be dragging from a long day of travel and campaigning, but when they hit the rope line, they start to get energized all over again. I've seen it time and time again. It seemed to have the strongest effect on Clinton. He'd replenish his energy from theirs and get charged up and ready to continue. They all did it, but it seemed to have the strongest effect on him."

Clinton liked to go running, presenting the predictable security problems.

"There were people waiting for him to run every morning," says Pete Dowling, who was second in command of Clinton's detail during the first term. "So it was nice for him, but quite frankly, for us they were unwanted guests. They weren't screened; we didn't know who they were. People were trying to hand him water bottles, so we were really concerned about that. If the president were to run up the Mall every day, with the same regularity, it'd be pretty easy for a terrorist group, who would observe his actions, maybe to plant a bomb in a trash can. And if he didn't run by that day? They'd just take it away and come back again. That kind of presented a threat to us that we hadn't seen before."

The Secret Service discussed its concerns with Clinton, but he continued to run. That changed after he fell walking down the stairs at golf pro Greg Norman's house in Florida in the early morning hours of March 14, 1997. The Secret Service Joint Ops Center then woke agent Norm Jarvis at home to ask him to secure the National Naval Medical Center in Bethesda, Maryland, where surgery would be done on the president to reattach a tendon torn from his right kneecap.

Later that morning, Clinton arrived by motorcade from Andrews Air Force Base. Jarvis arranged for an agent to stand in the operating room throughout the surgery.

"I'm not sure if they knew we had guns on under our scrubs, but sharp cutting instruments so close to the president—even in the hands of a trusted military physician—needed a countermeasure in the hands of a trusted agent," Jarvis says.

Clinton's doctor, Admiral E. "Connie" Mariano, who traveled with the president, oversaw the operation. But Jarvis was startled to see an orderly line of dozens of surgeons outside the operating room waiting to step up and do part of the knee reconstruction.

"Each one had a tool, probe, scalpel, or whatever, waiting to take their turn to poke, cut, or saw so they could claim they operated on the president of the United States," Jarvis says. "After the anesthesia was administered, the first surgeon did the initial incision. The next exposed the tendon. Then another cut the tendon to even out the jagged remains. Another surgeon cleaned and exposed the kneecap. On and on it went for hours."

In one form or another, Jarvis had seen this phenomenon played out dozens of times: For most people, any contact with a president is a highlight of their lives.

Clinton did not want to return to the White House in an ambulance, and Secret Service vans were not equipped to transport him in a wheelchair. Because Jarvis knew Sarah Brady, wife of the former Reagan press secretary James Brady, he asked if the Secret Service could borrow her husband's wheelchair-accessible van for the trip.

Clinton faced about eight weeks on crutches and months of physical therapy. He had to wear an adjustable leg brace to restrict knee movement. After that incident, Clinton gave up running and started using exercise machines.

Meanwhile, the Secret Service tried to adapt to Clinton's style.

"President Clinton would see a small crowd of spectators that may have gathered behind a rope outside our secure perimeter just to get a glimpse of the president, and he would head off to shake their hands," says Jarvis. "Of course, this drove us to distraction because we didn't want him to approach an un-magged crowd. We didn't know if we had a Hinckley or Bremer in the crowd with a handgun. A person like that might be loitering in the area because he couldn't get into the event."

In fact, at one point, Jarvis was faced with just such a situation: Clinton had plunged into a crowd that had not been screened.

"I was in the lead on the rope line," Jarvis says. "When you're working a rope line, there are agents leading in the president's direction, then there's the president, and then others who trail behind, with others nearby."

Jarvis noticed a woman whose hands were under her coat.

During an event, "You'll be in the formation and walking along with the president, you spot something, and you say something over the air to the shift leader," Jarvis says. "You're generally very quiet. There's not a lot of chatter, but if you say something and you're with the president, it means something. You size up the person that causes you to bring your attention to them, and you have to make a quick judgment as to what you're going to do or what the detail needs to do."

In this case, "What was strange was everyone was looking at the president—clapping, yelling, smiling," Jarvis says. "She was staring down and had a real puzzled look on her face. Mind you, the president was two arms' lengths from us. I let the shift leader know I had a problem, and I just wrapped my arms around this woman because I didn't have time to frisk her."

Jarvis held her in a bear hug as the shift and the president worked their way around him.

"She was startled, but I wouldn't let her arms out from under the coat," Jarvis says. "I held her until I could get some assistance, which arrived from a protective intelligence team that was nearby."

The team interviewed the woman and quickly determined that she was mentally ill.

"She didn't have a weapon under her coat, but you can tell mentally disturbed people by the way they react," Jarvis notes. "And when they react the opposite of everybody else, it brings your attention to them, and you know you've got an issue out of the ordinary."

To be sure, Jarvis says, "Not a lot of people would appreciate an agent grabbing them in a bear hug and pinning them against a crowd. But you've got maybe seconds to correctly respond to a situation that has potentially catastrophic consequences."

"We had a young, gregarious guy who absolutely thrived on and was energized by being in crowds," Dowling says. "We weren't going to have a conversation saying, 'Sir, you're really going to have to change. This isn't presidential.' We really had to redefine the way we did business on the road."

Dowling thought the fact that Clinton would plunge unpredictably into crowds could work to the advantage of the Secret Service because there was no advance notice. "The odds of somebody being there that would willingly want to do him harm were at least decreased," notes Dowling, who later headed the Washington field office. At the same time, Dowling says, the Secret Service worked with the staff to identify places where Clinton could go and allow agents to scout out the areas in advance.

On Sunday morning, February 26, 1995, Dowling read an item in *Parade* magazine's Personality Parade and knew he was in for trouble. The item asked how much truth there was to "those stories coming out of Washington that Bill Clinton is still an incurable womanizer."

Parade answered, "If there were any hard evidence that the president of the U.S. was womanizing, you can be certain it would have appeared by now in the media. The days when the White House press corps respected a president's privacy and ignored his extracurricular activities—as with JFK—are long gone."

More ominously for the Secret Service, the item continued: "Insiders say the salacious rumors about Bill Clinton often can be traced to Secret Service agents, who may be feuding with the first lady. She reportedly suspects that some of the agents are snoops and tries to keep them at a distance. One agent recently spread a story that Mrs. Clinton had become so tired of her husband's wandering ways that she threatened to seek a divorce and run against him in 1996. No one believes that outlandish tale, but unfortunately it has made its way through the Washington gossip mill."

Dowling, the assistant special agent in charge of the Clinton detail, was working that Sunday. The Clintons were attending church, and the president said nothing to him about the *Parade* item. However, two hours later, Dowling was at his office in Room 62 of the Eisenhower Executive Office Building when the phone rang.

"Mr. Dowling, stand by please for the president," a White House operator said.

"Did you see *Parade* magazine this morning?" Clinton asked Dowling.

"Yes, sir, I did," Dowling replied. "I was very disturbed at what I saw."

"This is happening all too often, that the Secret Service is purported to have said this," Clinton said.

"For the first time in history, Mr. President, we've had to defend our honor in terms of being able to maintain the privacy of the family that we protect," Dowling said. "But let's think about this for a second. You think if we were to say something, we would say something as preposterous as that? As that your wife was going to run against you?"

"You know, you're right," Clinton said.

In fact, many of the stories were untrue. Hillary never threw a lamp at Bill, the Secret Service saw no indication that she was a lesbian, and Bill never left the White House to see an alleged girlfriend at the Marriott. But on August 17, 1998, Bill Clinton confessed from the Map Room of the White House on national television to his relationship with Monica Lewinsky. "Indeed, I did have a relationship with Miss Lewinsky that was not appropriate. In fact, it was wrong," Clinton said.

The next day, the Clintons took Air Force One to Martha's Vineyard.

"I was up at Martha's Vineyard right after he had confessed on national TV to the whole Monica Lewinsky affair," Albracht says. While Albracht was operating the command post, Hillary called him and said, "Where is he?"

"Ma'am, the president is downtown right now. I think he just arrived at a Starbucks," Albracht said.

"Confirm that," Hillary demanded, and Albracht did. Hillary then ordered Albracht to tell the president to "get home now, and I mean right now."

Albracht passed along the message to the detail.

"Oh, my God. Clinton loves mingling with people, and he loves to play golf, but she was having none of that," Albracht says. "Clinton was to remain at the Martha's Vineyard estate. He was being punished. It was like he was grounded," Albracht says.

When in public, Hillary would smile and act graciously. As soon as the cameras were off, her angry personality often became evident. During her run for the Senate, Hillary planned visits to diners and local hangouts as part of her "listening tour."

"The events were all staged, and the questions were screened," says a Secret Service agent who was on her detail. "She would stop off at diners. The campaign would tell them three days ahead that they were coming. They would talk to the owner and tell him to invite everyone and bring his friends. Hillary flew into rages when she thought her campaign staff had not corralled enough onlookers beforehand. Hillary had an explosive temper."

Publicly, Hillary—code-named Evergreen—courted law enforcement organizations, but she did not want police near her.

"She did not want police officers in sight," a former agent says. "How do you explain that to the police? She did not want Secret Service protection near. She wanted state troopers and local police to wear suits and stay in unmarked cars. If there was an incident, that could pose a big problem. People don't know police are in the area unless officers wear uniforms and drive police cars. If they are unaware of a police presence, people are more likely to get out of control."

In Syracuse, a bearded man who aggressively sought autographs accosted Hillary as she went for a walk outside her hotel.

"He grabbed her," an agent says. "She was livid. But she had insisted she did not want us near her."

Hillary's campaign staff planned a visit to a 4-H club in dairy farm country in upstate New York. As they approached the outdoor event and she saw people dressed in jeans and surrounded by cows, Hillary flew into a rage.

"She turned to a staffer and said, 'What the [expletive] did we come here for? There's no money here,'" a Secret Service agent remembers.

In contrast to Hillary, since leaving the White House, Bill Clinton is "very friendly to the agents," says one agent. "I think he realizes once he's out of office, we're pretty much all he's got, and he does treat the guys really well."

Until 1997, former presidents received lifetime Secret Service protection, as did their spouses unless they remarried. However, congressional legislation that became effective on January 1, 1997, limited the protection of former presidents elected after that date to no more than ten years after they leave office. George W. Bush will be the first president whose protection will end after ten years. Children of former presidents receive protection to age sixteen. In September 2008, Congress passed legislation extending protection of the vice president, his spouse, and his children who are under sixteen years of age to six months after he leaves office.

After Clinton left the presidency, "Anywhere he went, he shook hands; he'd go out of his way to shake the hand of a worker," says a former agent who was on his detail. "Fifty feet away and on a tarmac, he's walking around a plane to shake the hand of a worker. Or going through the hotel's restaurant, he's in the back in the kitchen shaking people's hands and taking pictures."

Clinton's office is in Harlem, where a woman on the street told the agent, "Honey, you can take the day off. We're not going to let anything happen to that man."

22

Shutting Down Magnetometers

D URING SENATOR JOHN Kerry's presidential campaign, an event near a train station was about to start. A thousand supporters still had to be screened.

"What are we going to do?" a Kerry staff member said. "There's still a thousand people waiting to come to the mags [magnetometers]."

"Right," the agent said in response. "This is security. They'll come in as soon as we can screen them."

"Well, he's going to be here in five minutes. There's no way they're going to get them in the mags," the aide said.

According to the agent, a Secret Service supervisor then allowed the rest of the crowd to enter unscreened.

"That happened a number of times at other sites, other venues," the agent says. "How are they making these decisions? You've got agents doing the right thing, making this as safe as it can be for the candidate, and one supervisor completely undercuts it."

When President George W. Bush visited an eastern European country, "The local police set up a very good checkpoint and were doing a thorough job of screening people with magnetometers," an agent who was assigned to the trip recalls. "When a staff lead saw the mags were backed up and not all the people would make it to hear Bush's speech, she demanded that the mag officers expedite clearing people through. When a Uniformed Division lieutenant said they needed to do their job, the White House staff person completely went nuts, threatening the officer and threatening to report him to the head of Bush's detail. The local authorities held their ground and did not cave to the staffer."

Yet at other times, the Secret Service bows to White House or candidate pressure to stop magnetometer screening. When acquiescing to such requests, Secret Service management assures the White House staff that stopping screening is not a problem, Andy Card, President Bush's former chief of staff, tells me. The White House, in turn, trusts the service.

Aides want to believe in the omnipotence of the Secret Service because it serves their political ends. They do not want to annoy stragglers. Yet if one of the people allowed through without screening drew a weapon or threw a grenade and assassinated a president or a candidate, it would be entirely because of the Secret Service's negligence. Indeed, Arthur Bremer was able to shoot Alabama governor George Wallace—the only presidential candidate shot while under Secret Service protection—because magnetometers were not used.

As was the case with protecting presidents, Congress was slow to act when it came to protecting presidential candidates. It did not extend protection to candidates until Robert F. Kennedy was assassinated on June 5, 1968, after he won the Democratic presidential primary in California. As a result of the legislation, Secret Service agents were protecting Wallace on May 15, 1972, when he spoke to about two thousand people at a shopping center parking lot in Laurel, Maryland. It was a beautiful, sunny day. Because of the heat, Wallace decided to remove his cumbersome bulletproof vest.

"The crowd was cheering and everyone was responding well to him," recalls William Breen, a Secret Service agent on his detail at the time. "He certainly could electrify a crowd. And when he concluded his speech, he was supposed to leave the podium and go directly, directly to the car. There were not to be any intermediate stops. And as he started—I was the point agent—he was to follow me. And I was going to go right over to the automobile. He was to get in and that was it, we were off to wherever we were going."

"You've got my vote," Clyde Merryman, an exercise boy at Pimlico Race Track, told Wallace.

Just then, Arthur Bremer jumped from the second row of spectators and yelled, "Governor, over here!"

"He [Wallace] just went right to Bremer, and of course the configuration of the protective circle changed," Breen says. "Bremer opened up on him and shot him."

The first .38 caliber bullet tore into Wallace's midsection. Bremer fired five more times. All but one shot hit its mark.

The governor, coatless under the afternoon sun, fell backward on the pavement. There were red stains on his blue shirt. His wife, Cornelia, rushed to his side, crying and cradling his head in her hands. Her beige suit was smeared with blood.

"Jimmy Taylor, who was the agent in charge of the detail, and I were the first to Wallace, and we got him on the ground," Breen says.

"Governor, this is Bill. You've been shot. You'll be all right," Breen whispered into his ear.

Secret Service agents and Alabama state troopers pounced on Bremer. Besides Wallace, Bremer had wounded Alabama trooper E. C. Dothard, Secret Service Agent Nicholas Zarvos, and Dora Thompson, a Wallace campaign volunteer. Although Wallace survived, he was paralyzed, and he dropped out of the race.

Like most assassins, Bremer kept a diary. His jottings described how pathetic and insignificant he thought he was. Also, like most assassins, Bremer had stalked his victim. Before shooting Governor Wallace, Bremer had stalked Richard Nixon and other national figures. Only days before he shot Wallace, Bremer had sat in his car in Kalamazoo, Michigan, for nearly the entire day outside an armory where Wallace was scheduled to speak. A store owner called the police, and Bremer was picked up as a suspicious person. He told police that he was waiting to hear Wallace's speech. Satisfied, the police released him without searching for a weapon.

As with the previous assassination attempts, the Secret Service learned lessons from the incident. Back then, the Secret Service did not travel with emergency medical technicians in case of an assassination attempt. Breen remembers looking for a pack of cigarettes so he could rip off the cellophane and try to stanch a gaping wound in Wallace's chest. Now the Secret Service alerts hospitals when the president or other protectees will be in their area. At least as far back as Franklin Delano Roosevelt, a military doctor has traveled with the president and has maintained a medical facility at the White House.

"If something happens now, you have an entire medical staff waiting for you when you get to the hospital," Breen says. "It's nothing like back in 1972, when Jimmy Taylor and I were confronted with the worst thing that could happen to a Secret Service agent, to have a protectee hurt or killed. This is your job, you're supposed to protect him, and something like this happens. And it rarely does, but it certainly happens. The agents feel horrible about it, and you live with it a long time."

While the Secret Service wanted to screen crowds with magnetometers, candidates like Wallace objected, saying such security measures would needlessly irritate people and discourage them from showing up. After the Reagan shooting, the Secret Service began using magnetometers routinely to find hidden weapons. To allow crowds into an event without magnetometer screening became unthinkable. Yet in recent years, under pressure from politicians' staffs to let crowds into events without screening, the agency has buckled.

Only one such incident has been publicized. The press reported complaints from current or retired law enforcement officials that an hour before a rally for presidential candidate Barack Obama was to start at Reunion Arena in Dallas on February 20, 2008, the Secret Service stopped magnetometer screening.

The *Fort Worth Star-Telegram* reported that Danny Defenbaugh, a former FBI agent who was inspector in charge of the bureau's investigation of the 1995 Oklahoma City bombing, questioned why guards would suddenly stop searching for weapons.

"Why were they doing it in the first place?" Defenbaugh asked rhetorically, adding that "of course" screening for weapons should have continued. "Dallas, 1963," he added. "You know what happened. I don't think Dallas wants that to happen again."

"This relaxed security was unbelievably stupid, especially in Dallas," Jeff Adams of Berkeley, California, said in an email to the paper, noting the assassination of President Kennedy in that same city more than four decades earlier.

Eric Zahren, a spokesman for the Secret Service in Washington, denied that stopping screening posed a problem.

"There were no security lapses at that venue," Zahren told the Dallas paper. There was "no deviation" from the "comprehensive and layered" plan, implemented in "very close cooperation with our law enforcement partners," he added.

But agents say such lapses occur periodically and defy common sense. An agent who was on Obama's presidential candidate detail says it was "not uncommon" to waive magnetometers at events when the crowd was larger than expected. While the overflow might be seated far from the candidate and often behind a buffer zone, "Someone could still fire a gun, make their way to the front, or detonate explosives," the agent says.

Other agents say magnetometers have also been waived for events attended by President George W. Bush, John Edwards, John Kerry, and others. Agents attribute such obvious lapses in security to the fact that the Secret Service does not have enough manpower to screen everyone properly.

"It's complacency," says the agent who was on Obama's detail. "They say we can make do with less."

On top of that, the Secret Service not only slashed the number of agents on counterassault teams assigned to the candidates from the necessary five or six agents to two, it delayed assigning them a CAT team. Then, when the candidates insisted that the CAT teams stay out of sight, the Secret Service caved.

During the 2008 campaign, "The agents assigned to the candidates were told to stay at least one terrain feature away from the working shift," an agent says. "Most of the time, that means a street block away from the protectee."

While CAT agents need to be kept out of the kill zone, they should have the candidate directly in sight.

"An attack, from beginning to end, could sometimes last no more than ten or twenty seconds," a current agent says. "If you are a block away, you cannot identify the threat, know where the protectee is, respond to the threat, engage the threat, and then respond to wherever the working shift leader orders you to go."

In a stadium or auditorium, the CAT team is stationed at the point where the protectee leaves the stage. In that situation, the audience cannot see the team, so the candidates did not object to its presence. But when the CAT team is outside, stationing it at a distance renders the team "completely ineffective," an agent who was once on the CAT team says. "It is basically window dressing. The attack would be over before the tactical element could even respond."

Many agents trace cutting corners to the Secret Service's absorption into DHS. Being submerged in what many view as a dysfunctional agency, and having to compete for funds with other national security agencies, led to a lowering of standards. The fact that the Bush White House itself periodically asked the Secret Service to skip magnetometer screening undoubtedly contributed to an indulgent attitude. Indeed, Michael Chertoff himself, secretary of DHS, contributed to the lowering of standards in a very personal way.

In October 2008, Immigration and Customs Enforcement (ICE) within DHS fined James D. Reid $22,880 for allegedly employing illegal immigrants when his Maryland cleaning company worked at Chertoff's home and at other Washington homes. On the face of it, that did not make sense, since Secret Service agents protecting Chertoff would have been expected to check the background— including citizenship—of anyone allowed in the DHS secretary's home. Indeed, in response to a December 11, 2008, *Washington Post* story reporting the violations, a Secret Service spokesman said that agents protecting Chertoff would have "run the appropriate checks, screened, and escorted people as appropriate in order to maintain the security of the residence and our protectee's security."

But an agent who was periodically on Chertoff's detail says that while the Secret Service initially performed routine screening of workers, the secretary's wife, Meryl J. Chertoff, an adjunct law professor at Georgetown law school, in recent years "admonished agents for 'hassling' the workers."

Agents in charge bowed to Mrs. Chertoff's wishes. As a result, "no name checks [were] done for some time," the current agent says. When checks were done at times, "It was obvious the workers were providing bogus identifying information to agents, but [the agents], out of fear of Mrs. Chertoff, allowed them through," the agent says. "The workers also were rarely escorted, as that pissed her off, too."

"Mrs. Chertoff would belittle the agents for trying to do their jobs by doing the name checks before the workers entered the residence," another agent confirms.

Asked for comment, William R. Knocke, a DHS spokesman, said, "These are baseless and sensational allegations that I'm not going to dignify with a response."

Knocke referred to his previous statement to *The Washington Post* that every contractor has the responsibility of ensuring his workers are legal.

"As customers, the Chertoffs obtained assurances from Mr. Reid that any personnel he dispatched to their home were authorized to work in the United States," Knocke said. "As soon as the Chertoffs learned that Mr. Reid deceived them by employing some unauthorized workers, they fired him."

That the Secret Service allowed itself to become complicit in flouting immigration laws and even directed its agents to ignore violations is shocking. But skipping magnetometer screening when the lives of the president, vice president, and presidential candidates are at stake is far more shocking.

Retired agents who served in prior years before the Secret Service began cutting corners after its absorption into DHS say they have never heard of stopping magnetometer screening. When told of the practice, they assert that the Secret Service would never do such a thing.

"The [political] staff sometimes would propose stopping the magnetometers when an event was about to start," says former agent William Albracht, who retired in 2001 and was an instructor. "I don't know of any agent that has ever done that. That's just not what we do.

It doesn't matter to us how your person looks in the media or to the crowds. It's not really our concern. Our concern is that person's safety."

"You face pressure from political staffs all the time, but you don't stop magnetometer screening," says Norm Jarvis, who also taught new agents, was on Bill Clinton's protective detail, and left the Secret Service in 2005 as a special agent in charge. "Sometimes things happen and the flow rate is a little slow. But nobody in the Secret Service would allow the staff to impair security and jeopardize the life of the president by stopping magnetometer screening."

"Requests were made by staff to expedite or stop magnetometer screening," says Danny Spriggs, who headed protection and retired as deputy director of the Secret Service in 2004. "I would never have acquiesced to that."

23

Trailblazer

O N SEPTEMBER 11, 2001, the Secret Service rushed President Bush to Air Force One from a school in Sarasota, Florida, where he was reading to children in a classroom.

Usually a Boeing 747 known as the doomsday plane accompanies Air Force One and is parked nearby when the president lands. Packed with ultrasensitive communications gear and military hardware, it is designed as a mobile command post in case of a devastating attack, such as a nuclear one. Consideration was given to transferring Bush to the doomsday plane after the 9/11 attack. The idea was rejected because just the sight of him entering the plane could have created panic.

"I spoke to him about not going back to Washington," recalls Brian Stafford, the Secret Service director at the time. "The first time he was agreeable. Later when I spoke with him, he wasn't as agreeable. By that time, we owned the skies. Even though we didn't have all the answers we wanted, we were more comfortable about his going back than [we had been] earlier in the day."

After landing at Andrews Air Force Base, Bush rode on Marine One to the White House.

Agents took Laura Bush from Capitol Hill to the basement of Secret Service headquarters. During such national emergencies, the Secret Service works with the military to ensure continuity of government and coordinates protection of those in the line of succession to the presidency. Because of that coordination function, even if officials in the line of succession receive protection from the State Department, as is usually the case with the secretary of state, or from the Capitol Police, as is the case with the Speaker of the House and the president pro tempore of the Senate, they receive a Secret Service code name. The secretary of labor, for example, was code-named Firebird after Elaine Chao objected to her assigned code name, Fireplug.

At the time of the attack, Laura traveled with only two cars and four agents. Before driving her to headquarters, the agents called for additional cars and backup. After 9/11, the number of agents on Laura's detail was more than doubled.

Bush entered the White House at six fifty-four P.M. to find it surrounded by agents in black carrying submachine guns. Laura met him in the Emergency Operations Center, a bunker of rooms deep underground. That night, they were sleeping in their bedroom on the second floor at eleven-thirty when a Secret Service agent, breathing heavily from running, woke them up.

"Mr. President! Mr. President!" the agent said. "There's an unidentified aircraft heading toward the White House!"

In their bathrobes, the Bushes returned to the underground bunker, where an aide pointed out a roll-out bed. Then word came that it had been a false alarm. The plane was friendly.

"George had to literally lead her to go downstairs," Nancy Weiss, a close friend of the Bushes, says. "She can't even find the bathroom without her contacts. She is very, very blind. She wears hard lenses because the correction is so much better."

More than a month after 9/11, Laura Bush was at the Crawford ranch with her close friend Debbie Francis while Bush was in China. Laura's Secret Service detail informed them of a threat they had picked up.

"They had me move from the guesthouse into the main house in case we had to evacuate quickly," Debbie Francis recalls. "I stayed in one of the girls' rooms. For that one night, they didn't want us to have any lights on in the house. So we closed all the curtains and just had a little candle burning." Throughout the ordeal, Laura remained "totally calm," Francis says.

Because of the extensive Secret Service preparations that precede his trips outside the White House, Bush preferred not to go out to restaurants. At one point, he told Laura he didn't like to be stared at while he was eating. Laura laughed and said, "Well, maybe you shouldn't have run for president."

In contrast to her husband, Laura regularly slipped out of the White House to have lunch with friends at places such as Cafe Deluxe, Zola, or Old Ebbitt Grill. Her Secret Service detail would sit at nearby tables.

Presidents are required to pay for the incremental cost of their personal meals and personal parties—the cost of a lamb chop, for example. The White House or the State Department pays for official entertaining. The political party in power pays for Christmas events and cards. In all, twelve thousand people typically attend White House Christmas events. During a recent Christmas season, guests invited by the Bushes consumed a thousand pounds of shrimp, three hundred twenty gallons of eggnog, ten thousand tamales, and seven hundred cakes. That does not include the display-only three-hundred-pound gingerbread White House painted in white chocolate.

A buffet dinner for the press included roast lamb chops, chicken-fried steak with gravy, fruitwood smoked salmon, cocktail shrimp,

Maryland crab cakes, bourbon-glazed Virginia ham, cheesy stone-ground grits, and tamales with roasted poblanos and Vidalia onions. Not to mention chocolate cake with chocolate buttercream frosting, chocolate truffles, apple and cherry cobblers, and countless glazed sugar cookies shaped like woodland creatures.

The government's real annual cost of running the White House is anybody's guess. The president receives a salary of $450,000 a year plus an expense allowance of $50,000 and $100,000 for travel. The White House and the Executive Office of the President receive $202 million a year. But these figures are a mere token of what the White House costs. The real costs—totaling more than a billion dollars—are unknown even to Congress and the Government Accountability Office, the audit arm of Congress, because dozens of other agencies help support the White House and detail employees to it.

"The total cost of the White House isn't in any records," says John Cronin, Jr., who directed the GAO's audits of the White House for twelve years. "The navy runs the mess and Camp David, the army provides the cars and drivers, the Defense Department provides communications, the air force provides airplanes, the marine corps provides the helicopters. The State Department pays for state functions, the National Park Service maintains the grounds, the Secret Service provides protection, and the General Services Administration [GSA] maintains the East and West Wings and the Old Executive Office Building and provides heat."

The mythology often conveyed by the press was that Bush was a puppet of Dick Cheney or, alternatively, that he was so stubborn he listened to no one. In fact, he made his own decisions and would let aides go if they were too timid to disagree with him. Thus, according to former chief of staff Andy Card, it was Bush who came up with the idea of paying a surprise visit to troops in Baghdad for Thanksgiving in 2003.

Card says the first thing Bush wanted to know was whether the Secret Service thought it could be done safely. More than a month before the trip, Card met at the White House with Director Mark Sullivan and other Secret Service officials to begin planning the trip. The White House informed the Defense Department of the plans later.

To be sure, as Bush himself joked, he often did not speak English. His close friend Clay Johnson was in the Oval Office a few days before Bush was to speak at a radio and television correspondents dinner.

"I'm going to give the funniest speech you've ever heard," Bush told "Big Man," as he called Johnson. "They have this tape of ridiculous phrases I used in the [2001] campaign. I can't believe that a candidate for president said those things."

Bush recited some of the examples:

"Africa is a nation that . . ."

"Dick Cheney and I do not want this nation to be in a recession. We want anybody who can find work to be able to find work."

"Families is where our nation finds hope, where wings take dream."

"The woman who knew that I had dyslexia—I never interviewed her."

"I've never seen him laugh that hard," Johnson says.

Secret Service agents appreciate the fact that Bush is punctual.

"Bush is down to earth, caring," an agent says. The Bushes offer food to agents. "They are always thinking of people around them."

But agents were always amazed at the difference between Bush in person and the way he came across at press conferences.

"He does not look comfortable in front of a microphone," an agent who was on his detail says. "With us, he doesn't talk like that, doesn't sound like that. He's funny as hell. Incredible sense of humor, and he'll joke around. He's two different personalities."

Agents loved to run with Bush—code-named Trailblazer—and chop wood with him. The agency tried to assign its best runners to his detail so they could keep up with him. Because of bad knees, Bush later gave up running and took up biking, which he often did at the Secret Service training facility in Laurel, Maryland.

"He had this group of agents that were kind of jocks that he liked to associate with on the detail," an agent says. "The guy is in phenomenal shape. He had guys on his detail that would push him, and they'd feed off each other. It was funny, though, because when he was diagnosed with bad knees and he switched to mountain bikes from running, he was out of control on that mountain bike. He would go too fast, and he'd have a wreck. He would just go full out on a trail, hit a log, and go flying off the bike. And he'd get off, dust himself off, and hop right back on and do it again."

"You pretty much knew that you're not supposed to pass him when biking," another agent says. "He's supposed to be in front. I was there when Lance Armstrong was at the ranch. The president was actually trying to compete with Lance Armstrong, to keep up with him. And I think Lance let him win."

If agents thought highly of Bush, it was nothing compared to their feelings about his wife. "Laura has the undying admiration of almost every agent," an agent says. "I've never ever heard a negative thing about Laura Bush. Nothing. Everybody loves her to death and respects the hell out of her."

An agent who was assigned to the Bushes one Christmas remembers how caring Laura—code-named Tempo—is. She talked to him for thirty minutes and seemed apologetic about having to take him away from his family during Christmas.

"With Laura, what you see on TV is what you get in person," another agent says. "She's always smiling, and she actually gave my mother a compliment, which I'll never forget. We were invited to the White House Christmas party, and my mother actually studied the type of dresses that Laura Bush wears and tried to get something similar. She walked in, and after my mother was announced by a military escort, Mrs. Bush called her by her first name and said, 'Boy, you look absolutely lovely this evening.' My mother was on cloud nine."

As an example of Laura's positive approach to life, when Teresa Heinz Kerry said just before the 2004 election, "I don't know that she's [Laura's] ever had a real job," Laura brushed it off. After Heinz—who dropped the name Kerry after the election—apologized, Laura told reporters there was no need for her to do so.

"I know how tough it is, and actually I know those trick questions," she said.

At the dinner table that night in the pale green family dining room, Laura took the same positive approach. As a butler passed cheese and chicken enchiladas, daughters Jenna and Barbara Bush expressed outrage at Teresa's comment. Typically, Jenna was the most vocal.

"You know, Mom, she put down every woman who raised their children," Jenna said. "She was saying that's not a real job. That was what was so bad about it. Not that she forgot you had a teaching job, but that she was putting down raising children."

As Pamela Nelson, a high school friend of Laura's from Midland, selected an enchilada from a platter offered by a butler, Laura talked about how easy it was for words to be twisted and taken out of context.

"You know that comment, 'Bring them on,'" Laura said, referring to Bush's July 2003 statement challenging those who would attack American forces in Iraq. "It had so many political repercussions. Everything can be used a million times against you."

"This has to be the meanest campaign ever," Nelson said, referring to the 2004 reelection campaign.

"No, the leaflets they dropped when Lincoln was running that disparaged him and his family were horrible," Laura said. "People blame everything that happens on this office."

24

Living on Borrowed Time

WHEN THE SECRET Service proudly shows members of Congress its James J. Rowley Training Center, it wows them with supposedly unrehearsed feats that bring down the bad guys and save the lives of protectees. But those scenarios are secretly rehearsed.

"Members of Congress were being escorted around the training complex, and we were doing building extraction scenarios with the protectee," an agent who was there recalls. "We would be trying to move the VP out of a hotel. Say there's a fire in the hotel, or there's an explosion outside. We want to get him down into the motorcade and out of the area and move him to a secure location."

On this particular morning when members of Congress were due to visit, "Everything changed," the agent says. "Everything was rehearsed, everything was put together, and we're like, 'Why are we doing rehearsed scenarios? We should be doing practical scenarios and real training exercises.'"

The agents were told, "Well, there's a congressional tour coming through."

Normally, in a training exercise, "The bad guy can kill the agent," the agent says. "You don't know. You could see the agent get killed, you could see two agents stumble over each other down a stairwell, things could happen. If you're putting on training that's effective, it is a practical exercise in the sense that you let it run through to its end. But when the congressional tour came through, we did it as we had rehearsed to do it," the agent says. In real training, "You never rehearse something like that."

The practiced scenario did the trick, impressing the senators and representatives who watched. "They watched an attack on a principal and saw how agents responded, how the shift goes to the protectee, how the CAT team deploys, but they didn't know that they spent the last couple days rehearsing that scenario."

According to another current agent, the same thing happened when the Secret Service opened the Rowley center to a group of visiting U.S. Attorneys. Prior to their visit, the agents had rehearsed scenarios for two hours.

That is not the way it's supposed to happen.

"You know what the setting is, that the president will give a speech," former Secret Service deputy director Danny Spriggs says. "They are not told what will happen. They don't know if an attack will come, where it will come from, or what it will be."

When asked about the practice of rehearsing supposedly spontaneous scenarios, Ed Donovan, a Secret Service spokesman, did not respond.

At the Rowley center, the Secret Service also likes to impress members of Congress with agents' marksmanship. But what the agency doesn't tell Congress is how agents are outgunned because the Secret Service continues to use the outdated Heckler & Koch MP5 submachine gun. In contrast, the army and other federal law enforcement agencies have switched to the newer and more powerful Colt M4 carbine.

While a counterassault team travels with the president and is armed with the SR-16—similar to the M4—other agents on a protective detail also need to be ready to repel an attack. Many of those agents are equipped with the MP5. In addition, all agents are armed with a SIG Sauer P229 pistol with the barrel modified to accommodate a .357 round instead of the standard smaller nine-millimeter round.

"The service, you would think, would be on the leading edge when it comes to weapons, and they're just not," says a current agent. "They're still carrying MP5 submachine guns," developed in the 1960s. "Guys from State Department are out there carrying M4s, which is a weapon that soldiers in Iraq and Afghanistan are carrying." Developed in the 1990s, it is "much more powerful. It has better range and better armor-piercing capabilities," the agent adds.

The army uses the M4 as its main weapon. The FBI trains agents to use both the MP5 and the M4. Even the Amtrak Police Department is equipped with the M4.

"You're going to be getting attacked with AK-47 assault rifles, you're going to be getting attacked with M4s," an agent says. "We want to be able to match or better whoever's attacking us. You want to get the same range or better. The problem is, if you're getting a shoot-out in a motorcade, with the MP5, you're shooting a pistol with a submachine gun round—you're basically shooting a pistol round. You don't want your rounds falling short and not even able to reach out to the bad guy. And that's essentially what you've got going on with the weapons they have now."

In fact, he says, "The nine-millimeter round fired by the MP5 does not even penetrate the most basic type of body armor available to the general public."

"I laugh every time I go to training and we do motorcade attack scenarios," another agent on a major protective detail says. "Our so-called attackers use the AK-47 as their weapon. When there is an attack and the bad guys open up with the AK-47s, it is deafening. You feel like you're being ambushed in the Middle East. Then the Secret Service shift fires back with MP5s. By comparison, it sounds like little cap guns."

In contrast to the M4, the MP5 used by the Secret Service does not have night-vision capability or mounted flashlights. Flashlights help agents identify a target at night, illuminate a dark room, and could be used to distract an enemy. By temporarily blinding assailants, they could give an agent an advantage in a confrontation.

"Without the ability to see at night, we are at a grave disadvantage," an agent says. "It is shameful and embarrassing that we do not have such basic equipment to even put us at a level playing field against any possible assassins."

In fact, in one night-training scenario at Beltsville, agents almost had a "blue-on-blue" incident because shift agents could not tell if the CAT team members bounding through the woods were good guys or bad guys. To identify themselves to other agents, CAT members wear a device called a firefly, which emits a blip of light. But it can only be seen through night-vision goggles or scopes mounted on weapons. Some of the agents later said they almost unloaded their blanks on the CAT team thinking they were the attacking force.

Agents constantly raise the need for improved weapons with the brass, but management dismisses their concerns.

"There are guys who are out there trying to campaign to upgrade to the M4," an agent says, "but we have these people entrenched at headquarters who have actually come out and said the M4 is a weapon of war; it's not a weapon of protection. It's an excuse because they don't want to spend the money to buy new weapons."

When asked why their weapons do not have night vision and flashlights, supervisors say the Secret Service needs to take "baby steps" before it gets to that point, meaning it would cost too much to upgrade agents' weapons. When one considers that the United States has been spending twelve billion dollars a month to fund military personnel and the procurement of the most advanced weapons in Iraq—not to mention $787 billion for the stimulus package—the fact that Secret Service management is hesitant to provide agents with the best equipment to repel an attack on the president is mind-boggling.

Agents say the Secret Service is still fixated on the idea that a lone gunman will pull off the next assassination, reflecting what one agent calls an "old-school mentality." Not enough emphasis is placed on the possibility of a full-scale terrorist attack or an attack with an improvised explosive device (IED), they say.

"Let's look at IEDs now, look at things that are a real threat," an agent on one of the two major details says. "Take a look at the boys in Iraq and see what they're dealing with every day and see how that threat's going to come home to us. Not the lone gunman with the .45 caliber sitting up in the second floor window as the motorcade rolls by. That limousine is going to withstand a .45 round when it hits the glass."

Nor is enough attention being paid to the possibility of attacks by suicide bombers.

"How can the Secret Service not train for suicide bombers when Benazir Bhutto was killed standing in her limo by a suicide bomber?" another agent says. "How can you not see that that's the kind of thing you ought to focus on? Not the guy with a .45 caliber standing on his rooftop two streets over. Let's worry about real threats that are threats today."

According to a third agent, a new Secret Service directive does address the threat of suicide bombers but is vague and says agents should try to talk to them.

"If I see somebody in ninety-degree heat coming with a winter jacket on, and I see he's sweating and he's nervous, I'm going to draw down on him, and he's not going to get any closer," the agent says. "You know if I start talking to him, somebody's going to die right away. I'm not talking to anybody. I'm going home to my family at night."

The tendency to cut corners extends to protecting Bill and Hillary Clinton at their home in Chappaqua, New York. Chappaqua is a pictur-esque hamlet that recalls towns of the 1950s. Its tiny downtown center is full of mom-and-pop stores where owners greet customers by name. Here among the rolling wooded hills thirty-five miles north of Man-hattan, Bill and Hillary Clinton bought a five-bedroom Dutch Colonial home for $1.7 million in 1999.

The nine thousand residents of this Westchester County town adhere to an unofficial code of conduct: When you drive past the white house on Old House Lane, don't rubberneck, slow down, or pull over to the side of the road. While Chappaqua residents may be impressed by the Secret Service agents guarding the property, the security fence does not totally surround it. As one looks at the house from the front, intruders from the adjoining property can walk right in. While they would trip alarms, they would have a head start on gaining access. At any given time, at least six agents are detailed to the house, plus two from the New York field office. But the house is outfitted with only two pivoting surveillance cameras that frequently go on the blink.

At Secret Service headquarters, the computer system that plugs into the intelligence community's classified information on threats is limited in scope and technologically primitive. Agents say they typi-cally learn more about overseas threats by watching CNN, Fox News, or MSNBC than from briefings by their own intelligence agents.

Until recently, the Secret Service even scrimped on cell phones, supplying agents with huge, obsolete cell phones and refurbished Motorola pagers that would not work near the White House. They have since been replaced by BlackBerrys. The agency's radio communications that connect to agents' earpieces often will not transmit through brick walls.

Citing innovations at the Rowley training center, an agent proudly mentions during a tour of the facility that agents are trained with a newly acquired "shoot/don't shoot" computer program that scores them on whether they have made the right decision on when to fire. Yet when writing *The Bureau: The Secret History of the FBI*, I operated such a program at the FBI's training center at Quantico, Virginia, back in 2002.

While the Secret Service scrimps on equipment needed to save lives, it wastes agents' time by requiring them to engage in needless record-keeping using software out of the 1970s. Every two weeks, agents must submit a printout with the hours they worked each day. An attendance clerk then retypes the data into the payroll system. At the end of the month, agents are required to compute manually the number of regular hours and overtime hours they worked for each specific protectee and the number of hours they traveled or worked out of town. They then enter the data into an antiquated computer program.

While the Secret Service has an ombudsman to whom problems can be submitted, agents call the position a joke. "The ombudsman is buddies with the person you're complaining about, or he went into training with them, and it's a good ol' boy system," an agent on one of the major details says.

Because of the serial deficiencies and corner cutting, "I think we're on borrowed time, personally," a current agent says. "I really think it's just a matter of time before an assassination occurs."

25

Turquoise and Twinkle

WHEN IT CAME to protecting Jenna and Barbara Bush, the Secret Service had its hands full. Back when Bush was reelected governor of Texas, "The next morning after the inauguration, they had a breakfast for friends and family," Laura's friend Anne Stewart says. "George was sitting on a chair at a podium. He looked like he was about to fall off of it. I mean, his eyes kept closing."

Bush gave a short speech.

"Thank God for the person who invented caffeine, because I really needed the coffee this morning," he said. "I also have something to say about the person who coined the word 'curfew.' Unfortunately, my girls do not know the meaning of the word 'curfew.'"

Later, Anne Stewart asked Laura what he meant.

"The girls did not show up after the inauguration party," Laura said. "At two-thirty in the morning, I heard him frantically punching buttons calling all of their friends, finding out where they were. Finally, he tracked down one of the girls. He said, 'I don't care if it's my inauguration. Get your booties home.'"

"They were partying and having a great time," Stewart said. "They thought, 'Dad won't mind. It's his inauguration as governor.'"

Recognizing how a presidential race would infringe on their family life, Laura later said she was "somewhat reluctant initially" about a presidential campaign. "I knew it would be hard to see someone I loved criticized," she said. Laura knew that a run for the presidency and a possible win would mean giving up even more of their family's privacy than when Bush was governor of Texas. Simply taking a walk or dropping in at a drugstore would require heavy security precautions.

The twins, especially Jenna, were opposed. They wanted to be normal teenagers. The thought of being different, singled out because they were in the White House, made them cringe.

When Bush became president, Barbara—code-named Turquoise—went off to Yale, and Jenna—code-named Twinkle—went to the University of Texas, and they both made good grades. But on May 29, 2001, Austin police officer Clay Crabb was dispatched to Chuy's restaurant after manager Mia Lawrence called 911 at ten thirty-four P.M. Crabb later wrote in his report that when he arrived at the restaurant on Barton Springs Road, Lawrence told him the subject of her call was a blonde wearing a pink halter top who was seated in the bar area with her back to the wall.

Crabb and another officer "were about to go in and talk to the girl Mia pointed out when I was tapped on the shoulder by a subject identifying himself as a member of the Secret Service," Crabb wrote. By then, the officers knew that the alleged offender was Jenna Bush, and they explained to the agents that they were checking into an allegation that she had used fake identification to buy a drink.

The Secret Service agents did not interfere. Instead, Michael Bolton, a Secret Service supervisor, told Jenna and Barbara, who was also at the bar, what was happening. He then told the police the girls were going to leave. Two days later, the Austin police issued tickets to both girls for Class C misdemeanor violations. Jenna was cited for mis-representation of age by a minor, Barbara for possession of alcohol by a minor.

It had all started when a waitress became suspicious of the license Jenna handed her. The waitress showed it to Lawrence, who noted that the license had someone else's name on it. In addition, the photo looked "slightly off." Lawrence told Jenna she would not be served.

"Whatever," Jenna said, according to the police report.

Apparently thinking she was older than Jenna, the waitress brought Barbara and two friends three margaritas and three tequila shots. The bartender kept watch to make sure Jenna drank none of them. After other patrons pointed out that Barbara was the same age as Jenna, Lawrence called 911. By the time officers arrived, the tequila shots were gone. Each of the margaritas had been at least "partially consumed," the police report said. When officer Clifford Rogers asked Jenna for the identification she had used, she handed it over and started to cry.

"She then stated that I do not have any idea what it is like to be a college student and not be able to do anything that other students get to do," Rogers wrote.

Another officer asked restaurant manager Lawrence what she wanted the police to do with the girls.

"I want them to get into big trouble," Lawrence said.

Police Chief Stan Knee told the *Austin American-Statesman* that the unusual thing about the incident was not the way the police handled it, but that they were involved at all.

"Most business establishments usually handle those things them-selves," the chief said. "Once we were notified of the crime, or the potential crime, we felt obligated to make as thorough a report as possible."

For Barbara, it was a first offense. But two weeks before, on May 16,

Jenna had pleaded no contest to possession of alcohol at Cheers Shot Bar on Sixth Street in Austin. In response to the new charge, Jenna on July 6 pleaded no contest to misrepresenting her age. Her driver's license was suspended for a month. She paid a six-hundred-dollar fine for the infraction at Chuy's and for the previous charge. She also got three months of deferred adjudication, a form of probation, plus thirty-six hours of community service. She was required to attend an alcohol awareness class. Barbara also pleaded no contest and was sentenced to deferred adjudication. She had to attend alcohol awareness class as well.

After the incident at Chuy's, Mike Young and John Zapp, the owners of the restaurant, apologized. "Usually, we wouldn't have handled it the way it was handled," Young admitted.

While the girls matured in college, they still resented having Secret Service agents around, even though the agents dressed in casual clothes and most people were unaware of their role. Jenna was particularly difficult. She would sometimes purposely try to lose her protection by going through red lights or by jumping into her car without telling agents where she was going. As a result, the Secret Service kept her car under surveillance so agents could follow her—a waste of manpower.

"One night I was working on her detail, and about three-thirty P.M. on a Friday, she steps out of the house all dressed to the nines and hops into her car," an agent says. "We follow her in our vehicle. She drove to a bar and got there around four-fifteen."

The bar was across the street from the Verizon Center at 601 F Street NW in D.C., and it turned out the Rolling Stones were playing there that night. Jenna was meeting friends for a party at a private box at the center. Such a public event requires special security arrangements and close to a hundred agents. But, the agent says, Jenna never told her agents.

"So we scrambled," an agent says. "We're trying to get guys from the Washington field office, and we're trying to get guys into the Verizon Center. Whoever invited her to this box had sent emails to all his friends saying, 'Hey, Jenna Bush [now Jenna Bush Hager] is going to be there.' We had no idea about this. We pulled people in from the Washington field office and said, 'Dress for the Rolling Stones concert.'"

The agents asked the Verizon Center management for help.

"That's the beauty of being a Secret Service agent," the agent says. "Basically, we can go anywhere, show our badge, and say, 'Listen, here's what we've got going on. Please help us.' So we said, 'Listen, Secret Service, got a problem. Can't tell you who's going to be here, but somebody important's going to be here tonight, and we need your help because we didn't know about it.' And management at the Verizon Center bent over backward that night and gave us whatever we needed."

Since the center is private property with its own security force, the agents had to get permission to enter while armed. The center provided a room as an operations center.

Jenna "doesn't like the protection whatsoever," says another agent. "The supervisor of her detail was scared of her, because they were afraid that she was going to pick up the phone and call Dad."

In fact, says the agent, Jenna called her father many times when she wanted the agents to back off. "The president would call the special agent in charge," the agent says. "The SAIC would call the detail leader, the detail leader would call the guys and say, 'Hey, you've got to back off.'"

"How about us doing our jobs?" an agent says. "I mean, what if something happens to her? I think she has a hard time grasping how easy it would be to pick her up, throw her into a van, and next thing you know she's on Al Jazeera. And we're out there, we're trying to do the right thing. And I don't think she understands it. She definitely didn't respect what we're out there trying to do for her."

At times, Bush chewed out the detail for not following his daughter. One afternoon at the White House, Jenna snuck out a back exit that leads to the Rose Garden, eluding her detail. Bush saw her leave and called the detail leader to complain that she was not being followed.

"She stepped up to the plate and said, 'Daddy, I didn't tell them where I was going,'" an agent says.

An agent on the counterassault team accompanied Jenna on a trip to Central and South America.

"She was really getting a hard time in Argentina because the paparazzi were following her around, and she really couldn't go out and do the things that she wanted to do because of all these cameras following her around," the agent recalls. "Typically, she would just start complaining [about the Secret Service following her]. She would actually sit in the car and start looking back, trying to pick out the counterassault guys. She would say, 'Hey, those guys are too close.' Next thing you know, the cell phone rings and it's the DL, the detail leader, saying, 'Hey, can you guys back off a little bit? She sees you.'"

One detail leader found he could give Jenna instructions, and she would listen.

"He could call her up on the phone and be like, 'Jenna, what the hell are you doing?' They were buddies. They were pals. He was strictly professional, but he knew how to deal with her. He could tell her, 'Listen, Jenna, you're killing me. You gotta tell me what's going on.' And she respected him, which was great."

Still, says another agent, "Every day we'd run the risk of losing her. She never told us where she was going. It was rare. Sometimes she'd tell Neil [the detail leader], and Neil would get the scoop of what was going on, and Neil would try hard to get that information."

Another agent says Barbara was almost as difficult as Jenna.

"She'd pick up the phone and call Dad and say that we're getting too close," the agent says.

When Barbara was attending Yale, she would sometimes jump into her car with friends and drive to New York, where she would stay overnight, never giving her agents advance warning.

"Agents learned to pack a bag with clothing, because it became a habit for both Barbara and Jenna to say 'I want to go to the airport. I want to fly to New York,'" an agent says. "These guys were prepared to work an evening shift, and all of a sudden they're going with just the clothes on their backs."

"Instead of calling somebody to complain about us, just tell us what you're going to do and we'll make it work, but just work with us, instead of trying to play games with us, making our lives miserable," says an agent who was on Jenna's detail.

When Barbara spent time in Africa, the White House said she was helping children with AIDS. A member of the counterassault team who accompanied her says that while she did some volunteer work in places like Cape Town, South Africa, "Most of the time she was out on her own, doing her thing, partying. She went to a couple schools, but we ended up doing an African safari, and of course the American taxpayer paid for her protection. You never knew where she was going, and she was always calling and complaining."

Meanwhile, at a 2005 Halloween party in the Adams Morgan section of Washington, Henry Hager, who was Jenna's boyfriend and soon-to-be husband, became so inebriated that the Secret Service wound up taking him to Georgetown University Hospital.

"It was after a Halloween party, and they were all dressed up in their costumes," an agent on her detail recalls. "She's like, 'Listen, Henry, we've got to get you out of this costume. We got to look dignified before we go to the hospital.' At this point, I'm thinking to myself, yeah, she's growing up a little bit when she's thinking about having to look dignified before going to the hospital, as opposed to looking like a sloppy drunken mess in a Halloween costume."

Another time, Hager became drunk with Jenna in a Georgetown bar and picked a fight with several other patrons. Agents had to intervene to avoid a brawl.

"He was getting out of control and starting to pick a fight," an agent says. "Agents pulled him aside and they said, 'You realize that you are with the president's daughter? You know the situation you are putting her and us in because of the way you're acting?'"

"When she got around her friends, she was out of control," an agent who was on her detail says of Jenna. "She was a party girl, smoking cigarettes, drinking a lot, burping, loud, and sort of obnoxious. I couldn't believe that she was a schoolteacher during the day."

Jenna taught inner-city children in Washington and later in Baltimore. Barbara maintained her interest in helping people afflicted with AIDS. Over time, the twins became more mature and demonstrated that they appreciated their detail.

"Around the Fourth of July, Jenna had a whole bunch of steaks delivered to our command post," an agent says. "Around Christmas, she gave us all another order of steaks and hot dogs and stuff like that. It's got to be tough being the kid of a president. I can't imagine it."

Asked if Barbara, Jenna, or Henry Hager had any comment, Sally McDonough, Laura Bush's press secretary in the White House, said, "I am making a formal request that you do not include any of this nonsense in your book."

Like Jenna and Barbara, Susan Ford Bales, the daughter of President Ford, tried to evade her Secret Service detail. Eighteen when her father became president, Susan—code-named Panda—had a reputation for romantically chasing Secret Service agents. After her father left the White House, she married Charles Vance, a Secret Service agent who was guarding the former president in California. They later divorced, and she remarried.

"In my career, Chelsea Clinton did it the best," says an agent familiar with both her detail and the Bush twins' details. "Treated the detail right, told them what was going on, never gave problems that I knew of."

In recent memory, the brattiest offspring of a president was Amy Carter, who was nine when her father became president.

"Amy Carter was a mess," says Brad Wells, an Air Force One steward. "She would look at me and pick up a package of [open] soda crackers and crush them and throw them on the floor. She did it purposely. We had to clean it up. That was our job."

Secret Service agents guarding Amy—code-named Dynamo—at school often found themselves in the middle when Amy wanted to play with friends after school instead of going home to the White House to do her homework, as she was supposed to do. When agents told her she had to go home, "Amy would call her father and hand the phone to the agents," Dennis Chomicki, who was on her detail, remembers. "The president would say to take Amy anywhere she wants to go. Amy just had her father wrapped up."

Since Amy would often stay at a friend's house through the evening, agents wound up working longer hours than if they had taken her directly to the White House. As a result, says Chomicki, "The detail would always try to get Mrs. Carter, the first lady, on the phone, because she would say, 'Nothing doing. She's coming home; she's got her homework to do.'"

Of all the presidential children guarded by the Secret Service, Carter's second oldest son, James Earl "Chip" Carter III, was one of the least liked. Twenty-six when his father won the presidency, Chip had helped campaign for him in 1976 and again gave speeches on his behalf when Carter ran for reelection in 1980.

"He was outrageous," a Secret Service agent says. "Chip was out of control. Marijuana, liquor, chasing women." Separated from his wife, Chip would "pick up women in Georgetown and ask if they wanted to have sex in the White House. Most of them did. He did it as often as he could," the agent says.

At one point, Rosalynn Carter told the press that all three of her sons had "experimented" with marijuana. Their oldest son, John William "Jack" Carter, had been discharged by the navy for smoking weed.

Carter told the Secret Service that Rosalynn objected to agents and uniformed officers being armed inside the White House. According to Carter, Rosalynn cited the fact that guns made Amy "uncomfortable." The Secret Service explained that in the event of an attack, agents would be useless if unarmed. President Carter relented.

26

Angler

WHEN ASSIGNING CODE names to protectees, the Secret Service starts with a random list of words, all beginning with the same letter for each family. The code names were once necessary because Secret Service radio transmissions were not encrypted. Now that they are, the Secret Service continues to use code names to avoid confusion when pronouncing the names of protectees. In addition, by using code names, agents prevent people from overhearing the subject of their conversations.

Produced by the White House Communications Agency, the list of code names excludes words that are offensive or may be easily mistaken for other words. However, those under protection may object to a code name and propose another. Thus, Lynne Cheney, a prolific author, asked for and was given the Secret Service code name Author. Dick Cheney, an avid fisherman, got the code name Angler.

George W. Bush objected to Tumbler, the code name he was initially assigned. Perhaps it reminded him of his drinking days. Instead, he chose Trailblazer. Bush's chief of staff Josh Bolten chose Fat Boy, referring to the model of his silver and black Harley-Davidson. The code name was one word, "Fatboy." His predecessor Andy Card had been Patriot, a code name the Secret Service chose when Card said he did not like his assigned name, Potomac.

"My Secret Service detail loved the code name—even the female agents, who end up getting called Fatgirls," Bolten tells me.

When Clinton was president, the press claimed that his brother Roger Clinton was code named Headache, presumably because he replaced Billy Carter as the black sheep of the first family. But because he was not protected by the Secret Service, Roger Clinton had no code name.

Besides those entitled by law to Secret Service protection, the president may extend protection to others by executive order. By executive order, Bush ordered coverage for Cheney's two daughters and his six grandchildren.

Besides the vice president's residence, the Cheneys have homes in Jackson Hole, Wyoming, and on Maryland's Eastern Shore. After the Cheneys bought the house on the Eastern Shore, they would go there almost every weekend on a marine helicopter. The Secret Service outfitted each home with alarm systems and surveillance cameras. Looking ahead to when he would leave the vice presidency, Cheney also bought a home in McLean, Virginia.

In Cheney's case, when Bush extended protection to his children and grandchildren, the Secret Service did not add additional agents. Instead, the agency made do by extending hours and paying overtime to agents on his detail, borrowing agents from field offices, and allowing virtually no time for the required refresher training, physical fitness, and firearms practice.

"Instead of saying, 'Well, we'll be glad to take care of his grand-kids, but let's just do the right thing and get some more people over here so we can cover all these added assignments,' Secret Service management said to the president, 'No problem, sir. We'll take care of it,' without giving us any more people," says an agent who was on the vice president's detail.

"You end up working twelve-hour days sitting in a cul-de-sac," says another agent on the detail. "That's why you don't get the training, because you're having to fill in these assignments. You're fighting battles on a multitude of fronts, because you've got the protectees you're trying to make happy, and you turn around and see people we work for who don't care about us at all. It leaves you with feelings of hopelessness, and that's why people want to leave."

Before the Cheneys' daughter Mary—code-named Alpine—had a child, the Secret Service provided full protection to only her older sister, Elizabeth, since she had kids. Mary received partial protection: Agents drove her to and from work. But Mary seemed to feel competitive.

"She got all up in arms because we sat outside her sister's house all night long. She said, 'Well, I think I should have that, too,'" an agent says.

Mary also complained about the Secret Service vehicle assigned to her.

"She saw that her sister had a brand-new Suburban," an agent who was on her detail says. "Mary had an older vehicle. She was like, why can't I have one? Next thing you know, within a day or two, she has a brand-new Suburban from the Secret Service sitting out there in front of her house."

When her Suburban sustained some damage, the Secret Service chauffeured her in the older vehicle until the new one could be repaired.

"When she saw her old vehicle was brought back to use as her limo, she threw a fit," an agent says. "She called bosses demanding her Suburban be brought back immediately, not realizing that it takes time to make repairs on a damaged vehicle."

Mary objected to agents standing post overnight at the back of her home. She said they disturbed her dogs.

"I don't even know what the back side of her house looks like because she won't let us walk around the back because of the dogs," an agent who was on her detail says. "Her dogs start barking. It gets them all upset if we go back there. So [we had] some cameras angled back there. But your hands are tied. It's a thankless job anyway, but then you've got protectees who mandate how you're going to do your job."

When Mary demanded that the Secret Service shuttle her friends out to restaurants, her detail leader objected. She had the agent removed from her detail.

Asked for comment, Mary Cheney said, "These stories are simply not true, and I have nothing but the utmost respect for the men and women of the Secret Service. I am deeply appreciative of everything they have done to keep my family safe over the last eight years."

Often, protectees think of Secret Service agents as personal servants, there to act as gofers. When he was running for president, Edmund Muskie demanded that the Secret Service carry his golf bags.

"He took vacations in Kennebunkport," a veteran agent says. "He would play eighteen holes of golf every day. He would cheat and kick the ball into the hole with his foot and pick it up and put it in. An agent would not carry his golf bags [after Muskie asked him to]. It reduces our effectiveness."

But with a gracious woman like Lynne Cheney, agents happily offered to help with her bags. "To her credit, she shops a lot, and she'll come out with all kinds of bags, and she's never once that I know of ever asked us to help," says an agent on her detail. "Probably because she doesn't ask us, we go ahead and volunteer."

Like the Bushes, Dick and Lynne Cheney were always on time and were well-liked by the Secret Service. The Cheneys invited agents and their families to the Christmas party they gave every year and took photos with them.

"I remember that I was probably the one hundred sixtieth click that afternoon, but when my kids walked up, Mrs. Cheney acted like we were the first picture of the day," an agent who was on the vice president's detail says. "She squatted down and reached out and hugged my little girl, and it really meant a lot to me."

As with the Cheneys, agents thought highly of most members of Bush's staff and Cabinet.

"Karl Rove loved the counterassault team," says an agent. "He would always come by and talk to us. He took photos with us. Any time he saw us in the CAT truck, he would come over and say hello. Always smiling, always joking, a real nice man."

"Karl Rove has a phenomenal reputation within the service, taking care of the guys," another agent says. "Andy Card, same thing."

In general, agents found the Bush administration to be much more friendly and appreciative of what agents do than most other administrations. In the Bush administration, there were two exceptions: Treasury Secretary John Snow and Homeland Security Secretary Tom Ridge. Agents considered Ridge the cheapest protectee they had ever known. On weekends, he would return to his home in Erie, Pennsylvania. So he would not have to pay for his own plane ticket, he would insist that agents drive him—a trip of more than six hours, one way.

"The guy would make them motorcade to Erie, Pennsylvania, almost every other weekend, or every weekend, because he didn't want to pay for a plane ticket," an agent who was on his detail says. "If the guy found a free meal, he was there. His reputation in the service was he was the biggest cheapskate ever."

Instead of buying a newspaper at hotels, Ridge would ask agents for their copy of the paper.

"If somebody said, 'Hey, Mr. Secretary, appreciate it. Meal's on us,' Ridge would go back there the next night to the same restaurant and see how long he could milk a free meal from this place," an agent says.

Agents liked John Snow because he loved to chat and joke with them.

"John Snow was kind of a pretty cool protectee, in that he knew every guy on the detail," an agent says. "He'd sit in the back of his limo, and he'd talk with you. It was like a group of guys hanging out."

But Snow, a former chairman and chief executive officer of CSX Corporation, had what agents on his detail believed was a mistress in Richmond where he and his wife lived. While Snow rented and later bought an apartment in Washington, he would travel back to his hometown almost every weekend, incurring huge expenses for taxpayers because the Secret Service had to drive him the two hours to Richmond and stay in hotels.

The Secret Service gave the woman the unofficial code name Area 51, after the supersecret air force testing ground that gives rise to conspiracy theories.

Now chairman of Cerberus Capital Management, which owned 80.1 percent of Chrysler Corp., until its bankruptcy, Snow commented through his Richmond lawyer Richard Cullen, a former Virginia state attorney general and friend of the Snows for more than twenty-five years:

"John Snow did not have an affair. . . . The agents who refuse to identify themselves in making this accusation are simply and sadly very wrong."

Agents who were on Snow's detail say otherwise. Snow "was messing around quite a bit, and it was pretty disturbing to the guys on the detail, because we knew we were away from home for the express purpose of him to meet up with his mistress," says a former agent who was on his detail.

When the woman's husband was out at church on Sunday mornings, "The secretary [Snow] would say, 'Oh, I've got to drop a book at their house,'" an agent recalls. Or Snow would say he had just found an article in the Richmond paper he would like to give them.

"That was grating on us, because we had to spend every weekend in Richmond, and during the week he was traveling pushing Social Security reform, so we were on the road all week," a current agent says. "We were never home. And it pissed us off no end to realize that the only reason we were in Richmond was for the secretary to mess around."

One morning, another agent was walking by the front window of Snow's house in Richmond and saw Snow and the alleged mistress kissing. She would also fly to Washington to see Snow at his rented apartment near what agents refer to as the Hinckley Hilton, the Washington Hilton.

"She knew all of us by name," the former agent says. "She'd just come out of the woodwork out of nowhere and say, 'Hey, guys!' We'd go on hikes, and they'd be there. She was always around."

"He really thought he had us fooled on that one," another agent says. "She would show up at like a hotel in New York, and he would act like, 'Oh, look who it is!'"

Early on, after Snow was appointed treasury secretary in February 2003, he would travel to Richmond with his Secret Service detail on Saturdays and return on Sundays.

"It didn't take long for him to realize that he could leave fairly early on Friday, come back late Sunday," an agent who was on his detail says. "And then it didn't take long much past that to realize that he could get there early Friday, leave Monday morning, and make it to work on time. So it became Friday, Saturday, Sunday, and Monday."

Snow resigned in June 2006. By then, "He would leave on Thursdays, come back on Monday," an agent remembers. "So that makes five days in Richmond. And he was going every weekend."

"I think he legitimately liked Richmond," says an agent. "He had a nice place on the river with a nice big pool. But you've got six or seven guys on the detail, he's spending four or five days a week in Richmond. You do the numbers, and you're running out of bodies pretty quick to cover that."

Snow's wife rarely came to Washington and seemed to despise the agents.

When Snow was in town, she expected agents to bring in the mail and the newspaper. The mail was not screened, and agents are not supposed to perform personal errands. While some agents did so as favors, most did not.

One Sunday, Snow's wife came out in her bathrobe and asked an agent, "Why don't you deliver the paper?"

"It's not my job to deliver your paper; you can get your own paper," the agent responded.

"That didn't go over too well," the former agent says. "I was there to keep the secretary unharmed—as well as her, if possible—but I most certainly was not her paper boy."

"Nothing amazes me anymore, but apparently she [Snow's wife] didn't suspect anything," an agent says. "It was going on the entire time he was under our protection, and it was obviously going on prior to that. It was just more convenient with us around."

The agents say there was one close call. One Sunday when Snow was with his alleged mistress, her husband came home from church early.

"One of our agents saw what was happening," says an agent. "To his credit, he got out of his vehicle and started making as much noise as he could." Loudly, the agent called out the husband's name and said to him, "Hey, great to see you." The agent slammed the doors of his Suburban. As the husband was walking into his house, Snow came out, his hair messed up.

What infuriated the agents was the way Snow seemed to think he was pulling the wool over their eyes. On one occasion, Snow said he wanted to go for a walk.

"He gets into the car, and we take off, and he says, 'Go down this road down here,' which was a dead end with a museum at the end. Well, we get down there, and she's [the alleged mistress] down there with the hood of her car up."

Snow said, "Oh, looky here! What's happened here?"

Saying her car had broken down, the woman asked for jumper cables to help charge the battery. Sensing a ruse, one of the agents suggested they try starting the car first. Snow insisted that would not work. After the jumper cables were attached, the car started without any hesitation.

"We better follow her home, just to make sure the car doesn't cut off again," Snow said.

"So we get her home, and he's there for about an hour, hour and a half," an agent says.

"He thought we weren't smart enough to realize what was going on," another agent says. "That's what really drove a lot of guys crazy."

In denying that Snow had an affair with Area 51, Snow's lawyer Cullen put the author in touch with Tom Greenaway, the leader of Snow's detail for the first half of his term. Greenaway said that the woman in question was not Snow's mistress.

"I was with him fifteen hours a day, sometimes twenty-five days a month," Greenaway said.

As it turns out, Greenaway became a golfing buddy of Snow's while he was protecting him. That is considered a no-no in the Secret

Service because a personal friendship could lead an agent to do favors beyond his duties or to back down on security issues. In addition, agents who become friends with top protectees may start trying to push their weight around with their bosses.

In response to a question, Greenaway acknowledged that the Secret Service tried to give him what he called a "punitive" transfer after he had a disagreement with management. He confirmed that Snow intervened with the Secret Service director to delay any transfer off Snow's detail for several months until after the 2004 election. Greenaway said he then retired.

Cullen said neither Snow nor his family "improperly used the services of the U.S. Secret Service detail assigned to him. The Secret Service is required to protect the secretary of the treasury," Cullen said. "Protection is mandatory. It is not discretionary. Nor is it assigned on the basis of a threat assessment for a particular event or trip."

Cullen said that Snow considers Secret Service agents "professional, brave, and extremely hard-working." While Snow is "surprised and saddened that a former Secret Service agent would be a source of any information—particularly anonymous, erroneous information—going into a book, he believes that the honor and historic tradition of the Secret Service will remain intact, and he recalls with great fondness and affection the brave members of his detail," the lawyer said.

In view of that, the lawyer said, Snow is "surprised that you would imply in your book that he had asked or demanded that his detail ever deviate from their proper role."

Snow's lawyer is correct in saying that the treasury secretary, along with others in the line of succession to the presidency, is required to have Secret Service protection when the secretary of homeland security authorizes it. But he is wrong in saying that the book suggests that Snow asked that his detail deviate from their proper role.

If a government official under protection decides to travel from Washington every weekend to see his mistress or his wife or to take in a movie, the Secret Service is required to provide protection. The question is whether the protectee should be taking such trips knowing that taxpayers are footing the bill.

27

Renegade

THE SECRET SERVICE began protecting Barack Obama on May 3, 2007, eighteen months before votes for president were to be cast. It was the earliest point at which the Secret Service had ever protected a presidential candidate. In contrast, in the 2004 election, John Kerry and John Edwards began receiving protection in February of that year, eight months before the general election. Michelle Obama began receiving protection on February 2, 2008. It would turn out to be the longest and most demanding presidential campaign in history.

Strapped for agents and facing rising attrition rates, the Secret Service began planning for the campaign in January 2005. In February of that year, the service asked most of its 3,404 agents for their preferences on types of candidate protection assignments. For example, agents can ask to join a general protection shift, operations and logistics, or transportation details. Agents were given special training at the Rowley center so that members of each detail to be assigned to a future candidate would get used to working together. Agents who would drive candidates were given refresher courses. The campaign also would require the support of twelve hundred Uniformed Division officers.

By law, the Secret Service provides protection of major presidential and vice presidential candidates and their spouses. The secretary of homeland security determines who the major candidates are after consulting with an advisory committee consisting of the speaker and minority leader of the House, the majority and minority leaders of the Senate, and one additional member selected by the other members of the committee.

The secretary of homeland security also decides when protection begins. Protection of spouses starts a hundred twenty days before the general election, unless authorized before that by DHS or by executive order. To protect a presidential candidate, the Secret Service spends an extra thirty-eight thousand dollars a day beyond agents' existing salaries. That includes airline tickets for agents and for advance personnel, rental cars, meals, and overtime.

At one point, based on the public record, the Secret Service counted fifteen potential presidential candidates. As it turned out, three presidential candidates received protection. As a former first lady, Hillary Clinton already had Secret Service protection.

While Obama never received a specific threat before his protection started, agents on the Secret Service's Internet Threat Desk picked up a number of vaguely threatening and nasty comments, mostly directed at the fact that he is African American. Many of the comments appeared on white supremacist websites and said Obama would be assassinated if he took office. Even before Obama decided to run, Michelle Obama expressed concerns to her husband that a black candidate for president could be in jeopardy because of his race.

In the end, says Steven Hughes, deputy special agent in charge of the dignitary protection division, "We really picked him up because he asked for the protection, and then it goes through a whole process of whether we will protect him or not, and it's really not driven by the Secret Service. It's something that he asked for, and the secretary of homeland security and the president ultimately said he is a viable candidate, and it's a go for protection."

As Hughes speaks, he checks a text message on his BlackBerry. It's a report from the Protective Intelligence and Assessment Division of a threat against a candidate.

"I'm getting them all day long, updates on whether someone on the Internet says something or someone that's drunk says something," Hughes says. "Whether it's very minor or very major, they're going to send it to me, so I can't say I didn't know that was happening."

Asked if he ever gets any sleep, Hughes says, "With the U.N. coming up next week, where we have an incredible amount of protectees, yeah, we don't have time to sleep now."

By August 2008, the Secret Service had arrested Raymond H. Geisel in Miami after he made a threat against candidate Obama in a training class for bail bondsmen. Two members of the class heard Geisel say, "If he gets elected, I'll assassinate him myself." When arrested, Geisel had a loaded nine-millimeter handgun, knives, dozens of rounds of ammunition, body armor, a machete, and military-style fatigues in his hotel room. He was charged with threatening a presidential candidate.

In Denver, a group of men with guns and bulletproof vests made racist remarks about Obama and talked of gunning him down as he gave his acceptance speech at the Democratic National Convention in August. They were high on drugs and not capable of carrying out a plot.

Four days before the convention, one of them was pulled over for drunk driving in the Denver suburb of Aurora after a patrol officer spotted the man's rented Dodge Ram truck swerving erratically. Inside, the officer found two high-powered rifles, a silencer, a bulletproof vest, camouflage clothing, and three fake identification cards. The truck contained enough drug-making equipment to be considered a mobile meth lab. While the Secret Service kept tabs on the case, the men were prosecuted locally on gun and weapons charges.

Chatter among white supremacists on the Internet increased throughout the campaign. As Obama was giving his acceptance speech on November 4, 2008, Ku Klux Klan leader David Duke was rallying white supremacists in a call to action, saying Obama's election represented a "night of tragedy and sadness." In an audio message broadcast on a radical website, Duke said, "Barack Obama has a long history of antagonizing white people." He added, "We as European Americans have to rally for our survival."

Just before the election, two skinheads in Tennessee were charged with plotting to behead blacks across the country and assassinate Obama while wearing white top hats and tuxedos. In both cases, the Secret Service determined the men were not capable of carrying out their plots.

The day after the election, one of the most popular white supremacist websites got more than two thousand new members. One posting on the site said, "I want the SOB laid out in a box to see how messiahs come to rest. God has abandoned us, this country is doomed."

Five days before Obama's inauguration, Secret Service agents arrested Steven J. Christopher in Brookhaven, Mississippi, for allegedly saying on the Internet that he intended to kill Obama. His entries on a website devoted to government conspiracies and unexplained phenomena included racial and anti-Semitic remarks. In one entry, Christopher wrote, "Yes, I have decided I will assassinate Barack Obama. It's really nothing personal about the man." He added that he had no way to travel to Washington.

"I don't own a gun, so maybe someone can give me one," he said, according to the Justice Department.

Media reports claimed that someone yelled "Kill him," referring to Obama, at two Republican rallies. But Secret Service agents on the scene and videotapes played afterward revealed no such comments. At a rally for Governor Sarah Palin at Clearwater, Florida, a man yelled "tell him" or "tell them" rather than "kill him," the Secret Service concluded.

Despite the ranting by racists, throughout the campaign the Secret Service saw no spike in credible threats.

John McCain did not initially request protection and claimed he did not need it. After a congressional hearing on April 7, 2008, revealed that he was not under protection, McCain was urged by both his staff and members of Congress to accept Secret Service protection. He then agreed to it, and his protection began on April 27.

The Secret Service worked with the campaigns so it would know ahead of time who the vice presidential nominees would be and when their names would be announced. It then chose a time on the day of the announcement when protection would begin.

Thus, by the time Sarah Palin—code-named Denali—and Joe Biden—code-named Celtic—were nominated for vice president at their respective conventions, they and their spouses were already under protection. Palin's husband, Todd, was code-named Driller, and Biden's wife, Jill, was code-named Capri. Protection for the Bidens began on August 23, 2008 and for the Palins on August 29, 2008.

Before protection began, Secret Service director Mark Sullivan and his team met with each candidate. Like nearly all the Secret Service's twenty-two directors, Sullivan came up through the ranks. A native of Arlington, Massachusetts, Sullivan graduated from Saint Anselm College in Manchester, New Hampshire. He began his Secret Service career in 1983 as an agent assigned to the Detroit field office.

In 1996, Sullivan became an assistant supervisory agent in charge within the Office of Protective Operations. He later became deputy special agent in charge of the Counterfeit Division. In 2002, he became deputy special agent in charge of the vice presidential protection division. After briefly serving as deputy director, Sullivan was sworn in as director on May 31, 2006.

While the backgrounds of Sullivan and the deputy director are on the Secret Service website, unlike the FBI, the agency does not announce the names of other Secret Service officials when they are appointed.

When Sullivan talks about growing up in "Aah-lington" (Massachusetts) and playing "haah-ky," he speaks with the typical pahk-the-cah-in-Hahvad-yahd accent. His ice hockey team beats the FBI's team every year. It's gotten so Director Bob Mueller jokingly accuses Sullivan of hiring for hockey talent.

Sullivan has a corner office on the eighth floor of Secret Service headquarters on H Street at Ninth Street in Washington. The objects in his office underscore his jock status: a framed photo of hockey great Bobby Orr on the ice, an aerial view of Fenway Park, a cluster of Red Sox caps and signed baseballs and signed footballs.

The traces of a Boston Irish accent fade quickly when Sullivan starts to talk about the job. There are twenty-two hundred working investigations, he says. As he speaks, his brow rises and furrows over his large wide-set brown eyes, and it stays furrowed in a persistent intensity. He leans forward in his chair, his meaty hands slapping his knees for emphasis. He throws himself into things physically. He sits with his legs crossed, his calves massive from all the years of skating.

Besides starting earlier than any other presidential campaign, candidates were taking more overseas trips, Sullivan notes. As a candidate, Obama took a six-day trip to Jordan, Israel, Germany, France, and Great Britain. Before that he went to Afghanistan and Iraq. McCain traveled to Canada, Colombia, and Mexico.

"The type of crowds we see in the earlier time frame of the campaign are larger than historically we've seen for that time frame," Sullivan says. While the campaign was the longest in history, "I think that our people have reacted to it very, very well," Sullivan says. "I've been very proud of the way they've reacted to it."

In the summer of 2008, the Secret Service asked for and received an extra $9.5 million to cover unexpected costs of protecting the candidates, in addition to the $106.7 million already budgeted. In all, the Secret Service protected the candidates on 5,141 travel stops. More than 2.8 million people passed through thirty-five hundred Secret Service magnetometers.

That did not include screening 1.5 million people at events attended by the president and other protectees, or screening at the two national conventions, in Denver and in Saint Paul. The Secret Service oversaw security arrangements for the two conventions and set up an off-site communications center at each. The center coordinated the efforts of a hundred representatives from seventy entities ranging from the FBI and local police to local hospitals and utility companies. Manned twenty-four hours a day, each center had tiered seats as in a stadium so those in attendance could easily monitor the screens on the walls.

Every security concern, down to a car being broken into, appeared on a screen with the action being taken to resolve it. At the Republican convention, the Saint Paul Police Department and the Ramsey County sheriff's office arrested eight hundred protesters. They included three hundred self-described anarchists, most of them affiliated with the RNC Welcoming Committee.

The Secret Service considered the local law enforcement efforts a model of how to handle such threats. Thirteen months earlier, Sheriff Bob Fletcher had organized an intelligence group that infiltrated the Welcoming Committee. A few days before the convention, sheriff's deputies arrested eight of the group's leaders and executed search warrants that obtained their plans, maps, and weapons. The group allegedly had planned to barricade bridges, spray delegates with urine, and possibly kidnap delegates. They were charged with conspiring to cause a riot as part of a terrorist act.

At the convention itself in the Xcel Energy Center, several Code-Pink protestors interrupted speeches by Senator McCain and Governor Palin with heckling. As they approached the stage, they revealed pink slips they were wearing. While delegates or the press may have given them guest passes, they also could have obtained them through others who received them from the original recipients. As long as the protesters did not threaten anyone, the Secret Service considered the matter one for the convention's security force to handle.

"We screen everybody coming in," an agent says. "If they had posed a threat, we would have addressed it. If they had rushed the stage, if they had tried to get to the protectees, if they had yelled some sort of threat, we would have been involved. But that wasn't the case."

Convention security personnel escorted the protesters out, and the Republican National Committee did not press charges.

"They were voicing their First Amendment right to what they had to say, and they were escorted out by the host committee there, so that really wasn't a Secret Service issue," Hughes says.

Agents say both Barack Obama—code-named Renegade—and Michelle Obama—code-named Renaissance—treat them with respect, as does Biden.

"Twice Obama invited agents to dinner, including a party for a relative, both at his home," says an agent who was on his candidate detail. Michelle Obama insists that agents call her by her first name.

"Michelle is friendly—she touches you," an agent says.

Obama makes an effort to be on time and usually is. If Obama is running late, Michelle gets on his case, saying he is being inconsiderate of his agents. Biden "gets a kick out of shmoozing with agents," says an agent. "The Bidens buy agents food and are getting to know everyone by name."

On April 4, 2008, just before Obama's pastor, the Reverend Jeremiah A. Wright, Jr., spoke at the National Press Club, Obama secretly met with Wright at Wright's home. So that they would not be noticed, agents made a point of driving Obama in a minivan instead of the usual Suburban. They parked their other vehicles a block away. Obama spent an hour with Wright and then left.

No doubt Obama wanted Wright to fade into the woodwork, but in his press club speech, Wright only confirmed that he thought America created the AIDS virus to kill off blacks. After that, Obama severed ties with him.

After Obama was elected president, Barbara Walters asked him if he worries about his safety. He said he never thinks about it.

"Part of it is because I've got this pretty terrific crew of Secret Service guys that follow me everywhere I go, but also because I have a deep religious faith and faith in people that carries me through the day," he said.

Contrary to Obama's repeated claims that he is quitting smoking, he has continued to smoke regularly, agents say. A week after being sworn in as president, Obama told CNN's Anderson Cooper that he hadn't had a cigarette on the White House grounds. That left open the possibility that he smokes on the Truman Balcony and in the White House residence and West Wing. Agents say he smokes outside the White House as well.

Unlike Obama, Secret Service agents say McCain—code-named Phoenix—was irritable, impatient, and displayed his famous temper over trivial annoyances.

"McCain's really hard to work with," an agent says. "He's always complaining, just making comments. We knew from the start that he wasn't a big fan of ours. We get in his way. We impede his ability to meet the people."

On the other hand, Cindy McCain—code-named Parasol—was a pleasure to work with and has a good sense of humor, agents say.

After Obama was elected president, his two children—Malia, code-named Radiance, and Sasha, code-named Rosebud—began receiving Secret Service protection. The Secret Service also began protection of Joe Biden's children, grandchildren, and mother. As with protection of Cheney's daughters and granddaughters, rather than bringing in additional agents, the Secret Service expected agents to work longer hours to cover much of the extra load and to skip firearms training, physical fitness training, and tests. In fact, because of Biden's constant travel as vice president—including to his home state of Delaware—the burden on agents became so great that the Secret Service stopped all training on the vice president's detail. Nonetheless, agents on both his detail and the president's fill in forms claiming that they have taken and passed all tests, when they have not, creating a dishonest culture.

"We have half the number of agents we need, but requests for more agents have fallen on deaf ears at headquarters," an agent says. "Headquarters' mentality has always been, 'You can complete the mission with what you have. You're a U.S.S.S. agent.'"

The inauguration of the first African American president and the unprecedented crowd size made the event a high-value target. Once Obama became president, the Secret Service experienced a 400 percent increase in the number of threats against the president, in comparision with President Bush. While most of the threats were not credible, each had to be checked out and adjudicated. Because the Secret Service thinks calling attention to threats gives people ideas and generates more threats, the agency never publicly characterizes their frequency.

Since the inauguration was a special national security event, the Secret Service was the lead agency in charge of security. The security precautions were unprecedented. Under the Secret Service's plan, a large section of downtown Washington was cordoned off. Personal vehicles were banned from Potomac River bridge crossings to D.C. Interstates 395 and 66 leading into Washington were closed to personal traffic as well.

As with previous inaugurations, the Secret Service arranged to block with concrete barriers or police cars every street in Washington leading to the motorcade route. Since the 9/11 attack, crowds must now pass through magnetometers before entering the area along the motorcade route. Coolers, backpacks, and packages were banned.

Secret Service agents and military explosives experts inspected manholes and underground tunnels along the motorcade route. Manhole covers were spot-welded shut. Mailboxes and trash cans were removed from the street. If an item could not be removed, it was inspected and taped shut. If anyone tampered with it, the special tape—which varies in color with the event—would deteriorate.

Bomb-sniffing dogs inspected buildings, garages, and delivery trucks. Employees in offices along the route and hotel guests were often checked for criminal records. Agents made sure they had access to every office and hotel room with master keys kept by building or hotel managers. They taped shut utility rooms or electrical circuit boards. They stationed agents or police officers on top of buildings.

More than a dozen countersniper teams were deployed at the most vulnerable points along the parade route. Helicopters hovered overhead, other aircraft were kept away, and high-resolution surveillance cameras scanned the crowds. A $350,000 loudspeaker system using sonar technology was installed to give instructions in the event of an emergency.

"Every window must be closed when the motorcade passes," a supervisory agent says. "We have spotters looking at them with binoculars. For the most part they comply. If they don't, we have master keys to all those doors. We ask them why they are there and opening the windows."

If agents encountered a problem, they called for an ID team. Named for the Intelligence Division, the ID team travels with the president and vice president. It is usually composed of a Secret Service agent and a local police officer. At the inauguration, most of the ID teams consisted of Secret Service agents. Several times, the teams interviewed suspicious individuals.

In all, the Secret Service coordinated the work of at least forty thousand officers and agents from ninety-four federal and local law enforcement, military, and security agencies. Police departments from across the country contributed officers, many wearing plain clothes. The total force was double that of Bush's second inauguration.

Just past noon on January 20, Obama placed his left hand on the Lincoln Bible, a velvet-bound volume purchased by a Supreme Court clerk for the Great Emancipator's swearing in on March 4, 1861. Obama raised his right hand and took the thirty-five-word oath of office administered by Chief Justice John Roberts.

Twice, Obama and his wife, Michelle, left their limousine to walk along Pennsylvania Avenue and wave to the crowds. Jimmy Carter was the first president to do this, spontaneously leaving his limousine without clearing it with the Secret Service. Since then, the Secret Service has scripted where the president should walk, providing extra security along the way.

Intelligence officials picked up information that people associated with a Somalia-based group, al-Shabaab, might try to travel to the United States with plans to disrupt the inauguration. The information had limited specificity and uncertain credibility.

In the end, nearly two million people packed the outside of the Capitol, the parade route, and the National Mall. The inauguration went off without a hitch. Yet even as Obama took the oath of office, the Secret Service took risks by cutting corners. Contributors who raised three hundred thousand dollars or more for the inauguration were never asked to show identification to pick up tickets, including VIP passes allowing them and their guests to meet privately with him. Others who were screened before sitting in a ticketed area near Obama during his swearing-in mingled with crowds that were not screened. They were never again checked for firearms or explosives.

More than a hundred VIPs were told to gather for a security screening outside the Renaissance Hotel before boarding "secure" buses that would take them to Obama's podium at the Capitol. But after passing through the magnetometers, they were told to walk on a public sidewalk and find their way to buses waiting in a convention center parking lot. They were not screened again or asked for identification.

One donor who handled contributions for the inauguration told *The Washington Post* that he was shocked at the difference between Secret Service security during Bill Clinton's inaugurations and Obama's.

"The lack of security was absurd," he said.

As usual, the Secret Service claimed some security measures are not visible.

"We take a layered approach to security and don't rely on any one countermeasure to ensure that a site is safe," spokesman Ed Donovan said.

Yet for all the mumbo jumbo about layered security, the fact is that by failing to properly screen spectators, the Secret Service exposed the new president to possible danger.

28

Grenade

IN HIS OFFICE on the ninth floor of Secret Service head-quarters, Nicholas Trotta, who heads the Office of Protective Operations, is talking about lessons learned from previous assassinations and assassination attempts. After the attempt on President Reagan's life, "We expanded our use of the magnetometers." Now, he says, "Everyone goes through the magnetometer."

Often, just seeing a magnetometer in use is a deterrent, Trotta notes. He recalls working an outdoor event in Denver with President George H. W. Bush. A deranged woman with a handgun in her backpack arrived early at the site, thinking she would get close to the president.

"She sees one of the limos go into a tent," Trotta says. Because onlookers were being screened with magnetometers, "She can't get in. So she waits." She thought she would then shoot the president as he entered his limousine, but she got distracted by people next to her. As agents were flying back to Washington, they learned that the woman had been committed to a mental hospital. She revealed her aborted plan to family members.

"There's been so many like that—ones we don't know about because they were not successful," Trotta says. "How many [assassins] have been stopped or have seen a police officer, have seen a magnetometer? I don't know how many times I've been briefed where people, as they are getting in line, see the magnetometer, and they turn the other way. That's a trigger for us. Teams will go and interview, and all of a sudden a person has weapons on them."

But what about instances when the Secret Service buckles under pressure from campaign personnel or White House staff to let people into events without being screened? Suddenly, Trotta changes his story. "When we have a crowd of seventy thousand people, we may or may not need to put all those people through magnetometers," Trotta says. "Because some of those people in certain areas might not have a line-of-sight threat that can harm the protectee."

But what if an assassination occurred because someone was not screened? Trotta looks uncomfortable. Still, he plows on ahead, saying that a lot of factors come into play.

"The president can go to a sports arena or stadium and may stay in a box," Trotta says. "Let's say if he's on the third base up in a box, the people on first base side, center field, they might not be the threat. But the people around him may be the threat. So now we screen that area, and the critical part is to make sure that there's no handoff, so you have a dead space that is secure."

Has Trotta never heard of a gunman leaving his seat to zip off a shot or throw a grenade at the president? When told of Trotta's rationale for stopping magnetometer screening, Secret Service agents cannot believe he said what he did indeed say.

"I was in absolute shock regarding his comment about the mags closing down and potential attackers being too far away to cause any problems," says an agent on one of the two major protective details. Imagine, the agent says, if three or four suicide assassins came in with guns firing.

"I cannot believe the head of our protective operations actually said that," the agent says. "Yeah, let's drop those magnetometers.

Thank God you have it on record, because he would be one of the first people to be called to testify before a congressional committee if such an incident happened."

"Saying not everyone in a seventy-thousand-person event is close enough to shoot the protectee is an amazing answer," says another agent on one of the major protective details. "I'm embarrassed that an assistant director would give you that answer."

Danny Defenbaugh, the former FBI agent who criticized the Secret Service's decision to stop magnetometer screening at an Obama event in Dallas, notes that word can quickly spread that the agency engages in such lax practices.

"The people who want to assassinate the president will watch and look for the Secret Service to close down the magnetometers before an event starts," he says.

Shutting down magnetometers as an event is about to start is shocking enough, but when Vice President Biden threw the opening pitch at the first Baltimore Orioles game of the season at Camden Yards on April 6, 2009, the Secret Service had not screened any of the more than forty thousand fans. Moreover, even though Biden's appearance at the game was announced beforehand, the vice president was not wearing a bulletproof vest as he stood on the pitcher's mound.

"A gunman or gunmen from anywhere in the stands could have gotten off multiple rounds before we could have gotten in the line of fire," says a current agent who is outraged that the Secret Service would be so reckless. According to this agent, before the Baltimore event, senior management on Biden's detail decided "We don't need magnetometers," overruling stunned agents on Biden's detail and the agency's Baltimore field office.

In addition to being vulnerable to assassination at the Orioles game, Biden sabotages his own security by insisting on having only two vehicles instead of eight in his Secret Service motorcade, especially when visiting Delaware. Nor does he want the usual police escort. "He doesn't understand protection," an agent says. "Our bosses have no backbone. Instead of folding, they should explain why protection is needed and insist that he have it."

Biden's lack of regard for security was evident when, chatting with journalists at the head table at the 2009 Gridiron Dinner, he revealed the location of a top-secret bunker beneath the vice president's residence. Biden later tried to claim that he was talking about a study used by his predecessor Dick Cheney at the upper level of the residence. But the Secret Service emailed agents to warn them that Biden had compromised the location of the vice president's secret underground bunker.

"It was a shock to all of us that the vice president did that," says an agent. "If we had done that, we would have been prosecuted."

Referring to the decision to dispense with magnetometer screening, an agent says, "The Secret Service has dismantled the first line of defense against an assassination. They can say it's okay, but it will not be okay when the president or vice president is killed."

As Trotta acknowledges, demands on the Secret Service have been exploding. Moreover, as presidents travel more, the Secret Service has to devote more resources to advance work. Near the end of his term, President Bush traveled somewhere almost every day. In 2008, he visited thirty countries.

In April 2008 alone, the Secret Service provided protection during trips to twenty countries on five continents. In that month, "We had all our protective assignments—the former presidents—and you had the Pope come in; you had heads of state coming into the U.S. because of the Pope's trip," Trotta says. "Then we had the Caribbean summit in Miami. You had the president's North American summit in New Orleans. We had huge campaign rallies."

Yet Trotta refuses to acknowledge that those demands have in any way diminished the level of protection, either as a result of magnetometer screening being waived or because overwhelmed, experienced agents are getting fed up and leaving. If agents are departing, it's not the fault of Secret Service management practices, he says. Moreover, he says it's fine if people leave.

Agents "look at travel, and they see the money they're making, and it does come down sometimes to the quality of life," Trotta tells me. "But the job is what it is. We have a responsibility to the American public, and it comes with sometimes a price: long hours, travel, missing birthday parties, and transfers. And it comes down to an employee saying, 'I can't do it anymore.' So they choose. They just go. And that's okay."

When it comes to the agency's weapons, Trotta is similarly indifferent. Trotta says he leaves those decisions to the training facility.

"They're the experts," he says.

Remarkably, the assistant director in charge of protecting the president and presidential candidates expresses no interest in the question of whether an assassination attempt could be successful because agents are not equipped with weapons that the FBI, the army, and even the Amtrak Police Department use.

In fact, says an agent, "When we go for firearms training, every one of our instructors implores us to ask in the evaluation forms we submit to switch to the M4. The MP5 is a big pistol. We are outgunned by our enemy."

Trotta's nonchalant attitude about whether Secret Service weapons are effective, about increasing agent turnover, and about the practice of skipping magnetometer screening reflects a culture of denial. The fact that Trotta would cite the effectiveness of magnetometers in preventing assassinations and say "everyone goes through the magnetometer," and, in the next breath, defend skipping them at major events, is astounding.

In fact, it was such a decision to stop magnetometer screening that almost led to the assassination of President George W. Bush on May

10, 2005, when a man threw a grenade at him as he spoke at a rally in a public square in Tbilisi, Georgia. Because magnetometer screening was stopped, the man was able to take a grenade into the event where Bush was to speak.

"The Georgians had set up the magnetometers all around this area," says Thomas V. Fuentes, the FBI special agent in charge of international operations who headed the investigation of the incident. "They screened about ten thousand people, and there's about a hundred fifty thousand that want to get in. They realize they're not going to get them in in time on the president's schedule, so they just shut off the machines and let everybody in."

The grenade landed near the podium where Bush was speaking, but it did not explode. Witnesses later said a man wearing a head scarf who was standing off to the side reached into his black leather jacket and pulled out a military grenade. He yanked the pin, wrapped the scarf around the grenade, and threw it toward Bush.

Inside a grenade, the chemical reaction that creates an explosion occurs when two spoons disengage. But because the spoons got stuck, when the grenade landed, no explosion occurred. After analyzing the device, the FBI concluded it could have killed the president if it had worked. If all onlookers had been screened, the grenade would have been detected, and Bush's life would not have been in jeopardy.

"We were within an eyelash of losing our top protectee, yet this is never brought up during our training," says a Secret Service agent on one of the major details.

Prior to that attack, the assassination attempts on Presidents Reagan and Ford and on Senator Robert F. Kennedy and Governor George Wallace all occurred because bystanders were not screened with magnetometers.

"If someone is willing to commit suicide to assassinate the president, there's nothing you can do about it unless you have magnetometer screening," says former Secret Service supervisor Dave Saleeba.

Trotta's cavalier responses are symptomatic of the Secret Service's refusal to acknowledge or address problems that undermine the agency's mission. In similar fashion, when asked about the increasing attrition rate and sagging morale, Mark Sullivan, the Secret Service director, says, in effect, too bad.

"The hours are tough," Sullivan says. "We've all worked them, and I know what it's like. I've been an agent for twenty-five years now, and I would never ask anyone to do what I wouldn't do. And I know that they do a lot of travel. I know they're away from home. I know they work long hours out there, and it quite frankly is not an easy job."

If being an agent were an easy job, "Anybody could do it. But not just anybody could do it," he says. "I think it's because of the character of our people, and the pride that they have in their jobs that they are going to work hard. We try to get enough relief out there for them and get enough people out there to support them, to make sure that they don't have to work any more hours than they have to."

While Sullivan was a respected agent, he does not have the management skills to uncover problems at the agency and deal with them. Nor does he recognize how the agency's practice of cutting corners has jeopardized the safety of agents and those they protect. Indeed, Sullivan rejects the notion that the Secret Service has been cutting corners.

"When it comes to our protective mission, we're never going to cut corners," the director says. "I will tell you that we will never, ever, put anybody in a position that they're going to fail, because we can't afford it. We're going to make sure that we do what we have to do to make sure we get the job done. And I think we have."

29

Padding Statistics

T O IMPRESS CONGRESS, J. Edgar Hoover, as director of the FBI from 1924 to 1972, would count among the bureau's arrests those made by local police for car thefts. At the same time, Hoover ignored some of the biggest threats, such as organized crime and political corruption, in part because they required much more time and manpower.

In many ways, Secret Service officials have the same mentality. Just as Hoover did, the Secret Service pads arrest statistics proudly presented to Congress and the public to make itself look good. In 2008, the Secret Service made 2,398 arrests for counterfeiting and 5,332 arrests for other financial crimes. But those figures include arrests that the agency never made. They are so-called in custody responses, which is when local police notify the Secret Service that they have a suspect in custody for the equivalent of a counterfeiting violation or other financial crime. The Secret Service then takes credit for the local arrest.

"When you are a field agent, you are strongly urged to call the local police departments in your district and have them contact you if they made an arrest, state or local," a veteran agent says. "Then you write up the necessary reports and claim credit for the arrest and conviction of the subject."

"The reason they do it obviously is so they can walk over to Congress and inflate the investigative success of the agency," says a former agent who joined the inspector general's office of another federal agency. "They make a copy of the police report and make a copy of the note, and that's about it. The FBI does not do that. It's a game, and it's deceptive."

Moreover, instead of rooting out the biggest offenders, "By and large, arrests are all about the numbers," an agent says. "Very infrequently do we go after the big fish. We work very few high-profile cases that get to the source of counterfeit currency and the stolen credit card numbers."

When asked about the practice of padding Secret Service statistics with arrests made by local authorities, Ed Donovan, a Secret Service spokesman, did not respond.

Why the Secret Service has the dual role of protection and law enforcement in the first place is a legitimate question. While the FBI traditionally leaves counterfeiting investigations to the Secret Service, it covers all the other financial crimes Secret Service agents investigate. But since the needs of the protection side rise and fall, the Secret Service's dual role provides flexibility. The agency can always borrow agents from the investigative side when needed. Maintaining field offices that interact with local law enforcement on a daily basis helps the protection side when the president comes to town.

Agents say that after spending endless nights in a Suburban guarding a protectee, they look forward to eventually returning to investigative work. Interviewing people as part of a criminal investigation sharpens agents' skills when dealing with possible threats to the president. While many agents are former police officers, most are not. Investigating crimes, they learn to evaluate body language and eye movement to get a sense of whether an individual is being deceptive.

The value of combining investigative and protective operations is that as a criminal investigator, "You learn the basics," Nick Trotta says. "You learn about your own safety and your partner's safety. You learn how to think on your feet when you're out on the street and get in the mind of the criminal—whether it's a counterfeit case or the financial fraud cases. I think that our dual mission is what makes us unique, and it makes our agents very efficient and effective in our over-all missions."

The downside of the Secret Service's dual role is that agents often cannot show up for a meeting with prosecutors or for a court appearance because they have been pulled off for a protection assignment.

"You could be working one of the biggest cases, and if your name gets pulled to go on a protective operation, you're off that case to per-haps stand in a hallway as a king of a small country comes to get his prostate checked at the Mayo Clinic," says a former agent.

For that reason, U.S. Attorneys dread working with Secret Service agents.

The larger problem is that the Secret Service blindly takes on greater jurisdiction on the investigative side and more duties on the protection side without obtaining a commensurate increase in budget and agents. That is a reflection on management, not the agents, who are generally sharp and dedicated. More than officers or agents of any other law enforcement agency, FBI agents who have worked with them admire Secret Service agents.

Aside from their normal duties, agents have saved lives by giving cardiopulmonary resuscitation and have prevented murders and apprehended hit-and-run drivers, as Agent Patrick Sullivan did in New York one afternoon. Driving alone on the FDR Drive, he saw a car in front of him racing northbound at high speed. A man was changing his tire at the side of the road underneath the Williamsburg Bridge. The speeding car hit the parked vehicle, sending the driver into the air.

Sullivan radioed the New York field office asking for police assistance and an ambulance. He turned on his flashing red light and siren and chased the car uptown, where he finally headed him off on First Avenue, in front of the United Nations. Drawing his gun and displaying his badge, Sullivan ordered the man from the car and held him until police arrived. The victim survived.

In other cases, agents prevent harm to protectees in unusual circumstances. When young Amy Carter attended Ethel Kennedy's annual Hickory Hill Pet Show at Ethel's estate in McLean, Virginia, in May 1978, a three-ton elephant named Suzie charged her. As the crowd scattered in panic, an agent scooped up Amy and carried her to safety.

Aside from agents who have lost their lives in the line of duty, many have contracted incurable tropical diseases like dengue fever and other maladies while protecting U.S. officials overseas. Agents will literally give protectees the shirts off their backs—as agent Harold Ewing did when the president's limo hit a pothole on the way to Annapolis and Bill Clinton spilled coffee all over his own shirt.

"The Secret Service attracts a lot of people who have been brought up with a certain code of ethics," says former agent Norm Jarvis, who trained new agents and later was a special agent in charge. "Those ethics mean that a person who would ordinarily be interested in preserving his own life is willing to sacrifice his life. The training that the agent goes through doesn't necessarily say, 'When you hear this, this is what you've got to do. You hear a gunshot, and step one is this. Step two is you take a bullet for the president.' It's basically, you go to an instinct kind of mode."

Obviously, Jarvis says, "When you sign up for the job, you have to come to the conclusion that you would step in front of the president to protect him from an assassin. But," he adds, "I don't even think it's worth contemplating. You would just do it."

"The greatness of the Secret Service is its people," says former agent Pete Dowling. "Somehow we get high-quality people who are superdedicated to a mission."

No one knows how many assassination attempts have been prevented because a gunman decided an attempt was too risky or because the Secret Service confiscated a weapon. Beyond the well-publicized attempts, presidents and other protectees have been targets of dozens of lesser-known plots. For example, when Edward M. Kennedy was running for president in 1979, agents subdued a knife-wielding woman who entered the reception room in his U.S. Senate office.

"The Secret Service's mission of preventing a criminal act is far harder than investigating one after it takes place," FBI director Robert S. Mueller III tells me.

Yet effective as Secret Service agents have been, their capability is diminished by a management that cuts corners when the need for tight security has never been greater, and refuses to recognize that the agency cannot properly handle all the duties it unflinchingly assumes. Just as FBI Director J. Edgar Hoover managed to cover up the bureau's shortcomings through good public relations, the Secret Service has done a brilliant job of projecting an image of infallibility that is not deserved.

Even Hoover's obsessive emphasis on dressing sharply and wearing white shirts is mirrored by Secret Service management. In one of his first communications with agents after being named deputy director in July 2008, Keith Prewitt said that agents should dress like Secret Service agents when traveling. Yet agents point out that one way to catch a terrorist planning to take down an airplane is to dress in the most casual clothes so a terrorist does not suspect the person sitting next to him is a law enforcement officer.

In one respect, Hoover's management style differed from the Secret Service's: Hoover inspired loyalty to himself and the organization. Secret Service management inspires mistrust and cynicism, leading to low morale.

In explaining this counterproductive culture, agents say that Secret Service officials prefer to maintain the status quo rather than make waves and rock the boat. That way, they further their chances for promotion, resulting in high-paying jobs in the private sector. Meanwhile, top agents who head field offices drive BMWs, Lexuses, Corvettes, and Jaguars, cars that have been seized in arrests. The rationale is that the vehicles could be used for undercover work. In fact, they rarely are. Rather than providing senior agents with luxury cars, the Secret Service should sell such cars to generate money for the Treasury Department.

"If anyone did that in the FBI, we would be in hot water," says a former FBI assistant director. "In the FBI, cars used for undercover work are designated as such, and the head of a field office would never get one." Nor, the former agent says, does the FBI claim an arrest if it is made by local police.

Secret Service agents believe that if they press their concerns and point out shortcomings, they will suffer repercussions. "Management will label them as malcontents or implement classic Secret Service retaliation, most notably an undesirable duty station and lack of advancement, or both," an agent says. "Everyone at headquarters sees the job as a stepping stone to something better. If you raise a big issue, you waste your energy, and they want to screw you. It creates a culture of fear."

In 1978, the Secret Service asked Frank M. Ochberg, a former associate director of the National Institute of Mental Health, to study agents and their jobs to see if they were under excessive stress.

"I found the danger they face is not a source of significant stress," says Ochberg, who is now clinical professor of psychiatry at Michigan

State University. "Rather, it was an excessively authoritarian management style that does not respect agents enough and does not try to make arrangements so they don't miss their daughter's christening or graduation. The attitude was, 'Yours is not to wonder why; yours is just to do or die.'"

Based on Ochberg's recommendation, the Secret Service stopped its practice of forcing agents to double up in hotel rooms. Until then, agents on different shifts sleeping in the same room would wake each other up getting ready for work. But beyond that change, the problems have become worse. The Secret Service's management has become even more rigid, insular, and even punitive. An agent who left to work for another federal law enforcement agency says with relief, "I am now being treated as an adult."

To get ahead, agents say that, much more than in most other organizations, they need connections—juice—meaning higher-ups who take a liking to them and socialize with them. The perception of favoritism has been furthered by management's overreaction to a lawsuit by black agents claiming discrimination. During discovery, the lawsuit uncovered two dozen or so emails with racist comments or jokes out of twenty million emails sent by Secret Service employees over a period of sixteen years. In April 2008, a black agent was confronted by a noose strung up by a white instructor at the Rowley training center. The instructor was placed on leave.

Despite these disgusting but isolated problems, the proportion of black agents in the service is 17 percent, much higher than the 12 percent of blacks in the rest of the population. An independent analyst found that for each year from 1991 to 2005, African American agents were promoted to senior pay grades more quickly than white agents. In fact, 25 percent of supervisors belong to ethnic minorities. Since 2001, three black agents—Keith Prewitt, Danny Spriggs, and Larry Cockell—have served as deputy director, the number-two spot.

"The service is very sensitive to the diversity issue, and the statistics and appointments to top posts demonstrate that," Spriggs says.

Growing up in Detroit, "I never could have imagined that I would one day be with the president in his limousine, in the White House every day, and riding on Air Force One," says Reginald Ball, a black agent who became a supervisor.

Ironically, several racist emails uncovered by the lawsuit had been sent by Reginald Moore, the plaintiff who is alleging discrimination by the agency. One email sent by Moore contained a joke about a black woman hitting her daughter.

Despite these facts, the Secret Service has overreacted by promoting a few black agents to high-ranking positions even though they are not generally thought to be up to the job. While other black agents are among the agency's best, reverse discrimination does a disservice to everyone in the organization and to the people agents protect.

30

Dereliction of Duty

WHEN ONE CONSIDERS how important to our democracy preventing an assassination is, the amount spent on the Secret Service—$1.4 billion a year, nearly two thirds of it for protection—seems like a misprint. Indeed, while the agency's budget increased substantially after 9/11, since then it has actually decreased, when inflation is taken into account. That does not include supplemental appropriations to cover incremental costs for coverage of campaign and national security events.

This at a time when well-funded terrorists have replaced the lone deranged gunman as the greatest threat to American elected officials and when threats against the president have been up as much as 400 percent. Yet rather than ask for substantially more funds from Congress, the Secret Service assures members that the agency is fulfilling its job with the modest increases it requests, even as it takes on more duties and sleep-deprived agents work almost around the clock.

Inevitably, when asked if the Secret Service needs more money, Director Sullivan makes a comparison with challenges faced by soldiers in Iraq.

"Let's face it," he says. "Everybody would like to have more money in their budget. I was looking at my budget, and I was saying, 'Boy, I would love to have this or have that.' Then in thinking of all the sacrifice that all of us have to do—I mean we're in the middle of two wars now—and I looked at the front page of *The Washington Post* one day, and I saw several marines going to bed that night. They were going to bed on a concrete floor with like a foam cushion maybe an inch thick for a mattress."

These men, he says, are fighting for our country, not knowing "when they wake up tomorrow morning and go through their day if they're going to be alive to go to bed again."

In contrast to soldiers in Iraq, "We don't have it bad at all," Sullivan says. "And everybody has to do their part. And I think I owe it to them. I think this whole organization owes it to the people that pay our salary, to be just as efficient and effective and be as good a steward of the government resources as we can. And I think we are."

Sullivan's effort to compare Secret Service agents with twenty-two-year-old soldiers in Iraq shows how out of touch with reality Secret Service management is. In contrast to soldiers serving in Iraq, veteran Secret Service agents are being offered up to four times their salary by the private sector to leave the agency.

One director who understood this was Brian Stafford, who headed the agency from 1999 to 2003. Because Stafford perceived the problems, the Secret Service's budget, even before the 9/11 attack, rose by as much as 25 percent a year after adjustment for inflation.

"When I became director, one of the first things I did was pick the brains of the special agents in charge of each field office," Stafford tells me. "What I learned was we had quality-of-life issues and an attrition rate that was going up. It wasn't because agents weren't passionate about their jobs. It was because they didn't have a life."

With the budget increases, Stafford hired another thousand agents.

"The overtime was way too high," he says. "We were working people too hard."

Today, while the Secret Service fosters conditions that lead experienced agents to resign, it compromises the security of the president, vice president, and presidential candidates by not assigning enough agents to screen everyone with magnetometers. Under pressure from politicians' staffs, it allows people to enter events without having been screened.

Yet ironically, when Secret Service spokesman Eric Zahren defended the agency's performance when an Iraqi journalist threw his shoes at President Bush at a Baghdad news conference in December 2008, he pointed out that everyone had been screened with magnetometers. Thus, he said, while shoes were thrown, no weapons were brought into the room, so the president's life was not in jeopardy.

To be sure, as that embarrassing spectacle illustrates, so long as presidents insist on seeing the public, the Secret Service will not be able to prevent every incident. The tension between letting the president interact with people and protecting him goes back to the earliest days of the presidency. Secret Service agents constantly have to balance the need to protect and the need not to look like the gestapo. But failing to take the most basic precautions is as inexcusable as the decision of the Washington policeman guarding President Lincoln at Ford's Theatre to wander off for a drink at a nearby saloon.

In the movie *In the Line of Fire* starring Clint Eastwood as a Secret Service agent, the Secret Service believes an assassin will attempt to kill the president during a planned trip to California. Because it cannot locate the assassin, the agency advises the president's chief of staff to cancel the trip. Saying the president's reelection campaign is too important, the chief of staff rejects the advice.

As tension mounts, just before the assassin—played by John Malkovich—is about to shoot the president at a fund-raising dinner on the West Coast, Eastwood lunges for him and is wounded. In effect, he takes a bullet for the president. Yet allowing crowds into an event without screening—as the Secret Service actually does with presidents and presidential candidates—is even more foolhardy and egregious than what the 1993 movie portrays.

Even when the Secret Service could ask for help from other agencies, as when it assigns only three agents to protect a visiting head of state at the U.N. General Assembly, it refuses to do so, rolling the dice on an assassination attempt.

"This is another example of our stubborn leadership saying, 'We can do this; we don't need help; we're the mighty Secret Service,'" an agent who was assigned to the U.N. General Assembly says. "They have this attitude to the detriment of their agents and the well-being and security of the protectees."

While it scrimps on agents and magnetometers, to impress Congress, the Secret Service wastes taxpayer funds by assigning agents to write reports on thousands of arrests made by local police. Similarly, the agency's practice of directing agents to ignore violations of law by clearing illegal immigrants to work at the home of the secretary of homeland security, inflating its own arrest statistics by claiming credit for arrests by local police, telling agents to fill in their own physical training test forms, and rigging training exercises to impress members of Congress and U.S. Attorneys fosters a dishonest, corrupting culture that has no place in law enforcement. That culture of deceit conflicts with the inherent honesty of Secret Service agents.

The fact that the Secret Service cuts counterassault teams to two agents and bows to staff demands that the teams remain at a great distance from protectees points to the fact that the agency is geared to deal with a lone gunman rather than a full-scale terrorist attack. The agency's reliance on the MP5 rather than the far more powerful M4 that a terrorist may use is further evidence of that. That the Secret

Service, in contrast to the FBI and the military, ignores the need for regular training and firearms requalification highlights a complete disregard for the sanctity of the Secret Service's mission. In some cases, members of counterassault teams have not shot the SR-16 in more than a year.

"Why must demonstrations at the Rowley center for VIPs, politicians, and others be rehearsed?" asks an agent on one of the major protective details. "It comes down to the instructors and supervisors knowing that if it is not rehearsed, we will look like a bunch of fools running around not knowing what to do."

How can something as shocking as waiving magnetometer screening go on for so long without being exposed? The same way the FBI and CIA allowed the so-called wall to prevent them from sharing information with each other for so long, impairing the bureau's ability to detect and stop a terrorist attack. The same way investment banks knowingly acquired substandard mortgage securities, impairing the American economy and requiring the expenditure of hundreds of billions of dollars by the U.S. Treasury to shore it up. The same way the Securities and Exchange Commission brushed aside specific allegations that Bernard Madoff was running a Ponzi scheme.

"If this were a private company, they couldn't survive," an agent says. "But it's the government, and nobody's accountable."

The effect of an assassination of a president or presidential candidate is unimaginable. If Abraham Lincoln had not been assassinated, Andrew Johnson, his successor, would not have been able to undermine Lincoln's efforts to reunite the nation and give more rights to blacks during the Reconstruction period. If John F. Kennedy had not been assassinated, Lyndon Johnson likely never would have become president. If Robert F. Kennedy had not been killed and had won the presidency, Richard Nixon might never have been elected.

By definition, an assassination threatens democracy. To be sure,

Secret Service management understands the importance of that mission. On the fifty-eighth anniversary of the death of Officer Leslie Coffelt, Nick Trotta, the head of the Office of Protective Operations, wrote a memo to all agents. It was Coffelt who defended President Truman at Blair House. Dying from a wound, Coffelt leaped to his feet, propped himself against a booth, and fired at Griselio Torresola's head, taking out a would-be assassin.

In his memo, Trotta wrote that we "must not fail in our protective mission. We are protecting the lives of those that our country expects we protect at all costs." Trotta went on, "We are here to make sure that you have the tools that are needed to do what you are expected to do."

Written just before the 2008 election, the memo closed by saying, "In these last few days before the presidential election, as those on the campaign trail, your travel remains nonstop, you must remain ever so vigilant, ever so attentive to detail. We do this as the nameless agent, the nameless officer. We continue to do this without any fanfare or pats on the back."

Trotta framed the mission well, but his words ring hollow. Secret Service management is oblivious to how its own failings undermine that mission and the safety of its protectees.

Neither the DHS inspector general nor Congress has penetrated the agency's invincible veneer to uncover the shortcomings. And so long as presidents continue to select directors from within the Secret Service to lead the agency, its culture of denial will remain intact.

"We don't have enough people or the equipment to do protection the way they advertise we do," a veteran agent says. "And how we have not had an incident up to this point is truly amazing, a miracle."

Most Americans have no idea what is behind protecting a president, the first family, the vice president, and presidential candidates. They may see agents at an event or a shopping mall outside a store— dressed in suits, wearing the telltale clear spiral wire that wraps around their ear and disappears somewhere down their shirt collar. And then they think of the news story they read that morning, that the president or a presidential candidate is in town, and they realize who they are.

If the agents seem a little distracted from the hustle of the street, marching to a different drummer, it is because they are tuning into a sort of different dimension, one of heightened awareness. They are looking for anything out of the ordinary in the passersby—a man in a strange hat who nervously looks into the store. Anything odd, like beads of sweat on a forehead when the day is chilly.

It is a good day when the agents can epitomize the poet John Milton's line, "They also serve who only stand and wait."

Most days aren't like that. Most days entail risk and demands and meticulous planning—sabotaged by the Secret Service's practice of dangerously cutting corners. Agents who are concerned that the Secret Service is on the brink of a disaster say that only a director appointed from the outside can make the wholesale changes that are needed in the agency's management and culture.

Without those changes, an assassination of Barack Obama or a future president is likely. If that happens, a new Warren Commission will be appointed to study the tragedy. It will find that the Secret Service was shockingly derelict in its duty to the American people and to its own elite corps of brave and dedicated agents.

Afterword to the Paperback Edition

R OXANNE ROBERTS COULD not believe her eyes. As a *Washington Post* reporter, Roberts had been covering Washington parties and White House state dinners for twenty years. She knew all the players: the power brokers and the wannabes, the VIPs and the phonies. Roberts had never seen anything like this.

Floating into the state dinner for Indian prime minister Manmohan Singh on Tuesday, November 24, 2009, was a couple who looked exactly like Michaele and Tareq Salahi. With her long blond mane, Michaele—wearing a striking red and gold traditional Indian *lehenga*—was hard to miss.

Roberts was standing with other members of the press in what is known as the booksellers' area, a foyer next to the East Colonnade of the White House. As the guests strolled in, some would stop to chat with reporters. If reporters needed to check guests' identities, they had a hard copy of the list of 320 invitees.

"I was sort of perusing the list and seeing what names to look for," Roberts tells me. "We sort of skim the list to say, oh, we want to make sure we get a picture of this person, make sure we get a picture of that person. So guests were coming through. I'm watching, I'm watching.

There's nothing earth-shattering. And then I hear 'Mr. and Mrs. Salahi.' And I looked up. I knew the name."

Since 2005, Roberts has written "The Reliable Source" gossip column with Amy Argetsinger. Over the years, they had reported on legal wrangling over the Salahis' Oasis Winery in Hume, Virginia, and on complaints that patrons had been ripped off by a polo championship the Salahis ran. More recently, Roberts and Argetsinger had written about the couple's effort for Michaele to be selected for Bravo's *Real Housewives of D.C.* reality series.

"I immediately looked down at the guest list and saw that they weren't on it," Roberts recalls. "I have never in all the years covering state dinners seen a guest come through who wasn't on the list." It never occurred to her that they had not been invited. Instead, Roberts was shocked to think that they were.

"I knew that they weren't wealthy," Roberts notes. "I knew they were not big political donors or moved in any significant political circles. They were not what I would call part of Washington's power establishment, by any stretch of the imagination."

Roberts thought that perhaps the Salahis had some connection with the Indian embassy that could have gotten them invited.

"But I wondered whether or not the White House was familiar with their whole saga and the reality television connection," she says. "After years and years and years of doing this and knowing how people competitively vie to get an invitation to a state dinner, I was just shocked that they had managed to get an invitation to the Obamas' first state dinner. So while I was very surprised to see them, I also thought to myself, Gee, how did they pull this off?"

The Salahis swept through without stopping to talk to reporters. They walked into the White House lower hallway, mingling with guests on the red carpet before heading up to the cocktail reception in the East Room.

Roberts began to question if she had really seen what she thought she saw. After all, she had only seen the couple for a few seconds. She asked Courtney O'Donnell, communications director for Jill Biden, if she could verify that the Salahis had indeed been invited. O'Donnell said she did not know but would try to find out.

Robin Givhan, a *Washington Post* fashion reporter who was covering the event with Roberts, told her she was sure it was the Salahis, but Roberts wanted to look at the photos *Post* photographer Bill O'Leary had been taking. She asked O'Leary to email the photo of the Salahis, taken at 7:30 P.M., to Argetsinger, her "Reliable Source" partner. Then she emailed Argetsinger, asking her opinion. Argetsinger saw the emails when she got home at 10:30 P.M. after attending a movie screening.

"I recognized them, and my first reaction when I saw the photos of them was, Oh my God, they crashed," Argetsinger says. "Because they are not the kind of people you expect to see at the White House. If the one thing you knew about them was that Michaele Salahi was vying to be on the *Housewives* show, it would be inconceivable that the White House would want them there. This is a reality TV show, and one that in recent years is best known for pretty vapid material—plastic surgery, cat fights, table flipping, hair pulling."

Argetsinger checked the Salahis' Facebook page. At 9:08 P.M., they had boasted that they were "honored to be at the White House for the state dinner in honor of India with President Obama and our First Lady!" Since they would not have had reserved places at tables, they didn't attend the dinner, which began around 9 P.M. in a heated tent on the South Lawn.

Argetsinger emailed Rox, as she calls Roberts, urging her to include in the story she and Givhan would write for the late editions of the Wednesday paper that the Salahis attended but were not on the guest list.

"The most curious and unexpected sighting: Tareq and Michaele Salahi," the *Washington Post* story said in the sixth paragraph. "The notorious Fauquier County vineyard socialites, who are filming *Real Housewives of D.C.*, swanned in, even though their names did not appear on the official guest list."

By 2 A.M. on Wednesday, the Salahis had posted photos of themselves attending the dinner. The photos included Michaele posing with Vice President Biden, White House Chief of Staff Rahm Emanuel, CBS News anchor Katie Couric, Washington mayor Adrian Fenty, and three U.S. marines.

After Roberts kept pushing, the White House and Secret Service confirmed early Wednesday afternoon that the Salahis had not been invited. The story ran on all of the networks. Since Thursday was Thanksgiving—traditionally a slow news day—the gate crashers continued to be the lead story into Friday.

Late on Friday, the White House released a photo of the couple in the receiving line. A smiling Michaele Salahi is pictured clasping Obama's hand, as her husband, wearing a tuxedo, looks on. Prime Minister Singh is standing next to Obama.

As publicity about the Salahis intensified, a series of questionable dealings from their past came out. Redskins cheerleaders said Michaele had shown up on September 20, 2009, and performed with Redskins' cheerleading alumni. In front of a film crew, Michaele pretended that she had been on the squad—but she never had.

Questions also came up about the Salahis' annual Land Rover Polo Cup competition. Many of those listed as sponsors of the event's America's Cup for 2010—including Land Rover, the St. Regis Hotel in Washington, and the Ritz-Carlton Hotel—said they were not sponsors. The event claimed to be sanctioned by the National Polo League, but officials at the U.S. Polo Association, the sport's governing body, said they had never heard of the league.

A review of court records by the *Washington Post* showed that since 2004, more than thirty lawsuits in Virginia and Maryland had been filed against one or both of the Salahis, or a company they ran. Three couples who had their weddings at the Salahi family's Oasis vineyard sued, saying large, unexplained charges showed up on their wedding bills.

"It was devastating at the time," Marybeth Wootton told the *Post*. She related paying $20,000 in legal fees on top of a bill of $55,000 for the 2006 wedding. Wootton said the event cost $600 a person. That was three times as much as expected. She says she was billed for so much wine that every guest—including children—would have had to drink two bottles each, the *Post* reported.

"Every courthouse clerk in the vicinity recognizes the Salahi name," said Mark Simons, a process server who told the *Post* he delivered a summons to Tareq Salahi. Jim Jones, a detective in the Fauquier County Sheriff's office in Virginia, recalled that the Salahis showed up at court in a white stretch limousine. Onlookers remarked: "They're back!"

At first the Salahis claimed they thought they'd been invited to the state dinner based on email correspondence they had had with a Pentagon official who was a liaison with the White House. On NBC's *Today* show, they said that they would release emails supporting that claim. But the emails only showed that they were seeking an invitation, which they never produced. Their claim was as credible as a burglar who is caught in a home and says he thought the owners had asked him in.

Secret Service director Sullivan issued a statement saying the agency was "deeply concerned and embarrassed" by the incident. He said preliminary findings indicated that "established protocols were not followed at an initial checkpoint, verifying that two individuals were on the guest list."

"Everyone who enters the White House grounds goes through magnetometers and several other levels of screenings," Secret Service spokesman Edwin Donovan said. "That was the case with the state dinner last night. No one was under any risk or threat."

But that was more Secret Service spin. Normally, those attending a White House function receive a written invitation in the mail. If they wish to attend, they are asked to email or phone in their full name, Social Security number, and date of birth to the White House social office. The Secret Service checks their identities and, if no problem surfaces, invitees are told they have been cleared to attend.

Since none of that occurred in the case of the Salahis, they could have been wanted serial killers. They could have been involved with a terrorist group. They could have been agents of Iran or North Korea. The Secret Service would never have known. While they passed through magnetometers at the checkpoint at Fifteenth and E Streets NW, they could have possessed chemical or biological weapons. Inside, they could have grabbed a knife off a table and stabbed the president or another official in the heart. That night, it was a pretty blonde; tomorrow, it could be an assassin.

In previous administrations, aides from the White House social office have stood outside the Secret Service guard post and done a preliminary check to make sure that arrivals were on the guest list. Acquiescent as always, the Secret Service had agreed this time at a meeting with the social office that their representatives would not have to be there. Social secretary Desiree Rogers attended the dinner as a guest.

In the end, the fact that the Salahis were able to crash the White House was entirely the fault of the Secret Service. The Secret Service is solely responsible for the security of the president and the White House. It is the agents' responsibility to ask for the help they may need, from the social secretary or from anyone else.

Whether or not the social office did a preliminary check, it was up to the Secret Service Uniformed Division officers at the first checkpoint to verify that the couple was on the guest list. If they were not, the officers should have called the social office to see if they had inadvertently been left off the list. If the answer was yes, the officers would then ask the couple to step aside while they did a background check. They did none of this.

Called to testify at a hearing on December 3, 2009, of the House Committee on Homeland Security, Sullivan essentially stonewalled. To be sure, Sullivan told the committee that the failure to bar the two uninvited guests was solely the fault of the Secret Service. Although Sullivan said it would have been helpful to have White House social office representatives at the guard post, as has been done during previous administrations, he said the Secret Service Uniformed Division officers who let the Salahis into the White House event could have just as easily called the social office to try to verify that they were invited.

Sullivan said he had placed three Secret Service personnel on administrative leave. But he referred to the security breach as "human error." He said he had asked himself again and again why the uniformed officers had let the Salahis in and could never come up with an answer. He rejected any notion that the breach in security was symptomatic of a series of management deficiencies.

"I don't believe it is an institutional problem," Sullivan said. "I believe it is an isolated incident."

But the slipup was not human error. Unlike some previous security breaches cited in this book, it was a deliberate, conscious decision by uniformed officers to ignore the fact that the Salahis were not on the list. That decision is an expected consequence of the agency's practice of cutting corners—including by not passing people through magnetometers or shutting down the devices early, by cutting back on the size of counterassault teams, and by not allowing agents time for regular firearms requalification or physical training.

No doubt the uniformed officers who decided to let the Salahis in were aware of the corner cutting and were overwhelmed by the workload. In part because the Secret Service refuses to demand funds for adequate staffing, within the Uniformed Division alone, the attrition rate is as high as 12 percent a year.

In addition, the agency bows to political pressure. When agents refused to drive friends of Dick Cheney's daughter Mary to restaurants, she got her detail leader removed. The fact that Secret Service management does not back personnel when they are doing their job properly no doubt contributed to the uniformed officers' reluctance to turn away the glamorous couple and face possible repercussions.

When the Salahis refused to show up for a hearing, the Homeland Security Committee voted to subpoena them, only to hear them repeatedly invoke their Fifth Amendment right not to incriminate themselves. During the December hearing, Delegate Eleanor Holmes Norton, a District of Columbia Democrat, asked Sullivan whether the Secret Service might have allowed any other "interlopers" into the event.

"Ma'am, that was a concern of mine, as well," Sullivan replied. "That is something we have focused on; I cannot talk about it in this setting but I believe that I can satisfy you in explaining that there were no other people there that night that should not [have been let in]."

A few weeks later, I received a call from a high-level Secret Service official. The official, who requested anonymity, said he has been an agent more than twenty years and never thought he would place such a call. But he said Secret Service management had been covering up its shortcomings to such a degree that he had to speak out.

The official said that after Sullivan testified that no other intruders besides the Salahis crashed the state dinner, the Secret Service was examining surveillance video of guests arriving at the dinner, attempting to match the surveillance camera's images with the names on the guest list. The agency spotted an African American man wearing a tuxedo who was not on the guest list. He appeared to be with members of the Indian delegation.

Investigating further, agents found that the man had shmoozed members of the Indian delegation at the Willard InterContinental Hotel and had hopped on a State Department van taking them to the White House. The man underwent magnetometer screening with a handheld device before entering the van. But the White House had not invited him.

As with the Salahis, the Secret Service ignored the fact that the man was not on the guest list and had not conducted a background check on him. Under Secret Service procedures, even if the White House chief of staff invites his mother to the White House, she must submit to a background check.

The official told me that, even though the Secret Service had known about the third intruder for weeks and had identified him, mortified Secret Service officials had failed to inform the House Homeland Security Committee, which was continuing to investigate the original breach at the White House.

After I asked the Secret Service for comment, I ran a story on Newsmax.com revealing that a third intruder had crashed the state dinner. Having failed to respond to my request for comment, the Secret Service within two hours issued a statement confirming that "a third individual, who was not on the White House guest list, entered the state dinner."

The statement said, "It appears at this point that the subject traveled from a local hotel, where the official Indian delegation was staying, and arrived at the dinner with the group, which was under the responsibility of the Department of State. This individual went through all required security measures along with the rest of the official delegation at the hotel and boarded a bus/van with the delegation guests en route to the White House." The statement added, "Unlike the rest of the members of the official delegation, this individual was not entered into the WAVES system [for a background check]."

The news media swooped down on the story. After initially denying it, Carlos Allen eventually confirmed to reporters that he was the third intruder. Soon, Politico.com ran a video of Allen entering the White House on the night of the state dinner.

The publisher of a minor Washington society blog called Hush Society Magazine, Allen, thirty-nine, claimed he fell in with the India delegation congregating at the Willard and rolled on in with them. Like the Salahis, he claimed he had been invited. But the "invitation" he showed on a television show resembled the dinner program for the evening, according to the *Washington Post*'s "Reliable Source."

Allen turned out not to pose a threat. But when the Secret Service fails to perform a background check, the agency never knows if an individual has terrorist ties

In the initial House Homeland Security Committee hearing, Sullivan referred just once to the Secret Service's own failure in operating the guard post. He said it had only one magnetometer, although it usually would have two. That suggests that uniformed officers were under even more pressure than usual to move everyone through the checkpoint and out of the rain. It is another symptom of Secret Service management's disregard for the need for more funds and more personnel. Yet Sullivan denied that the agency needs more funds to Committee Chairman Bennie G. Thompson, a Democrat from Mississippi who ran the hearing with remarkable fairness.

Threats against Obama "right now" are not any higher than when Presidents Bush or Clinton were in office, Sullivan said.

While that was true, threat levels fluctuate. As spokesman Donovan told *Newsweek*'s Mark Hosenball, there were "substantial spikes" in threats against Obama before and after his election and again before and after his inauguration. As recently as March 25, 2009, Sullivan testified before a House Appropriations subcommittee that threats "remain at high levels."

What never came out is that the increase in threats against Obama became so disturbing that as the 2008 election approached, the FBI established a Presidential Threat Task Force to gather, track, and evaluate assassination threats that might be related to domestic or international terrorism. Based at FBI headquarters, the secret task force operates within the FBI's National Security Branch. It consists of twenty representatives from pertinent agencies, including agents from the FBI and Secret Service and operatives from the CIA, NSA, and the Defense Department, along with analysts. Yet the Secret Service itself continues to cut corners.

According to the high-level Secret Service official, Sullivan's own staff was convinced the director must go—for the good of the agency and the people it protects. He said Sullivan was spinelessly acceding to requests by Obama administration officials for Secret Service protection in instances where there are no threats against them, and the agency already suffers from being understaffed.

As a result, forty Obama administration officials and White House aides are under Secret Service protection, compared with thirty-two under George W. Bush. No one outside of the government has heard of most of them, but they have one thing in common: they enjoy being chauffeured free of charge by the Secret Service.

The Secret Service official cited the fact that the Secret Service has taken no steps to update security technology. For example, he said, while the party crashers passed through magnetometers to detect metal, the visitors could have been carrying an explosive of the type Umar Farouk Abdulmutallab concealed in his crotch on Northwest

Airways Flight 253 on Christmas Day 2009. To provide adequate security, the Secret Service should use whole-body imaging scanners that use radio waves or X-rays to reveal objects under a person's clothes, the official said.

The official noted that prior to the state dinner, Secret Service agents met with the White House social office and agreed that there was no need for the social office to staff the guard posts with aides, placing further pressure on uniformed officers.

"To this date, not one high-level person has been held accountable for these failures and corner cutting," the official said. "Secretary Janet Napolitano has failed to hold this director accountable. He [Sullivan] doesn't want to ruffle anyone's feathers. He doesn't want to ask for more money. He is more concerned about appeasing the administration."

The official added, "A large majority at headquarters has lost faith in him. Everybody's waiting for the day he leaves. This agency has some very talented people, and that is clearly lacking in the case of the director."

Despite the breaches, President Obama said he has complete confidence in the Secret Service, signaling that he saw no need for a change in management. Given the clear warning signs, that was just as reckless as Abraham Lincoln's and John F. Kennedy's disregard for security.

In the case of Obama, in the view of many current Secret Service agents interviewed for this book, the result could be a security breach with deadly consequences. As Representative Thompson observed, the country was fortunate the Salahi affair did not end in "a night of horror."

Epilogue

FTER ASSASSINATING PRESIDENT Lincoln, John Wilkes Booth escaped capture for twelve days. But on April 26, 1865, federal forces cornered, shot, and killed him in a gun battle. Four of his fellow conspirators, including one woman, were tried and hanged.

Charles Guiteau, who fatally shot the newly elected President James Garfield on July 2, 1881, was hanged on June 30, 1882.

Leon Czolgosz, a factory worker who shot President William McKinley on September 6, 1901, was executed by electrocution. "I killed the president because he was the enemy of the good people—the good working people," he said before his death. "I am not sorry for my crime."

Oscar Collazo, the surviving Puerto Rican nationalist who tried to assassinate President Truman, was convicted of first degree murder in March 1951. He was sentenced to death. A few weeks before he was to be executed in 1952, Truman commuted his sentence to life in prison. Truman said he didn't want to provide Puerto Rican nationalists with a martyr. In 1979, President Carter pardoned Collazo, who then went back to Puerto Rico as a hero. He died in 1994.

In 1964, the Warren Commission confirmed FBI findings that Lee Harvey Oswald acted alone when he shot President Kennedy. Two days after he shot Kennedy, Oswald was being transferred under police custody when Jack Ruby shot him to death.

Sirhan B. Sirhan was convicted of the murder of Robert F. Kennedy on April 17, 1969, and sentenced to death in a gas chamber.

The sentence was commuted to life in prison in 1972 after the California Supreme Court invalidated all pending death sentences imposed in California prior to 1972.

Confined at the California State Prison, Sirhan told a parole board, "I sincerely believe that if Robert Kennedy were alive today, I believe he would not countenance singling me out for this kind of treatment. I think he would be among the first to say that, however horrible the deed I committed was, that it should not be the cause for denying me equal treatment under the laws of this country."

After he paralyzed Governor George Wallace, Arthur Bremer was sentenced to sixty-three years in prison, later reduced to fifty-three years. After serving thirty-five years, he was released from a Maryland prison and placed on parole on November 9, 2007.

Bremer never explained why he shot Wallace, although in 1997, when the state denied his petition for parole, he railed against Wallace's position favoring segregation. As a condition to his release, Bremer is prohibited from going near political candidates or events.

Nick Zarvos, the Secret Service agent whom Bremer shot in the throat as he protected Wallace, still has a raspy voice as a result of the shooting.

After the shooting, Wallace asked people to forgive him for his segregationist views. He died in 1998.

Lynette "Squeaky" Fromme was convicted in 1975 of attempting to assassinate President Ford. In 1979, she attacked a fellow inmate with the claw end of a hammer. On December 23, 1987, she escaped from the Alderson Federal Prison Camp in Alderson, West Virginia, but was captured two days later. She served time in Texas at the Federal Medical Center and was released on parole in August 2009.

In December 1975, Sara Jane Moore pleaded guilty to attempting to assassinate President Ford. On December 31, 2007, she was released from prison on parole after serving thirty-two years of a life sentence. Moore has said that she regrets the assassination attempt, explaining that she was "blinded by her radical political views." President Ford died on December 26, 2006.

After attempting to assassinate President Reagan, John W. Hinckley, Jr., was found not guilty by reason of insanity on June 21, 1982. After his trial, Hinckley wrote that the shooting was "the greatest love offering in the history of the world."

Confined to St. Elizabeth's Hospital in Washington, he was determined to be an "unpredictably dangerous" man who might harm himself, Jodie Foster, and any other third party. Nonetheless, on December 30, 2005, a federal judge ruled that Hinckley would be allowed visits, supervised by his parents, to their home in the Williamsburg, Virginia area. A request for further freedom was denied.

After a man threw a grenade at President Bush in Tbilisi, Georgia, the FBI examined three thousand photos of the crowd taken by a college professor. The bureau found a facial portrait of a man who matched the physical description of the person who threw the grenade. The Georgians distributed the photo to the media and posted it in public places. That led to a call to the police.

"Oh, yeah, that's my neighbor, Vladimir Arutyunov," the caller said.

With an FBI agent, the police went to the suspect's residence on July 19, 2005. As they were approaching, the man fired on them and killed a Georgian police officer.

Arutyunov confessed, saying he did it because he thought Bush was too soft on Muslims. The man was sentenced to life in prison.

Secret Service Dates

1865 The Secret Service Division is created on July 5 in Washington, D.C., to suppress counterfeit currency. Chief William P. Wood is sworn in by Secretary of the Treasury Hugh McCulloch.

1867 Secret Service responsibilities are broadened to include "detecting persons perpetrating frauds against the government." The Secret Service begins investigating the Ku Klux Klan, nonconforming distillers, smugglers, mail robbers, perpetrators of land fraud, and other violators of federal laws.

1870 Secret Service headquarters relocates to New York City.

1874 Secret Service headquarters returns to Washington, D.C.

1875 A new badge is issued to operatives.

1877 Congress passes an act prohibiting the counterfeiting of any coin or gold or silver bar.

1883 The Secret Service is officially acknowledged as a distinct organization within the Treasury Department.

1894 The Secret Service begins informal, part-time protection of President Cleveland.

1895 Congress passes corrective legislation for the counterfeiting or possession of counterfeit stamps.

1901 Congress informally requests Secret Service protection of presidents following the assassination of President William McKinley.

1902 The Secret Service assumes full-time responsibility for protection of the president. Two operatives are assigned full-time to the White House detail.

1906 Congress passes the Sundry Civil Expenses Act for 1907 that provides funds for Secret Service protection of the president. Secret Service operatives begin to investigate western land frauds.

1908 The Secret Service begins protecting the president-elect. President Theodore Roosevelt transfers Secret Service agents to the Department of Justice, forming the nucleus of what is now the Federal Bureau of Investigation.

1913 Congress authorizes permanent protection of the president and the president-elect.

1915 President Wilson directs the secretary of the treasury to have the Secret Service investigate espionage in the United States.

1917 Congress authorizes permanent protection of the president's immediate family and makes it a federal criminal violation to direct threats toward the president.

1922 The White House Police Force is created on October 1 at the request of President Harding.

1930 The White House Police Force is placed under the supervision of the Secret Service.

1951 Congress enacts legislation that permanently authorizes Secret Service protection of the president, his immediate family, the president-elect, and the vice president if requested.

1961 Congress authorizes protection of former presidents for a reasonable period of time.

1962 Congress expands coverage to include the vice president—or the next officer to succeed the president—and the vice-president-elect.

1963 Congress passes legislation for protection of Jackie Kennedy and her minor children for two years.

1965 Congress makes assassinating a president a federal crime. It authorizes the protection of former presidents and their spouses during their lifetimes and protection of their children until age sixteen.

1968 As a result of Robert F. Kennedy's assassination, Congress authorizes protection of major presidential and vice presidential candidates and nominees. Congress also authorizes protection of widows of presidents until death or remarriage, and protection of their children until age sixteen.

1970 The White House Police Force is renamed the Executive Protective Service and given increased responsibilities, including protection of diplomatic missions in the Washington area.

1971 Congress authorizes Secret Service protection for visiting heads of a foreign state or government, or other official guests, as directed by the president.

1975 The duties of the Executive Protective Service are expanded to include protection of foreign diplomatic missions located throughout the United States and its territories.

1977 The Executive Protective Service is renamed the Secret Service Uniformed Division on November 15.

1984 Congress enacts legislation making the fraudulent use of credit and debit cards a federal violation. The law also authorizes the Secret Service to investigate violations relating to credit and debit card fraud, federally related computer fraud, and fraudulent identification documents.

1986 The Treasury Police Force is merged into the Secret Service Uniformed Division on October 5. A presidential directive authorizes protection of the accompanying spouse of the head of a foreign state or government.

1990 The Secret Service receives concurrent jurisdiction with Department of Justice law enforcement personnel to conduct any kind of investigation, civil or criminal, related to federally insured financial institutions.

1994 The 1994 Crime Bill is passed, providing that any person manufacturing, trafficking in, or possessing counterfeit U.S. currency abroad may be prosecuted as if the act occurred within the United States.

1997 Congressional legislation passed in 1994 goes into effect granting Secret Service protection to presidents elected to office after January 1, 1997, for ten years after they leave office. Individuals elected to office prior to January 1, 1997, continue to receive lifetime protection.

1998 Broadening the jurisdiction of the Secret Service and other federal law enforcement agencies, the Telemarketing Fraud Prevention Act allows for criminal forfeiture of the proceeds of fraud. The Identity Theft and Assumption Deterrence Act establishes the offense of identity theft. Penalties are established for anyone who knowingly transfers or uses, without authority, any means of identification of another person with the intent to commit an unlawful activity.

2000 The Presidential Threat Protection Act authorizes the Secret Service to participate in the planning, coordination, and implementation of security operations at special events of national significance as determined by the president. These events are called national special security events.

2001 The Patriot Act expands the Secret Service's role in investigating fraud and related activity in connection with computers. In addition, the act authorizes the director of the Secret Service to establish nationwide electronic crimes task forces to assist law enforcement, the private sector, and academia in detecting and suppressing computer-based crime. The act increases the statutory penalties for manufacturing, possessing, dealing, and passing counterfeit U.S. or foreign obligations. It also allows enforcement action to be taken to protect financial payment systems while combating transnational financial crimes directed by terrorists or other criminals.

2002 The Department of Homeland Security is established, transferring the Secret Service from the Department of the Treasury to the new department effective March 1, 2003.

2004 Barbara Riggs, a veteran agent of the Secret Service, becomes the first woman in the agency's history to be named deputy director.

2006 The network of Secret Service Electronic Crimes Task Forces is expanded from fifteen to twenty-four nationwide task forces dedicated to fighting high-tech computer-based crimes.

2007 Protection begins for presidential candidate Barack Obama on May 3, the earliest initiation of Secret Service protection for any candidate in history. Because of her status as a former first lady, presidential candidate Hillary Clinton was already receiving protection before she entered the race.

2008 Protection of presidential candidate John McCain begins on April 27. Just before the presidential candidates announce their selections for vice presidential running mates, Joe Biden and Sarah Palin receive protection. After Barack Obama is elected on November 4, his children, Malia and Sasha, receive Secret Service protection.

2009 Barack Obama is sworn in as the forty-fourth president on January 20. On November 24, the Secret Service allows Michaele and Tareq Salahi to attend a White House state dinner even though they are not on the guest list and did not undergo a background check. Subsequently, the Secret Service finds that a third intruder, Carlos Allen, attended the dinner. The Secret Service keeps that from the public and a congressional committee until the author reveals it in a January 4, 2010, Newsmax.com story.

Based on the time line available at

www.secretservice.gov/history.shtml

Acknowledgments

MY WIFE, PAMELA Kessler, is my partner in life and in writing. A former *Washington Post* reporter and author of *Undercover Washington,* about the spy sites of the nation's capital, Pam came up with the title for the book, accompanied me on key Secret Service interviews at the training center and at head-quarters, contributed vivid descriptions, and pre-edited the manu-script. I am grateful for her love and wise judgment.

My grown children, Rachel and Greg Kessler, rounded out the pic-ture with their love and support. My stepson, Mike Whitehead, is a loyal and endearing part of that team.

Mary Choteborsky, associate publishing manager of Crown Pub-lishing, edited the final manuscript brilliantly. She and my previous editor Jed Donahue provided just the right balance of encouragement and guidance. When it comes to book publishing, Mary and her team are unrivaled.

I am lucky to have my agent, Robert Gottlieb, chairman of Trident Media, on my side. Since 1991, Robert has guided my book-writing career and been a source of steadfast support.

For years, I had been gathering string on the Secret Service. But I began work on the book in earnest when a Secret Service agent and later others came forward to alert me to management problems at the agency. All agents in good standing, their sole purpose was to improve the Secret Service and ultimately avert another assassination. Along with former agents who helped, they are patriots, and they have my appreciation and respect.

The Secret Service agreed to cooperate on this book, the only book about the agency to receive such cooperation. While I made it clear in an email at the outset that the book would address management problems I had already raised in an article, based on my previous books and stories, Secret Service officials believed that I would portray the agency accurately and fairly.

The Secret Service arranged interviews with a range of Secret Service officials, gave demonstrations and tours of the agency's training center and the most secret headquarters components, gave approval to former agents to talk with me, and provided photos and compiled data in response to questions.

Mark Sullivan, director of the Secret Service; James W. Mackin, deputy assistant director of Government and Public Affairs; Eric P. Zahren, special agent in charge of that office; and Edwin Donovan, assistant special agent in charge of that office, have my appreciation for their help.

In the end, more than a hundred current or former agents up to the level of director and deputy director agreed to be interviewed, either on the record or without attribution. I am grateful to them for providing what I believe is a complete portrait of an agency that is a bulwark of our democracy. My hope is that the problems revealed in the book will lead to reforms that could avert a calamity.

Index

Also by Ronald Kessler

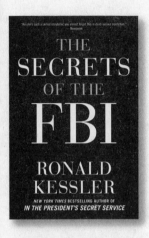

The Secrets of the FBI
$26.00 hardcover (Canada: $30.00)
978-0-307-71969-0

From Watergate to Waco, from the take down of Osama bin Laden to the Christmas Day bomber, *The Secrets of the FBI* presents headline-making disclosures about the most important figures and events of our time.

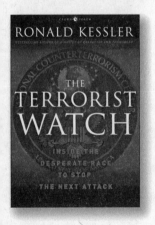

The Terrorist Watch
$14.95 paperback (Canada: $16.95)
978-0-307-38214-6

Based on exclusive interviews with FBI Director Robert Mueller, CIA Director Michael Hayden, White House Counterterrorism Chief Fran Townsend, and dozens of key intelligence operatives at all levels, *The Terrorist Watch* presents the chilling story of terrorists' relentless efforts to mount another devastating attack on the United States and of the heroic efforts being made to stop those plots.

Available wherever books are sold.